HIGH WITH THE MOST HIGH

VOL 1.

JONATHAN KANIA. D.D

High With the Most High, Copyright © 2023 by Jonathan, Kania

All rights reserved. No part of this publication should be reproduced, stored in a retrieval system, or transmitted in any form or by any means; electronic, mechanical, photocopying, recording, or otherwise without prior permission of the author and the publisher, Unmatched Publishing Inc.

For further publishing rights or publishing services, reach out to us today:

Unmatched Publishing Inc.

+233 (0) 5464 79 307

+233 (0) 5558 89 360

Email: unmatchedpublishing@gmail.com

ISBN Paperback: 979-8399-9-6109-5

Except otherwise stated, all scriptures are taken from the King James Version of the Holy Bible.

DEDICATION

To All Who Laugh In The Glory: Ruth Ward Heflin, Prophet Bob Jones, Dr Rodney Howard Browne, Kathy Walters, Todd Bentley, John Crowder, Matt Spinks, Royal Renee, Red Letter Ministries

Contents

Introduction: Sweet September..6.
Chapter 1: The Revelation...10
Chapter 2: The Milk And Honey Gate..................................16
Chapter 3: Dancing In The Pain!..26
Chapter 4: Six Wild Visions: Seeing Jesus!..........................32
Chapter 5: Pastoring In The Presence................................39
Chapter 6: Freedom To Travel -Prophetess Marie................50
Chapter 7: Clouds, Giants And Houses...............................54
Chapter 8: Praise During Persecution................................69
Chapter 9: My Sisters Dreams: Celebs Coming To Christ.........73
Chapter 10: Family Dreams : Restoration............................78
Chapter 11: Sounds Of Angels..84
Chapter 12: Prayers From Heaven: Revelation......................91
Chapter 13: Close To The Broken Hearted: Revelation............101
Chapter 14: You Didn't Miss It: Revelation..........................115
Chapter 15: Dreams And Portals..125
Chapter 16: Rejoice Always: Revelation..............................141
Chapter 17: Humiliation & Multiplication Vision & Revelation....153
Chapter 18: Realm Of Restoration......................................165
Chapter 19: God Honours Love!...172

Chapter 20: No Reliance On Old Understanding: Revelation........185

Chapter 21: Ministry Protection and Glory........................196

Chapter 22: Miracle Cafe: Different Dimensions..................200

Chapter 23: Fasting Vision: Gates Of Pearl!.....................208

Chapter 24: A New British Era...................................221

Chapter 25: Glory Is The New Drug!..............................225

Chapter 26: Forgiveness And Favour: Revelation..................235

Chapter 27: Throne Of Grace: Revelation.........................239

Chapter 28: Prophetess Marie....................................246

Chapter 29: Florida Confirmation................................251

Chapter 30: Wild Goose Oil......................................257

Chapter 31: Ascending In The Golden Glory.......................263

Chapter 32: Understanding Being Drunk In The Spirit.............271

Conclusion..275

Introduction
SWEET SEPTEMBER 22

It really was a 'sweet September.' That was the Rhema word the Lord gave me for that month in 2022 and He totally fulfilled it. This book is just half of that amazing month of my personal revival where God completely blew my mind with fresh revelation, impartation and encounters like I have never known before. These strange spiritual experiences have begun to reshape my thinking. How I feel about God, how I feel about His Kingdom and how I feel about Heaven all matters and I have found that all our thoughts are intertwined with a higher reality. Interesting right? Everything is supremely interconnected. These holy experiences have refreshed me and I pray that they will refresh and awaken you too.

To some people they may seem offensive and literally and metaphorically blow the old religious mindsets out of you. They sure did with me! I am still amazed and I have had to take almost a year to recover from these because they continued every single day!

INTRODUCTION

I can confidently say that I have begun to taste Gods goodness and this has all contributed to my online revival experiences and made me more of the supernatural man and minister of the Gospel that God wants me to be. He certainly wanted to blow my mind and show Himself to me in brand new ways. This book is only the beginning of my journey. God really has showed me a lot and spoken to me like a child, a friend but also a lover. It's one thing to claim revelations with your mind, which is very good, but it's another thing to experience these revelations, especially on a day to day basis. I call this the mystical path. It is something new and something ancient. We are supposed to ask for the ancient paths and we are supposed to wait on the Lord for the NEW. God loves to surprise His children. This is what I have found out, so some people will not like these revelations and they will be uncomfortable with them, so God has given me the grace and the space to experience them privately without being in a traditional church setting.

"But they that wait upon the Lord shall renew [their] strength; they shall mount up with wings as eagles; they shall run, and not be weary; [and] they shall walk, and not faint."

—Isaiah 40:31

Christians can have revivals and refreshing's in the church but they can also have them at home. Our home is a church. Every day we have to hear from God and I must pastor and help my family. Life isn't about just 'doing whatever the hell I want' that is a rebellious attitude and it leads to a hardened heart and a rebellious spiritual consciousness in the soul which does not add up to the full bliss kiss consciousness of Heaven's consciousness! We aren't to live from such a sinful limited and degraded mindset, nor a religious, dogmatic, stuck in the mud mindset. We are born of God and born for freedom. We are going to express that freedom by abiding in Gods fullness. We are going to enter new realms and have new experiences and a lot of these are going to surprise us. I am learning more and more about Gods higher ways and

HIGH WITH THE MOST HIGH

He is making the way smoother and clearer every day. We aren't supposed to put up with an anxious, defeated, victimised and sad disposition. We aren't supposed to be a people of misery but a powerful, supernatural, empowered, Holy Spirit filled, heaven flooded, open gateway of glory! We are spiritual, new creation, a people of praise and people of destiny! Are you with me on this journey of daily glory?

"Now the Lord is that Spirit: and where the Spirit of the Lord [is], there [is] liberty. But we all, with open face beholding as in a glass the glory of the Lord, are changed into the same image from glory to glory, [even] as by the Spirit of the Lord."

—2 Corinthians 3:17—18

A lot of people will misunderstand what I am saying because these realms are not for the first saved, new-born's, they are more mature, but that doesn't mean that you cannot grasp their essence by the Holy Spirit but you must be born again. You cannot say a quick prayer as a kid and then live however the hell you want because that is not salvation. Salvation must be worked out and we must work out our salvation with fear of God (awe) and trembling and laughing! So, get ready to laugh, get ready to smile more because God tells me that too many Christians are in the miseries daily just because they don't like or understand the trials they must go through for His names sake, so like it or not, you will be tested by God and you will have to learn spiritual contentment which will bring you into fresh realms of surprising liberty and spiritual revival consciousness clarity. It will be a cool journey if you learn to let go and stop trying to control and blocking the flow. So let's learn what it is to be high with the Most high and see things from a different perspective – a much higher perspective!

There are so many mysteries in Christ that are going to be unveiled and unravelled and worked through into our lives and we aren't always going to be in a weird competition in ministry a worldly, sinful, unloving, ungiving mode we are shifting out of survival mode into

INTRODUCTION

revival mode, so catch some fresh oil, catch the sun glow, be in the know and shine out and blaze on wherever you go! Be freshly imparted knowing that these revelations cost me my whole life and know that I lived on NO INCOME when I wrote this and I was not allowed to even sign on for a UK benefit or able to get a job so I assure you that this book cost me dearly.

But God is faithful and He is my provider and my source and I can and I will trust Him. Will you? Do you dare? Do you want to find out more about this strange drunken glory experience and what it can do for you? Do you dare to pray:

"Come Holy Spirit, blow the religion out of me by your fresh wind of revival consciousness. Please grant me a revival for my soul. Please help me to have your divine love as my only goal.

Please help me to understand this new movement and understand some of the old.

Lord, I confess, I do not really understand being drunk in the spirit, but I choose to trust you with this journey. Lord please help me to see you in a new way. I repent of not putting you first and for idolizing my own ideas and my old understanding. I lay down my whole life, every area to you now, and I ask for a revealing, a revival, a refreshing and an empowering.

Lord help me to have my eyes fully enlightened and seek you first as the lover of my soul. Lord help me to love myself by accepting the things that I cannot change about me or others as I surrender these things into your fully capable hands. Lord I trust you. I love you. Revive me, In Jesus Christ's, Yeshua' H'Meshiach's holy all powerful, all knowing, all seeing name. You are blessed now and good to go – so jump in the river to be in the flow!

All Glory is for King and Lord of the universe, Jesus Christ. The name above all names.

Chapter *One*
THE REVELATION

SEPTEMBER 2022.

REALMS OF ABUNDANT GLORY AND KEYS TO A NEW LIFE AND HOME IS COMING!

1st September

Happy blessed new month! PRAISE KING JESUS! The presence of God is overwhelming! Today I spent all day in praise and worship so the atmosphere was completely saturated! In fact, I can barely write - I'm so excited and happy! Forget

THE REVELATION

all the painful problems. A PRISM OF PRAISE has come out of the PRISON of PAIN! I saw a vision of meeting Benny Hinn and Alvin

slaughter that was awesome! We were together in praise concerts in America! God is putting everything together! Even though Mum and my sister Amy are still in pain, I will keep praying for them for total freedom! I see that Mum Priscilla will be dancing around on her new lawn with the Africans!

It's going to happen! She's going to be blessed for hosting me all these years I will see her dancing with her new eyes! No one will die - we are too blessed with great length of day! The presence is so strong right now! I am praying for so many people, so many prayer assignments just like in heaven and people are giving more and supporting the ministry! As God promised - We are all coming out of captivity this 2022! Amen.

Prophetic Word from Pastor Raza, Pakistan.

I see you as an international prophet travelling and preaching in America, Europe, India and Pakistan. You are going to get a big donation. In 2—3 years there is going to be no food and a famine. I am seeing God will raise you up like Joseph in 2024—2025.

SPIRITUAL MATCHES

Your spiritual father must match where your calling is going or be very similar. You must remember that spiritually you come from your father!

HIGH WITH THE MOST HIGH

Spiritual Father Notes

Some are in the flesh concerning spiritual fathering. There is a generational reward available in the spirit. With Elijah – Elisha, this illustrates that it has to be the right relationship. It will either be the Lord ordained by Spirit or by the flesh. If your spiritual father is not Christ-ordained, it will crush spiritual believers. There is a lot of insecurity of spiritual fathers. They are not biological, often they are organic vs being forced, it should not be an obligation.

Spiritual fathers are for adding value in relationships. Spiritual fathers have just learned to be sons themselves. This process can't be skipped. They should set a good example. They carry fire and different experiences. Their lives provide models, they are engaging the whole process, and this is not just read in books. (*See* Paul and Timothy)

"Paul, an apostle of Jesus Christ by the will of God, according to the promise of life which is in Christ Jesus, To Timothy, [my] dearly beloved son: Grace, mercy, [and] peace, from God the Father and Christ Jesus our Lord."

—*(2 Corinthians 1:1—2)*

Spiritual fathers don't just appear overnight. They are authentic and life transforming! They must endure an intense shifting of their faith. They must FIGHT the good fight and then be able to help their sons.

FREEDOM NOT CONTROL.

They must never seek to control or manipulate and especially for money! They must have personal integrity and value in themselves and others. It is not co-dependency, and it enhances our relationship with God. They bring a spiritual covering and protection. They add sanity and sound thinking by what they share. By having a Spiritual covering and protection, there are great changes in our lives from being fathered. They enhance our thinking and help us to see the bigger picture. They open up our life experience. They help us to lead towards maturity.

St Paul was an amazing father in the Faith. They provide a safe environment to go from adolescence to adulthood. Everyone gets older but not all mature. There is a big difference!

SPIRITUAL INJECTION

They should have a spirit of excellence and they will help you and give you instructions. They have an IMPARTATION. They can stir up the gifts, by laying on hands for example Impartation can often be misunderstood but it makes people's lives have impact. Spiritual fathers should be able to interact. You must watch how they handle people. You can tell by their spiritual father who identifies as their sons. They bring accountability and correction, therefore a son will be under their authority. They have an inheritance to give out for a blessing. (Pastor Prophet Raza. Pakistan)

My conclusion:

It is very important to have the right spiritual father and only submit to the right one otherwise all hell will rain down upon you and you can wind up with more problems than you can imagine and then feel very ostracised from the church! You can feel disconnected and afflicted if you submit to the wrong spiritual father! I know this from past experience. I know also that God has told me to be careful who I trust especially if your spiritual father lives in a different country or far away from you. You must be able to trust your spiritual Dad. Without trust, there is no relationship.

The Lord has also told me that I am able to have more spiritual fathers in each different nation as they can cause conflict because of the different cultures and countries. You need to be very prayerful when choosing your spiritual fathers covering. They have to be able to pray for you and you also have to be prayerful and be able to stand on your own two feet without constantly calling up your spiritual dad!

Some people have both a spiritual father and a spiritual mother. This is ok too. The aim is to create disciples and then let the disciples create more disciples. This leads to multiplication and with the right person at the right time and even in the right country a whole nation can be birthed in revival! Some choose to use the traditional terminology of disciple and others today use the term spiritual son, daughter or child.

You have to be very careful who you submit too so there will be no manipulation and especially financial control. Both the father and the son have to be able to manage his own household. This is very important and it cuts out the stress and also I believe that both the spiritual father and the son must at least learn to live by faith, dependent on God first before they can teach others more effectively and more empowered. God is looking at the heart of both individuals. The relationships between son and father can always be developed as more contact and wisdom is given out. If your spiritual father is very busy, do not always try to contact him. He needs his own time and space to pray and do his work and ministry and fulfil his relationship with his spouse or his partner.

In short, make sure you submit to the right person! When you do there are so many blessings that unfold and contacts with people you would not normally be able to access. Your spiritual father carries authority to open more and more doors of blessing for you. You will be very happy and a great relationship can be developed if you have the right spiritual father. You will feel loved and you may also, like me, be called 'Daddy' Praise Jesus! Remember your true spiritual father is Father God.

THE REVELATION

PERSECUTED BUT NOT DEFEATED

The Devil is such a LIAR! Even though we are being persecuted in lots of different ways, it doesn't mean that God is not faithful. I also have to live on no income! It is not easy! God has instructed me to live on faith at this point in my life and out of strict obedience I have had to do it! As Kathryn Kuhlman said 'If God has not called you, DON'T DO IT!! But if God has called you, DO IT!'

Friends of mine in Pakistan have extreme Muslims and even local Satanists targeting them preaching the Gospel and trying to beat them up with sticks. Sadly people do get hurt during persecution. Punches in the mouth, being nearly hit over the head - violence of all kinds it all happens and it's terrible! Jesus warned us that we would all be persecuted for his name's sake, but no one is saying that it doesn't hurt. Pain always hurts unless we are in a different dimension. It's painful, scary, troubling and traumatic and I just pray for the whole persecuted church in general. May God protect his children. Lord have mercy!

How people can rejoice in the midst of persecution and violence is beyond me! That is some shocking grace and I pray they see Jesus face!

"But you, oh Lord, be not far off, Oh my strength, come quickly to HELP me! Deliver (rescue) my life from the sword, my precious life from the power of the dogs."

Psalms 22:19—20, NIV

Please remember the cost of the cross! Please remember the daily cost of following Jesus!

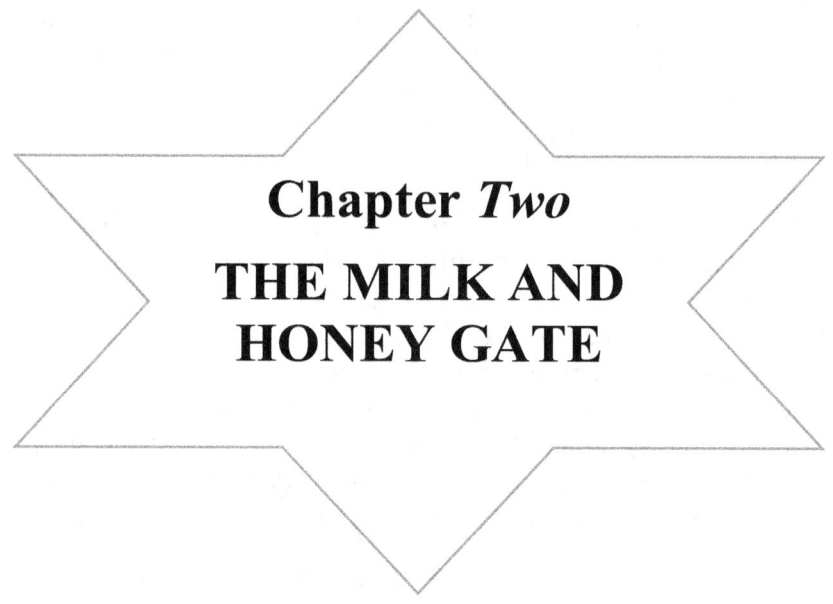

Chapter *Two*
THE MILK AND HONEY GATE

VISION OF JESUS TODAY

It was so awesome spending so much time today - just wasting it all by worshipping Jesus! I was amazed to see a glimpse of the river of life and then Jesus was swimming towards me - at that point I just couldn't stop crying! It was a heavy glory impartation.

And it's awesome too that my US friend Royal Renee had glory encounters by releasing the presence of God in Walmart and in order to get over a guy with split personality /demons in a past relationship, she got so full of joy she was laughing for 90 mins. So much that she gave herself a headache and had to rest. That's some Holy Ghost laughter!

Rodney Howard Browne would love her because she is so funny! I was laughing too as she cracks me up. So today I was crying and laughing and seeing visions of Benny Hinn and meeting Alvin Slaughter! The Devil must be getting really mad at me for wasting so much time, not even getting any of my writing work done! I was just laughing or crying with Jesus! This is such a supernatural funny life! I am still praying for my friend Milosch and for Kathie Walters move to North Georgia. Praise God! Satan the blood of Jesus is against you! I will give God all of my praise! PRAISE IS A WEAPON!! YOU CAN AND SHOULD PREACH TO THE DEVIL AND DEMONS AND FLESH!

They will bow the knee to the preaching of the Gospel as Jesus Christ is Lord!

- THANKSGIVING RELEASES THE PRAISE!
- PRAISE RELEASES THE REVELATION!
- WORSHIP RELEASES THE GLORY!

Especially when you don't feel like it! I then had another vision. People were standing in the sea and then big waves of glory came! I can see gold in the waves! During this time one of our Ministry sponsors gave me $100!

2nd September 2022

I was speaking to my friend Renee and I declared 'THE OIL GATE IS DRIPPING AND THE HONEY GATE IS OPENING' THIS IS SWEET SEPTEMBER BLESSINGS IN JESUS!! At night after all that time spent in worship the Lords presence was so thick and I saw an old man in the tent and God told me this was Abraham in the wilderness! It was like a movie clip. I'm going to start shouting if we as a body don't catch hold of the revelation that JESUS CHRIST MESSIAH LOVES US FOREVER AND NOTHING WE CAN DO CHANGES THAT!! ♥HONEYGATE SEPTEMBER SWEETNESS. REVELATION SHOCKS GLORY TO KING JESUS FOREVER! THIS OIL IS STICKY! PRAISE KING JESUS SOMEBODY!! HALLELUYAH! JESUS CHRIST WON! DID WE FORGET? HONEYGATE GLORY!

Never stop laughing. It's time to drive the devils wild and drive out the devils. Can I get an Amen?! FIREE! ♦My friend Renee is a laughing therapist! During this evening I was completely high on Christ!!

VISION OF ABRAHAM AND JESUS CHRIST.

That evening by surprise I saw Abraham in the Tent with the oaks of Bashan surrounding the scene. This spoke to me about receiving Gods strength. It is either to receive Gods Strength as my JOY vs Temporary abode with a heavy load. That made me laugh! I then saw 3 Angels and one next to them full of light was CHRIST! That was a great day seeing Jesus twice! I was absolutely whacked and I fell asleep laughing!

2nd September

Someone sent me this on WhatsApp – 5 CROWNS.

The FIVE Crowns to note and work towards:
1). CROWN 1.-- Crown of Righteousness -- Loved the Lord's Appearing -- **2 Tim. 4 : 8.**

2). CROWN 2 -- Incorruptible Crown -- Disciplined Bodies / Self Control – 1 Cor. 9:25—27.

THE MILK AND HONEY GATE

3). CROWN 3: -- Crown Of Life -- Endured Patiently Thru Trials-- James 1:12; Rev. 2:10.

4). CROWN 4: CROWN Of Glory --- Godly Leaders who were examples to flock -- 1 Peter.5: 2— 4.

5). CROWN 5 -- CROWN OF Rejoicing -- Soul Winners Crown -- 1 Thes. 2:19; Dan. 12: 3.

May the LORD help us to be found faithful in JESUS Name.

2nd SEPTEMBER

LOVE DRUNK/ LOVE DRUGGED

I have definitely caught a drunken with joy revelation since meeting Royal Renee. She carries so much in the Spirit! Which we are never separated I can barely write RED LETTER ministries. (This group I was involved with at the time) Glory honey gates are open! Other influences are Ruth Heflin and David Hogan who died literally! The revelation I have found is that we can be drunk and intoxicated on God.

Satan was keeping this revelation back from the whole church from becoming new wine! Wine was the DRUG of the time! God has the wine for the saints prepared! We can be drinkers as well as thinkers! We can be blessed to a blessing to others. We can get absolutely drunk on GOD! We are going to win souls now! This is NOW FAITH! Whether people like it or not, this revelation and experience will win souls and infuriate the religious!
OMG I feel so loaded!

HIGH WITH THE MOST HIGH

VISION OF COWS AND JESUS ENCOUNTER

Tonight God appeared to me through clouds and after seeing a whole tonne of cattle and then the clouds turned PINK and then I saw pills from the clouds float down as I floated up! The pills spelt the letters L.O.V.E on individual tablets and single letters. I saw other people floating up into the cloud realm with the holy drugs! They were wondering what they had been missing out on because God showed me deeply religious people in their robes floating up into the clouds. These are Glory fresh new realms! I am so excited! I had no idea God could drug me and I would experience ecstasies! The old Babylonian sorcerer's have had it now!

Now is the day to be SAVED and HIGH on GOD! Christ really has saved the best wine till last! Only the best can do! Simply the best! Rock on! Glory to God. Tina turner! Glory dome! I am going home! This is the LIFE Jesus promised us that we won't need any more drugs or alcohol etc. That is all imitation before the real thing! Heavenly bliss is intoxicating me now! No wonder why I can't sleep PRAISE JESUS! Revelation and intoxication!

I got hungry after the 'strange oil' encounters and I asked God if I should eat and He said 'Don't have a cow man! Don't be so religious my son!' Then after eating I laid on my bed and a massive cow mooing jumped over me and through my walls! Man, I was laughing so much and I bet you would be too! I am undone! That's the Bart Simpson and Sonic the Hedgehog anointing! Ha Ha! All I can hear now is cows mooing! I had seen Jesus right in front of me with a herd of cattle in a pink cloud laughing. It was so trippy! Is this what happens when the glory of God is in my bedroom stopping me from sleeping? I had no idea that God would honour 4 hours of worship so much! Now my hands heat up, tingle and shake in the anointing and they wouldn't stop either! I feel so blessed and so strangely selected!

THE MILK AND HONEY GATE

Then I kept seeing more cows and huge grapes everywhere. I was in the kitchen as high as a kite and all I could think was 'Oh man, I have got to juice those grapes before they perish!' I could NOT stop laughing. My whole world and perspective of reality was changed forever. I went back to my room and fell on the floor which turned into cow print in the Spirit! I had never had any drugs nor alcohol, all I had done from what I can gather was give God extra time in worship. I was both undone and overwhelmed!

Jesus said 'Every knee will bow that includes the cow!!' OMG MILK AND HONEY GATE!

(I even feel embarrassed to write this book – talk about 'die to self!')

Now I KNOW there is a HONEY GATE and MILK GATE IN THE SPIRIT! I laughed so much I fell on the floor. My spiritual family and myself had absolutely no grid for this encounter! Then God let me see a massive fat cow in my bed and there was money all around in the air and gold!! Is this a cash cow anointing? He said 'See, son, she's much more interesting to look at than you all the time, so she's got your bed for tonight!' ha-ha I was knocked out on my floor for another hour then eventually I crawled into bed without the huge cow!

In bed God still spoke 'We had so much fun tonight son didn't we? I gave you a gift in exchange for your worship as you are my living sacrifice and you spend so much time with me so I thought it would only be fair to spend time with you! And now you know how much time we can have inside and outside of time and space!'

REVELATION:

IN THE SPIRIT = UNDER THE INFLUENCE AND POSSIBLY DRUGGED BY GOD OR EVEN DRUNK OR INTOXICATED BY HEAVEN AND JESUS CHRIST LORD OVER ALL THINGS!

I can see the hippy drug culture is coming back and what the devil wants for evil, God will turn around for good! Romans 8:28 but this also means no more religious spirits or religious 'holy than thou' attitudes. God is literally shaking the Church and the nations! I see the Jesus People Movement coming back! It's going to be absolutely incredible. If the government legalize drugs then Jesus will have to drug the righteous. It might sound blasphemous or ridiculous but He did it to me as a prophetic sign! The revelation bombs are going off! I am riding that pink cloud so much that I cannot sleep! To 'have a cow' is defined 'to be very worried, upset or angry about something!'

OMG it is prophetic! The laughing cow. We had cheese adverts in the UK. All these funny British references to the 90's and God knows I love what is considered by lot of people as 'cheesy 90's music and pop culture' I am sure I will be laughing until the cows come home!

I had a revelation that even the darkness is not dark to God and that NIGHT CAN BECOME LIGHT! I had a total evening to night glory invasion. Are you sure you want the glory of God to visit you? Are you sure you want spiritual encounters? Ha-ha. I did!

After this crazy cow experience, I then saw Jesus face smiling at me in pink (YESU ADONAI PINK GLORY!) and then pink clouds were all over my room going through the walls so I no longer saw my room and I floated through the pink clouds over the earth into space into Heaven and then I fell asleep feeling like the world and all its desires had left me forever! I have never felt such bliss.

TOXIC VS TOXIN

A toxin is ok in the human body in small amounts.
- Intoxicated - toxicare ' to poison'
Poison Vs antidote
 - Antidote = A medicine taken or given to counter act a particular poison (Sin) = Something that counteracts an unpleasant feeling or situation (remedy)

THE MILK AND HONEY GATE

- Laughter is a good antidote to stress.

- Poison = potion, potio, potake (to drink)
A cure is the antidote and opposite to poison.
Lady Gaga 'The cure' vs Britney Spears 'Toxic!'

'Jesus made WINE that tasted so good the people at the wedding feast in Cana said it was better than the wine they had just drunk! Surely they would not have said this if it had tasted flat to them!'

Norman L. Geisler (from Covenant Keepers Alcoholic Beverages)

(God is a Covenant keeper even if you are alcoholic ha-ha)

This tells me that there are upgrades in the Spirit!

I was also contacted by the first Pakistan TV channel too called Chairman Six One One Foundation by Pastor Atiq, and other Healing TV YouTube channels because of the Pakistan flood which will be turned around into a flood of future glory! Then later I had more visionary encounters including seeing Jesus again!

3rd September

ANOTHER VISION

I woke up to God telling me something about a carpet shop and how I used to hide in them as kids could this be the secret place reference? I was overwhelmed last night/this morning and the last thing I saw with the Jesus trip was blue crystals and myself being shrunk into one wearing the same colourful clothes which are my terracotta trousers. I was wearing my Dreamers space rainbow T, and my loose open green check shirt this I saw all in miniature! Far out!

HIGH WITH THE MOST HIGH

Later on, I tried to process everything with a slightly more 'sober' spirit mind with Royal Renee, and in US time it was 4:30 am - so that was a bit too late and then later on I spoke to Mum Priscilla who heard me preaching about the NEARNESS and NOW REALM of God! I am not able to stop! It even hurts my throat, my stomach was so badly flared up in the natural I was full of poisons from my lax (awful I can tell you!) but I was supernaturally protected and kept in a holy bliss bubble with the wildest of drunken glory with Jesus and the cows !

Jesus had appeared to me and taken over my room where I saw Him and a field of cows and then I was completely high I didn't tell you this part I wanted it to be a great surprise!

The Lord keeps telling me to do my hair with more colours and I think he favours blue at this time! Most people will be saying that's not the Lord! but God keeps telling me to do wild things since August everything has shifted after a prophecy to be more 'flamboyant and not hide' and now we are in September 22, surely it's going to get even more wilder! I mean I asked for Wild fire encounters and liquid love and more oil and honey gate experiences! He's not going to give me a bunch of stones for asking for the children's bread when Heavenly Manna is our potion! Whoa I still feel whacked! God is truly good, surprising and wonderful. Glory to King Jesus!

He also keeps telling me to juice more grapes. (At this time I was harvesting our neighbours grapes and juicing them) It's like I'm making wine I feel the angels around when I do that.

HEAVENLY CHILDREN VISIONS

At first I saw big golden oil drops go through my ceiling and then massive sticky honey drops splashed and fell on my chest. This is God opening the realms of spiritual sight.

THE MILK AND HONEY GATE

I then saw kids in Heaven which appeared through my room which then just dissolved. At first I brushed this off as just my imagination until one of them came up to me with some sticky oil and slapped my forehead! They were touching each other like a game of 'Tag' and they ran off laughing! The sticky honey oil combination was stringy and it reminded me of melted cheese and the children were made of light. It was like I glimpsed Heaven afresh.

I heard father God: 'Son, You will be anointed by Heaven whether you are ready or not! God is saying 'Ready or not, here I come!' Then I had another vision although I was pretty whacked out I saw the same heavenly children and they were so happy all dressed in white made out of light crushing grapes on something shiny (a crystal floor) with their bare feet making new wine! Glory!

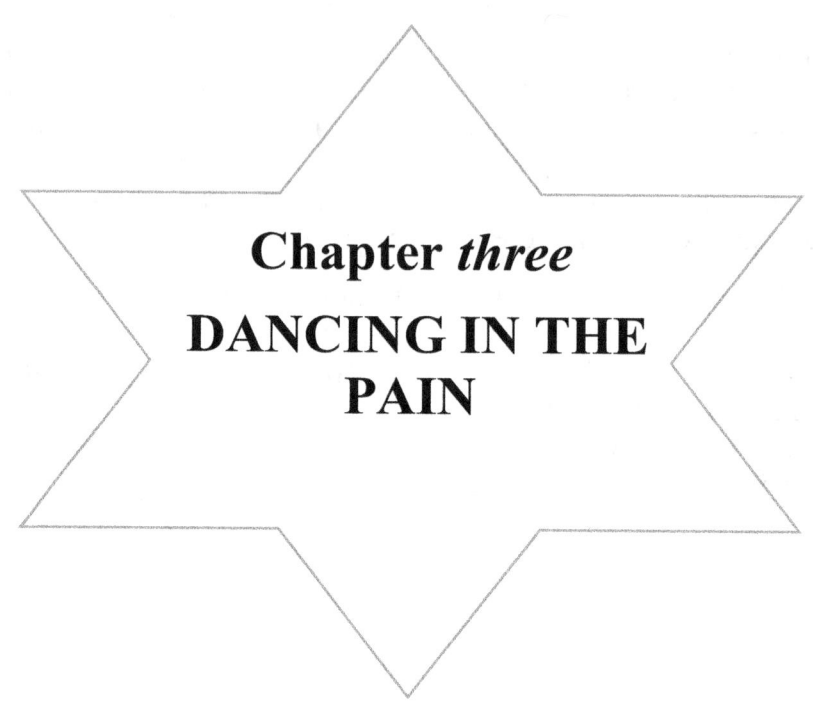

Chapter *three*
DANCING IN THE PAIN

3rd September

DANCING IN THE PAIN

Thanks to my wild Jesus trip last night I have awakened even more! And Christ clearly is saying a big fat ' WAKEY WAKEY, RISE AND SHINE! DON'T YOU REALIZE THAT YOU WILL ALWAYS BE MINE?!' He is saying this not just over me but over the whole Church. He has even made me a doctor of the Church Body of Christ. Can you believe it? This is GRACE!

From three different Bible universities I have an honorary Doctor of divinity from Dr. Blessing, Apostolos University and BA in ministry from Dr. Bishop Rudolph Kwanue, Grace International University and then I was also given the ability to do a free MA in Angelic theology that I don't even have time for yet from my friend Dr. Emeka from Revival Bible University, Nigeria. These amazing degrees are all perfect examples of God's kindness, compassion, grace, favour and plan! It's supernatural! I have been doing my best to write down my visions and experiences recently and I am praying into them even if they are considered wacky and far out! So praise God!

The Lord is telling me through these angelic visitations 'I am bringing outsiders in and some insiders will be outsiders that means are all in!' That's what I heard the other day from an angelic voice which wasn't God! So it's wakey wakey! RISE AND SHINE time

I saw another vision after my wacky pink cloud and cows night! So I conclude:

- The Oil Gate is open!
- The Honey Gate is open!
- The Wine Gate is open!
- The Milk Gate is open!

These are four multi-dimensional gateways of glory that we can bring into the earth to change the atmosphere to save souls. This is just the beginning of Heaven to Earth which is the name of our Ministry. Another sign that God is with me through all the pain and trials!

SONIC VISION

The next vision I saw was of the mega drive back in the 90'S with the well-known game Sonic the Hedgehog I saw Jesus fully robbed, full of light and He was playing the game like we all did as kids. This might not mean anything to you but it did to me because it gave me an impartation of my birth family healing for the future. This is the Lord's way of saying 'I was always there for you and I always will be!'

Despite what people say or do, God will always love me and you! Now that's a Revelation! Get excited and get blissful. It's time to kiss the son of glory! He is reversing the pain, bad memories and trauma and redeeming the years the serpent took and removing the cutting locusts! All Harvest years that were missed out on are about to be paid back in full in Jesus mighty name!

I was doing more grape juice making and feeling like electricity was pulsing through my body. I was barely able to stand. I am more aware of Heaven than before. These encounters are costly but worth it! I am seeing golden abundance glory all me! Abundance is everywhere! And I kept preaching the gospel and telling my stories, there are so many! I will have to record them as it's 'impossible' to write them all by hand! God bless my typists we are all team Jesus! Everyone will be blessed @ Heaven to Earth Apostolic Ministries international - PRAISE GOD.

Tonight I was listening to 5 mins of Justin Abraham on Podomatic and he said about 'Making pain our friend' which is exactly the same revelation God gives me and I hadn't heard that message yet and it was from 2012!

"For they call themselves of the holy city, and stay themselves upon the God of Israel; The Lord of hosts [is] his name."

—Isaiah 48:2

DANCING IN THE FIRE VISION

Then later I saw a vision of a flame and there was a figure dancing in the fire and I wondered who it was and they were spinning around and doing dance movements where their feet would be the centre of the flame - but their body would tilt away defying gravity, I flew in the Spirit closer and I heard Michael Jackson music and it was 'Billy Jean' and then 'Smooth Criminal' and there he was - but this time his hands were in the air praising God! Hallelujah! It was so funny, I told my sister Amy and we were laughing and it reminded me of the MJ dream I had once before.

MJ DREAM

I was drawing like a kid at the top of my landing just before my bedroom, a rather strange place, but dreams are weird! Suddenly in a cloud of smoke there was Michael Jackson and it was him alright as he flashed in with colourful smoke white and red, and his skin changed from black to white!

I got a revelation that some are singing his tunes in Heaven as he got completely saved in the door way of death where he met Jesus and went straight through the pearly gates! He told me God was real and that he knew I wanted to sing, that it was in my heart and not just to draw things and paint but that I was called by God to preach the Gospel and only say his messages. He also said my life was a message just like Joseph's and that God had big plans for me and that I was not to get distracted! He carried music in his heart and he had become part of musical choir and singers of Heaven!

He told me he had many regrets and fears on this earth and I spoke to him about love and healing and oneness, and I told him being filled with the Holy Spirit that we would all become one family and he was in full agreement saying he had God encounters growing up and when he was alone but was forced into the Illuminati who intimidated him, poisoned him with drugs, framed him and took his money but now he was very happy!

And wow he was shining like an angel! I asked him if he was an angel and he laughed really coyly and said NO WAY! Don't you know? God made us a little lower than the angels. I am SPIRIT! I am LOVE! We are LOVE! And with those final words God glorified his body in a flash bright light filled the landing and staircase and suddenly he had absolutely HUGE wings which took over the whole space and then he disappeared as if by magic but it was the glory of God into a puff of white smoke! Then I woke up!

Michael Jackson had become the absolute embodiment of love. He was so pure and angelic not like the media monster they invented. Jesus was in him, literally he had a brand new crystalline holy body. So prophetic! So many of Michael's songs are prophetic and profound and his talent, music, dancing and great love for healing the world will never ever be forgotten. Heaven is full of people that we would not expect as they didn't have conventional 'Religious' paths yet in their hearts, they knew God. We can't ever judge. CHRIST IS LORD!

3rd September

It was my birth father's birthday today, and I have not forgotten about him, even if he feels I don't care about him. I want him to feel and know the love of God and get saved. I don't want any of my family to accept an invitation to Hell! I am spiritually adopted and blessed in another family now but I am still praying for my birth family and prayer is extremely powerful and God answers my prayers in his own special way and in his own special timing. It will be well.

A lady from Colorado and Devon was staying in our village at this time and she was giving away the state from her cottage and me and mum prayed previously for slate for crazy paving stepping stones as that was exactly what she wanted and this lady was spiritual and boy did she give off that electrical energy. I told her that our village is a portal and I had encounters with God here and I have been given a healing gift. She may have been surprised but she still invited us in my sandals lol and so barefoot I gave the little home a spiritual blessing and thanked her for the free gift!

I thought I should tell her that she was part of the prayer being answered and she was quite pleased as she felt the energy of the home and asked the stones 'where would they like to go?' and 'could they go to someone in the village?' That was still a prayer and God answered it and now she knows it is King Jesus who answers prayers! Her name is Martr and I will be praying for her to be saved and have encounters with God too as she had childlike faith. She knew Mr Lewis Lewis, a wonderful man who lived here his whole life and he remembered the Welsh revival, he had an aura /an energetic glow about him and lots of peace. I wonder if he is praying for us in Heaven? I bet he is! His son Ivor still lives here and we are also praying for him as well as other villagers. This will be God's healing village. It is written in the spirit for the future as a highly prophetic, powerful and healing destination. Praise God!

We felt God's presence when praying in our kitchen and the glory bent my back double, it does this sometimes in churches such as the anointing and weight of glory that falls upon me in the most heavenly places I can really feel it and the anointing is JESUS!!

Chapter *Four*
SIX WILD VISIONS

I am going to take you deeper into my day with Jesus from the 2nd September 2022:

SIX WILD VISIONS!

I'm trying not to be whacked so that I cannot type! This day I woke up feeling an intense desire to spend time with Jesus. I was having a conversation with Him about how yesterday we went to the beach, it was social but I didn't get enough time with Him! I really need to spend a lot of time with God and I end up pushing away people if I dont get enough quality time with King Jesus. I hate the feeling of just rushing through a psalm or a verse in the morning and I refuse to live like that! I want to live saturated in the glory of God!!

SIX WILD VISIONS

He said to me 'Aww thanks son!' just like that it's really amazing how humanized Christ can be at times! So I responded 'OK that sounds cute Lord!' so I started reading the Bible I thought 'I can't take anymore!' The presence was very strong and I started to see a vision with the clouds and gold crowns being revealed through them and then all these gold coins were falling down in front of me! It was vivid like a hologram and it shocked me!

I was praying about a previous mermaid vision from August and I was like 'Lord it better not be some evil spirit and stopping me from seeing in the Spirit. I'm not dealing with that well right now, so it better be from you!' This was me asking to test the spirits! Well He didn't say anything and I was like OK and so I asked another question: 'God why am I seeing flashes of a person getting covered in oil all the time and then just flashes over and over of just a person covered in oil?' It's like seeing this glimpse of a person's face looking at me or that that they're looking up and they were worshiping and they were absolutely covered in oil! They were being completely covered so I asked Jesus 'what's going on? And I've been seeing this for the last week or so - wondering what was going on? And why every time when I start worshipping or sometimes I was reading the Bible and I saw it and I was like 'what's going on?' and I thought is there someone in the opposite field covered in oil or something because they suddenly sort of came really fast near to me and it was like a flash, it's a bit like a ghost, if you see a ghost it's that kind of sudden shock and then you are left questioning 'is there someone in front of me covered in oil for a second? Then all your reasoning comes in 'Nah, this can't be! I must be just seeing things! and you just reason it away, saying, 'no way, man!' and just brush it off and think, 'oh well.'

So yesterday I was a bit like 'Lord I need to catch up on my writing' so I thought I will go and do my work and so I said to God casually 'Actually you know what Lord, I can't even do my work! I can't even read the Bible today because this is too much of your presence! it's an effort because of the impartation grace! I hope you don't mind!' and then I said 'Well OK I will worship you for an hour.

HIGH WITH THE MOST HIGH

So after this hour I said 'Lord, I've given you an hour.' It was coming up over the hour and the Lord said to me 'just a little bit more son! Just spend time a bit more time with me!' Christ makes me laugh! So I'm worshipping and worshiping, meanwhile I am crying my eyes out as I'm in the second hour thinking 'this is so intense!'

Then I start to have visions. I start seeing myself with Benny Hinn and Alvin Slaughter and that was it - I was undone!! Alvin Slaughter is a great worshiper and I was listening to his music and I thought at that point 'I'm out of it! I'm done! I thought he's got so many angels and there's obviously an Angel around I'm going to start really crying really badly in a moment!' I tried to control myself but I just couldn't! All I could do was cry and this weeping in God's presence is just so intense and then Christ said to me 'I want to swim in your waters son!' and I thought wow and then I started to see the River of Life, I didn't see all of it, I just saw a glimpse of it and I saw this person swimming towards me and I thought 'who's that?' and He said 'It's me!!' I was like whoa, wow so at this point I was just completely undone even more than before and I saw Jesus coming for me- he was swimming towards me in these sparkling crystalline pure waters and He said to me 'I want to swim in your waters! I want to swim in your waters! I want everywhere you go to be spiritual waters! He was praying for me while He was swimming!' So I was amazed thinking 'what is that?!'

I can't brush off these things that I see so clearly in the Spirit as my imagination 'this is an encounter!' so I'm thinking 'I can't take anymore, I still can't take anymore!' and the Lord said to me 'Just one more hour!' He said to me 'Come on honey just one more hour, please I just want to spend time with you!'

I was amazed and laughing I got pretty high! I asked 'Lord are you serious?' to which He responded 'Yes! I'm in love with you! Come on, I want to spend time with you! You are really getting in my heart now!' So I was undone worshiping for 4 hours!!

I just wasted the whole day with God!!' I said 'Lord, now I can't do anything because I'm whacked! I'm trying to write up my book, by the grace of God I was able to write my journal. It took me all day just to

SIX WILD VISIONS

write my journal, talk to my friends and pray and try to do normal stuff and I was like 'this is just too much!'

Meanwhile the family household was miserable! We have got pain, everything going wrong, all the stupid attacks but contrasting in my room I had the glory! And I thought 'this is just immense!' but Jesus said to me like a command 'Worship!'

So tonight I'm just doing my normal thing and I thought well 'I better do my work now' but I started meditating again and suddenly I'm seeing this old man in a tent and I'm wondering 'what's going on?' and the Lord said to me 'Genesis 18 'I looked there and I saw Abraham and his three angels coming in while he was in the tent! 'Oh my goodness!' I was wondering I was seeing this old man in the tent. 'This is just Wild man!' So Jesus was showing me this man in a tent! I don't know how to explain it but when you start seeing these things it just really makes you overwhelmed and it makes you feel so undone and you can't do anything any anymore! You're like 'Jesus is a Wild man!' and this is what I'm saying to the church:

'This is the new normal!' we supposed to have supernatural life! This is what God wants!

I was telling Mum about my encounters and she said 'You are not going to get a lot of work done!' Lol. I said 'Lord if you keep doing these revival encounters every day…' and the Lord interrupted me with 'but you asked for it son – well come on now, you asked for it!' and He said 'You asked for money and I'm giving you money. You are living by complete faith with no income! I'm giving you donations so keep asking me I'm going to keep giving you what you need. That's how it works! Welcome to my Kingdom!'

We ask in faith and we're full of Thanksgiving and praise and worship and have a lifestyle of faith and then we will have a supernatural lifestyle! That is what God told me previously so I had to give up my income and a sickness benefit and yet I have the healing anointing for others! It does not make any sense to me!

HIGH WITH THE MOST HIGH

I've always known worship is so super-duper powerful, it's so powerful but this was so funny as God was trying to get getting another hour in with me! I was amazed laughing at His quirky sense of humour and I said 'My sweet Lord, I am not going to get anything done! I need to get this book done and I need to be with you at the same time and I just gave in and said 'Lord, you know what's best!' and I worship and worship even I can't see Him, I can't see anything yet, I'm just worshipping and then I start to see something and then that's it: 'I'm finished!' I'm crying and crying and just a complete mess or I am laughing.

Royal Renee my friend makes me laugh so much she's just absolutely hilarious so meanwhile she goes off to Walmart having encounters because I'm praying for her to have more encounters and it's happening at the same time as she's going into Walmart and she spoke to someone and this girl broke down on her and stuff like that and I don't know exactly what happened. She couldn't explain it all she was too out of it herself - but basically the Holy Spirit was doing some work in her with the presence which was everywhere!

Just imagine, so you are carrying the presence and when I came in to visit Mum in the sitting room I was laughing so much and I saw shimmering water on the floor instead! It was low shimmering water and I was again wondering 'what is that?!' Well it wasn't quite the River of life it was just that splash! The rivers flaming massive! The river is terrifying it's more like a sea. It has got a shoreline and everything that goes on for miles and miles and miles, it's incredible the River of life, is it's intimidating actually and there's all these reeds and they blow in the wind and Oh my goodness, if I see it again, I can't even talk about it it's just too much! So it's just beyond amazing and this is what we're supposed to do we're supposed to bring Heaven to Earth!

We're coming out of the misery, coming out of pain and the bloody captivity in Jesus name! You must know these encounters aren't happening for no reason so tonight I was like, 'who's this old man?' There he was, Abraham, in the tent looking out and then the three angels turn up. I was like, that is just astounding Lord! It was so strange and I could feel the heat of being in a tent, the humidity and I don't know how to

SIX WILD VISIONS

explain it. I was like 'what is that in the Desert?' I thought 'I haven't even turned on the radiator on in my room so what's going on?' so I discovered this is what life is supposed to be like! It's supposed to be full of joy and we can be intoxicated by God, not bogged down with terrible evil things and I'm still going through awful personal heartache- but you would never know it! The Bible is completely prophetic it says 'the Lord is close to the broken hearted' so I'm sure He is just using this broken heart just to get even closer to me and the Bible says 'draw near to Him and He will draw near to you' and it says 'He inhabits the praises of Israel.'

Well, we are we grafted into Israel so when we praise He inhabits those praises! So He is in my room!! So I was worshipping and worshiping and I thought 'Oh my goodness I am going to see God in a moment! I can't take anymore!' and then He started showing me Him swimming! I wondered 'who's this man swimming and splashing in front of me?!' I thought 'I think it's Jesus! He is swimming towards me' and He had this massive big smile and I thought 'I can't take anymore! I just can't take it! That's just too wild!' You don't expect it at all! That's what I'm saying it is the surprise of these things you encounter and 'you really surprise me Lord!' It was so wow—more than!! I'm praying for the whole family and I'm asking God 'why can't you do this with the rest of my family?'

But it's simply amazing and fulfilling prophecy because Prophet Ben from Ghana Podbean, Growing Together, said to me a few years ago 'Heaven to Earth you're going to be like the fountain for your family, it's going to be overflowing, it's going to revive the family! You're going to revive your family!'

So what's happening with me will start happening with them and they will be like 'pain? Whatever!' so it's all working for my good and you can catch the same revelation and you'll start to see stuff in the Spirit and Oh my goodness it's very sweet glory -praise Jesus, but please be aware there are also counter attacks too -oh well anyway, we praise God all the time. Can I get an amen?

HIGH WITH THE MOST HIGH

In summary I saw these 6 visions as part of my major encounter in September 2022:

1. Clouds, crowns and gold coins
2. Person covered in oil
3. Meeting Benny Hinn and Alvin Slaughter
4. Seeing Jesus swimming!
5. Abraham in the tent
6. The River of Life invasion

Glory to King Jesus who is full of surprises!

Chapter *Five*
PASTORING IN THE PRESENCE

Not only is it important to witness in God's presence, and not hide our light but it could be the last chance you ever get with that person! If angels are on assignment-then so are we! Now there's another revelation! God's been dishing out revelations as I pastor and preach to my family to encourage them and pull them out of pain and torments. My spiritual family have always been my first 'church' People need to know God, not just know about him - but really know him and we can! We really can know Jesus! Isn't that exciting? I spoke to a friend at the time called Debs and she let me minister as we prayed together the oil flowed and healing came to our souls and minds.

God's nearness came from releasing each revelation - and I am just loaded! Then my family needed my time so I ministered to them and I prayed on my knees on the kitchen floor until they felt the presence of God! Our whole home is a portal. This is why the enemy is so threatened by this future powerful family ministry. There were angels above me and all around me and in the village. Man, I really felt it then I ministered to my friend Renee and it always helps me to realize that God is doing all things for his Great glory! Amen.

So it's really important that we do not minister from our own strength if we give out oil - then we must go and get it back by spending more time with God and stay topped up all the time! This is biblical and it should be foundational and not revelational. We aren't supposed to forget the words of God that help us in every area. amen? That's why praying the scriptures is so powerful so we can meditate on what is already written and then think about this and speak it out knowing God is in control. With childlike faith we access the keys to the kingdom and turn into living sacrifices and then living gateways and portals of power through submission, surrender, and humility. We pray and we keep on praying.

"Pray without ceasing; in everything give thanks; for this is God's will for you in Christ Jesus,"

—1 Thessalonians 5:17—18

We renew our strength in the Lord and God is so faithful to top us up with His fresh oil! Glory! What a great exchange! So let's get all topped up again spending so much time with God, being led by Holy Spirit into great studies, great praying, great faith and great praises! Give God all the glory. Praise him in the pain and He will glorify his name!!! Even with a lot of my days over the last 20 years I have not felt well and I have just continued on, persistence is powerful and God's grace is sufficient for me.

Not that I speak in respect of want: for I have learned, in whatsoever state I am, [therewith] to be content. I know both how to be abased, and I know how to abound: every where and in all things

PASTORING IN THE PRESENCE

I am instructed both to be full and to be hungry, both to abound and to suffer need."

—(Philippians 4:11—12)

This was funny, I was just going into saying goodnight to my family here and 2 or 3 hours later after encouragement, revelations, fellowship and prayers we were done! I mean sometimes I minister to 3 am and let me tell you something that is God's grace! I am an unconditional lover because God is the unconditional lover through me. My life is laid down on the altar of surrender and I cannot minister from my own strength. It is all GOD and so He always gets all the glory but I must preach the Gospel! Is that zealous? Maybe to some but to me it's a necessary normality! Praise God despite problems! These are orders of the Heavenly army! I go and get a few minutes of fresh oil and that's it- then I am loaded and I now I must go and find someone to encourage and if you know me, you'll find out that I am a spirit man and I am just a weak little vessel with a beautiful big God. I am weakened by pain but I still preach the Gospel. This is how the Lord's power rests on me!

"Therefore I take pleasure in infirmities, in reproaches, in necessities, in persecutions, in distresses for Christ's sake: for when I am weak, then am I strong."

—2 Corinthians 12:10

"I counsel thee to buy of me gold tried in the fire, that thou mayest be rich; and white raiment, that thou mayest be clothed, and [that] the shame of thy nakedness do not appear; and anoint thine eyes with eyesalve, that thou mayest see."

—**Revelation 3:8**

Let's not spend our time and energy on things that don't satisfy us when only Christ will.

HIGH WITH THE MOST HIGH

Oh, someone praise Jesus! I can barely contain myself my cup runs over!

Everyday is different

Not every day I will feel as high as a kite with Jesus. I have learnt to take the rough with the smooth and there's been a lot of rough stuff but praise God-the Lord always sees me through-just like He will always see you through - you just have to let go, surrender and trust Him. Even when it feels like you don't have enough access to God - you still do! Now that's a revelation of the NOWNESS and the NEARNESS of God that we were discussing earlier on. We really need to know God is close, then we will feel cared for by Gods love despite our painful trials. God is unconditional love and He will always love us, obsess over us, sing over us, coo over us and woo us into his Bridal chambers!

Wow, we really are the bride of Christ, stop limiting yourself with limited negative unfaithful unbelieving thinking-We are God's bride to be and Christ will always love both you and me! You aren't a good person without God no one is, we are and were bad people, not good people but God has made us righteous. You cannot add your own righteousness (Good works) to your salvation. It must be GOD THOUGH YOU. You cannot do it.

"I will greatly rejoice in the Lord, my soul shall be joyful in my God; for he hath clothed me with the garments of salvation, he hath covered me with the robe of righteousness, as a bridegroom decketh [himself] with ornaments, and as a bride adorneth [herself] with her jewels."

—(Isaiah 61:10)

He looks at us with garments of righteousness on in the spirit realm in Heaven, even in the soul realm and He wants to ask us a question: 'Why aren't you wearing your garment of righteousness today my child?' God looks at you and sees holiness! That's just a fact and we better get used to it and stop being so religious thinking that we have to add anything to the completed Gospel that we ourselves could never complete- it was only God that could complete its prophecy and He never sinned, then he imputes that same righteous, that same faith and that same holiness to us - and it's accessible every day!

This is mind blowing and I can't keep quiet about it any longer, sure, I write books but I am also a public speaker a genuine preacher of the Heavenly Good News that is a saved child of God and who knows God and walks with Him by childlike faith every day! This is God's grace and every day is different full of all kinds of problems, pains, hardships and God is in the midst of it all, loving me, all the time, wanting to spend time with me it's enough to make anyone high and stay permanently high!

Are we really spending time every day giving God our time? Are we giving God all our attention, all our focus, not just because things are going wrong or right -but because we just desperately want to hang out with King Jesus! I LOVE HIM and My lover is mine!

He doesn't let me have any idols and guess what He loves me as I am! He is not trying to change me into something that other people say that I should be. I am being transformed by the renewal of my mind daily. I don't need to please people to come up to their standard when Christ is my standard and who is Christ? He is the judge, and unconditional Love is Christ!! Have we got that yet?

"Hereby perceive we the love [of God], because he laid down his life for us: and we ought to lay down [our] lives for the brethren. But whoso hath this world's good, and seeth his brother have need, and shutteth up his bowels [of compassion] from him, how dwelleth the love of God in him? My little children, let us not love in word, neither in tongue; but in deed and in truth."

—1 John 3:16—18

HIGH WITH THE MOST HIGH

He wants real laid down lovers, and partners! He wants to make us powerful ministers of the Gospel. This isn't my job it's my vocation and it's my utter prayerful dependence on God that keeps me feeling close to him despite problems!

"Who shall separate us from the love of Christ? [shall] tribulation, or distress, or persecution, or famine, or nakedness, or peril, or sword? As it is written, For thy sake we are killed all the day long; we are accounted as sheep for the slaughter. Nay, in all these things we are more than conquerors through him that loved us. For I am persuaded, that neither death, nor life, nor angels, nor principalities, nor powers, nor things present, nor things to come, Nor height, nor depth, nor any other creature, shall be able to separate us from the love of God, which is in Christ Jesus our Lord."

—Romans 8:35—39

So you have to pray every day. Lord show me who you really are! Show me your glory, show me your kingdom! Let me not be a stumbling block or have blockages. Repent daily, be sorry, and know you are already forgiven, with all humility. PRAISE GOD!

These revelations are rooted in the word of God which is our foundation, but know this God is bigger than the Bible! He is the Bible, He uses the Bible, but there is much more and we only have HALF a Bible! If that isn't a conspiracy then what is? Do we know half a God then? Hmmm, I am saying nothing. I just know that God and His fullness is fully accessible if we really want to know him. God will give you the desires of your heart, it won't be someone else heart, it will be what you truly need, and want, and crave that will manifest in your life at exactly the right time.

Until then, stay in the light, preach the Gospel and signs and wonders will follow you including great provisions. If people don't understand that's ok. Pray for them, pray for yourself and leave them to be. God owns them, not you! We do not have that much control, nor do we need to have it. Just be content where you are, if you are truly saved by God, then He is taking you somewhere. Do not try to rush ahead. Our hand doesn't need to be on the steering wheel, Daddy God is in that position! God gives us the responsibility for souls and He gives us his holy power, accessible by faith to help save them! Every day is different, good, bad, ugly days, we embrace them all because Jesus Christ is Lord, and He is in every single one of our days!

Sometimes the pain in my body is so bad I have to lay down and rest, and this is frustrating as it feels like wasted time but God gives his beloved rest. Also people do not understand! But God does wonderful things in every time and in every season. Rainy, windy, cold days are still God's days. They have a purpose and storms have a purpose. It's all happening, for a reason and a time and season. Don't try to figure everything all out-just let go and trust God. God never lies nor could he! He is only truth.

David prayed 'Lord you desire truth in me, in my inner parts.' All of David's body was given over to God as a living sacrifice even if he had to learn the hard way but it was all part of God's plan! The same is true for us, some days we will feel as high as a kite, others will be more stressful and feel much lower, but it doesn't mean God is not with you, nor will he forsake you. Try to have faith even when your oil supply seems to be lower and you feel dryer. The wilderness will end and it will burst into bloom.

He cannot leave you but you can leave Him, and he always will be there for you just like the prodigal sons father has his arms open wide just waiting for his son to return home. This is a picture for the church despite pain and problems! This is a picture of overcoming all rejection and betrayal of which I have had my fair share of tests! This is a picture of complete fatherly forgiveness and unconditional love. Let this not be a story, let the faith from these past encounters become your present encounters. You can experience this level of grace daily if you believe.

HIGH WITH THE MOST HIGH

5th – 9th September

I had some fellowship with Renee and others today and then a 3.5 hrs phone call with a friend from the USA and we were praying about a future trip to the USA and to confirm it, I ended with the surprise of gold dust on my fingers and my hands getting hotter as they even tingling as I write this! The gold shimmer appeared on my palm and it was not perspiration!

I was really drunk with bliss after that as God loves to surprise us! I had fasted all day and I knew this would stop tomorrow as go to the Miracle Café in Bangor, North Wales where I met Aliss Cresswell and her team before.

I was speaking with my Polish friend Milosz today who was on his way travelling. I knew God would open up the nations for him – and later He opened up the whole of America!

I am amazed as this is such a testimony of what God can do and no doubt he will tell his story one day. I am also friends with Prophetess Kathie Walters and this is how I met brother Milosz. Very cool how God connects the dots for our lives!

🔥: Thank God! He did everything wonderfully! I am going to Czestochowa today. I'm waiting for a train. I hope you are doing well. What book are you working on?

Milosz 🔥: Hello Friend, this morning I am going to the north of the country to Gdańsk. Being in Czestochowa, I felt very much to speak to one acquaintance I saw about 2 years ago. It's amazing, I found him on Facebook, he called him back, we talked and now I'm going there. It is awe-inspiring for God and for the Reformation. What the Highest is doing here is amazing ... driving all over the country relying only on Him

PASTORING IN THE PRESENCE

Milosz 🔥: Hey, I was in Gdansk, I was going there from Czestochowa probably 6 hours at 2 am to 8 am It was amazing. God was moving a lot and now I want to come back to Poznań. I need a place to stay there.

Around this time God was speaking to me about the spirits of self-destruction and self-hatred and despair and how sexual sins can entangle us and warp our consciousness and how God wants us to face all the dogs from hell and overcome them all. God wants to value ourselves in the light of His daily grace. Run ahead with your race not try to do others race! He will help you and strengthen you if you call on Him. Sex, money, status, success is not the answer—GOD IS THE ONLY ANSWER. Fellowship with Him will make you very happy and even high! I am proof of this!

Jesus was speaking to me about the spirit of dogs and I was reading a book on Kindle about it and this reminded me of a lady who saw wolf spirits in a book called 'Hell on Earth' and she really had to face her fears and overcome end time evils in advance! She even ended up in a mental home and God helped her overcome that and taught her about different dimensions. She got a new level of freedom from the revelation of prophetic suffering. I can relate!

The Ministry is getting more gifts thankfully so we are able to help the poor in Pakistan and Africa as God guides including an orphanage in Uganda whom we know all the people personally so it's perfectly safe to support us! I am also leading my friend from Ethiopia Biniyam to Christ!

I was also listening to Todd Bentley podcasts whom I also know on social media and I often pray for his Revive America events and his crusades in Pakistan. It seems we share a similar vision. I am also listening to Justin Abraham who is so anointed and mystical. I know this ministry is some sort of cross over between Apostolic Missionary and Prophetic Mystic.

I saw Todd Bentley live in a conference once with Ryan Wyatt who explains there is the Priestly life and the Kingly life and we can look at this subject more in the future.

Sadly, there were many family attacks over the weekend but God is faithful. I personally know God provides all we truly need at the right time. All this hardship is for God's glory and He will be glorified so I can experience mega joy and encounters despite all fall outs and misunderstandings!

We can have a lifestyle of supernatural and supernatural JOY is accessible whether we realize it or not! We aren't dependent on man nor money but on God almighty The Lord is the strength of my life. HE IS STRENGTH TO THE WEARY ONE!

"The Lord [is] my light and my salvation; whom shall I fear? the Lord [is] the strength of my life; of whom shall I be afraid? When the wicked, [even] mine enemies and my foes, came upon me to eat up my flesh, they stumbled and fell."

—(Psalm 27:1—2)

"Then he said unto them, Go your way, eat the fat, and drink the sweet, and send portions unto them for whom nothing is prepared: for [this] day [is] holy unto our Lord: neither be ye sorry; for the joy of the Lord is your strength."

—(Nehemiah 8:10)

7th September

Today Jesus told me that I can be:

PASTORING IN THE PRESENCE

Fortified with hope
Panelled with peace
Adorned with love

'My love is unconditional. It will always be this way and you have understood this revelation. All your time and energy spent with me is not in vain. I will never let go of you no matter how people treat you. I will make you so high you will wonder why!!'

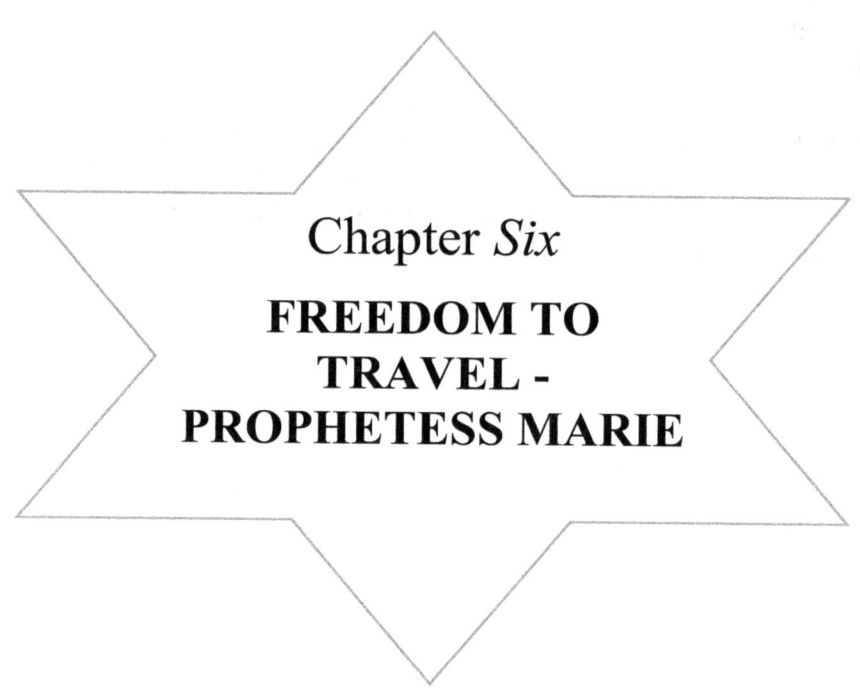

Chapter *Six*
FREEDOM TO TRAVEL - PROPHETESS MARIE

Prophetess Marie. (From Sat 3rd September)

Joy is filling your heart because of all those things God has given to you and the favour that God has given to be able to walk amongst people bringing together those things, knitting them together in a great and wonderful way. This has been a great service that has been given, you have overcome, that is why you are the living proof that all things can be overcome in the name of JESUS CHRIST. This has put a very strong position for you not only in England; Great Britain but also in other parts of the world. You are a traveller! God is sending you into

FREEDOM TO TRAVEL

different places to be able to spread the Good News of the Kingdom which knows no end! And the purposes that He has had, and the purposes he is going to have, the connection that we all have with each other being one family, the family of the living God we have one Father who art in heaven and his will be done, Kingdom come on earth as it is in heaven!

And so it does not matter what is happening to the world, we are in it, but not of it but the Kingdom comes! The kingdom suffers violence, but the violent take it by force! We are not fighting against flesh and blood but the principalities and powers of the darkness of this age but we win! We overcome all things through Christ because the Battle belongs to Him. The battle is the LORD'S!

This is why it is becoming easier, much more simpler, less to think about, more to do, not thinking about it, but getting on with it. This is the task that has been laid before you, to be able to fulfil what God has for your life in a great and powerful way. Nothing will be held back. Everything will go before you, He shows this now. The road is long but Jesus is on your side.

He teaches you how to overcome by faith in God who cannot fail. That is the living reality of a greater work which he has begun. As we preach out together, it's not even a team, it's a family! It's the family of God coming together with great love, not only to serve yourselves, but serve each other in the only way that the Lord can do.

The Holy Spirit shows us the times of the apostles when they worked together as a family with great love. The Lord is about to turn the world upside down again and we are privileged to be a part of that. So be prepared, so be bold, be strong for the Lord your God is with you, you are not afraid, you are not dismayed you are walking in faith and victory unto victory. His army he shall lead, every foe is vanquished in Christ, as Christ is Lord indeed.

So it's all part of a musical song which comes out in refreshing's and the ultimate understanding of the Lord your God in whom you put your trust faithfully pursuing on, pushing in, pushing forward into a greater and more powerful way which God is doing. Altogether we stand! We are all together so glad in the Lord. Amen.

The battle is going to be a long one and there will be persecution for His namesake, but the Lord our God he will help us to overcome by faith in God and the power of his Word. We have a God that cannot fail. That power of His Word is going to be our main steak! So the people understanding what the word of God says is going to be more important than anything else and you understand this fully.

So more and more nations are coming such as, Pakistan, India, Africa will be raised up for such a day and of course UK. The UK will come into her own again, oh yes she will! These nations which have been in the West will come into their own again. They have had a bit of a blow, a bit of putting down to raise them back up again in a great and powerful way. God is building His church and the gates of Hell will not prevail and no weapon formed against you will prosper! This is the understanding of a greater work.

Actually technology has opened up a way to the Christian Church and the Lord is showing that if we push it away we will not have the revelation of why it is being brought in! Because technology is being brought in by God not by mere man. They just think that they have the some hold over something, no they don't we do! Thank you Jesus!

And it's coming clear, and we are focusing keeping our eyes on Jesus, keeping them off ourselves, concentrating on him and then the living God in whom we put our trust arrives on the scene! At the coming of the living God every knee is going to bow, every tongue confess that JESUS CHRIST IS LORD! So we recognise everything that we are able to do is not of ourselves and this is what He is showing.

Soon, you are going to get your ticket and off you go again because you know that ticket is now open and you'll see and you go with it - but a time will come when you will have to go to America and the Lord

FREEDOM TO TRAVEL

shows you this because America has got something to do with the connection with the whole vision. Your bags will be packed and you will come into a place because He will show you - pre getting there.

The main thing that you are looking at is He is already working out the dreams, the visions and everything that is needed to do something in your life which brings you into a place in being able to recognise that He makes all the way clear. Because this is a point of contact which God gives us and at the point of contact it opens up realms! Realms of something that has never been seen before!

He is opening up ways which will not be understood to begin with but in due course we will fully realise what our duty is, what our purpose is. We still haven't quite gathered it, but it will be quite clear. The apostles knew what their mission was. Paul knew his mission, and even though he was a Pharisee of the Pharisees he was meant to go to the Jews because he was a Jew, but the Lord sent him to the Gentiles. Peter was more able to understand, you would have thought the Lord would have sent him to the Gentiles, but He didn't, He sent Peter to the Jews and Paul to the Gentiles.

This is opening up of the greatest time that's ever been! Great glory, great persecution for His namesake, but then this is where Christ's power rests in a very powerful way which is as yet to be seen. This love cannot be given, it cannot be bought, it has to be used in the name of Jesus, to love our enemy and to do good to those who despitefully used us!!

This has been a big journey for you to be able to go back to where you were and to forgive your enemy, what was done for you originally way back and overcoming that in Christ, knowing that it is a past thing and walking onto the mark of the higher call. To walk on with peace passing all understanding and rest in your heart. With those things that are to come and being a new creation in Christ, not the old man - that is buried under the waters of baptism. Thank you Jesus, joy fills your heart. You have come to the reconciliation to be reconciled to your Father who art in heaven! Amen. To God be the glory! I love you!

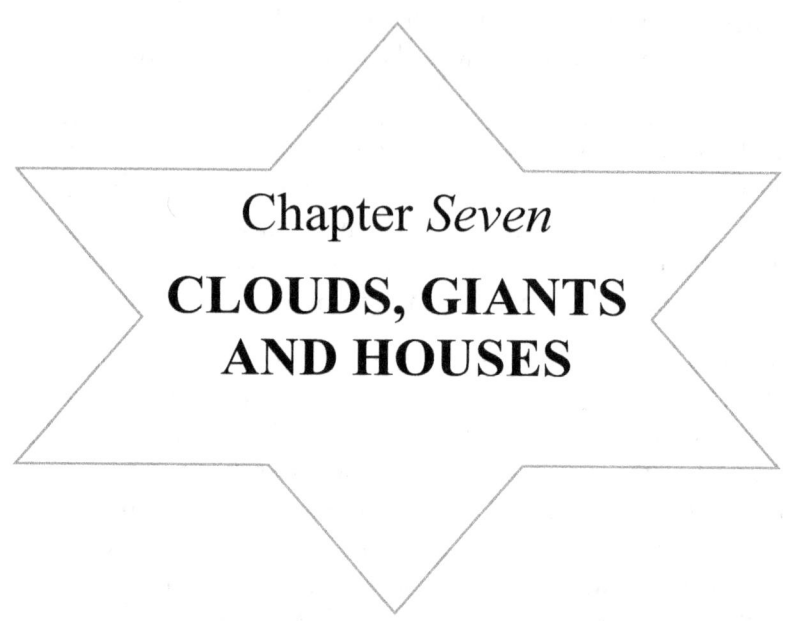

Chapter *Seven*
CLOUDS, GIANTS AND HOUSES

CLOUDS, GIANTS, AND HOUSES.

Conversation with Janet (From 3rd September.)

We were praying against any delay, any missing sales and all sabotage. We prayed for strength and I started to see a vision of Jack and the Beanstalk! 'There's this massive giant and you've got to go in the realm of the clouds to face your giant. You had your hair back looking quite boyish in a jacket in the Beanstalk style costume and you were climbing up the beanstalk (which made her laugh after the loss of a house sale) and you were on a mission!'

Prophetic warning! I didn't want to put my interpretation on it so it's advisable in prophetic seeing to just say what you saw and not analyse it otherwise you may miss direction and can be misleading to others. If you have this habit forming, please ask Holy Spirit to get rid of it and God will help. The spirit of Jezebel has destroyed prophecies and manipulated them and even Brandon from Red Letter Ministries (I later found out to rather difficult!) said that the spirit of Jezebel had destroyed thousands of ministers for lack of knowledge and manipulated, misguided prophecies, so we do have to take extra care in being aware of the devil's devices and praying with wisdom about them.

I have discovered many Christians are praying with fear or selfish motives and not the spirit of wisdom and revelation. We all make mistakes and these are covered by the Blood of the Lamb, but we need to be as wise as serpents, gentle as doves, vigilant and not lazy and certainly not saying any old thing that comes into our head! We must be daily guided and led by Holy Spirit and this becomes easier and easier when we let our agendas go, our feelings, thoughts, opinions and desires go and learn to pray selflessly. That is where the realm of victory is and we have Jesus as the perfect example of a prayer winner and intercessor.

"Who [is] he that condemneth? [It is] Christ that died, yea rather, that is risen again, who is even at the right hand of God, who also maketh intercession for us."

—**Romans 8:34**

"Ye lust, and have not: ye kill, and desire to have, and cannot obtain: ye fight and war, yet ye have not, because ye ask not. Ye ask, and receive not, because ye ask amiss, that ye may consume [it] upon your lusts."

—*James 4:2—3*

So to continue with Janet:

'You had to go to the cloud realm, where everything was clouds, but then suddenly the white cloud that you felt you were safe in all turned really grey and then really black.

Instantly you were just wondering around in that big black cloud in the darkness wondering 'What's going on?' You were crying and crying saying 'Oh God, I am lost! I am lost! I can't find my way!'

Suddenly you bump into this massive drawbridge and somehow your tears fell on the floor of the drawbridge and these opened it! It activated it by your brokenness opening the door way. As the drawbridge comes down, you get access to the door. The cloud starts to go a bit greyer so you can see a bit more in the light and Jesus said to me. 'In that castle is the giant of fear and you must conquer all your fears and you'll get all your dreams, but you've got to evict the giant from the castle because he doesn't belong in that castle, but you do!!!

Janet then said: 'I was afraid that God didn't help me before' and I answered 'Yes that's part of the dark cloud experience!' She continued, 'Yes it's when you feel like He's forgotten you. I will be 54 years not married and I don't think I would have made it (A very hard test, which I wrote about overcoming all kinds of tests, trials, fears, persecutions and desires in Tested by God VOL 1)

Me: Yes but you are a warrior Princess and in Christ you do make it. You will be incredibly successful as long you are honest and this means being true to yourself and others, not judgemental. The story is not over yet. God is giving you complete supernatural strength to face the giant of fear. This giant is a principality. You talk about principalities and Jezebel and I watched your Facebook video about it which is really good while praying for you, I knew the attacks were coming it was awful, I couldn't speak to you but I prayed 'Lord please strengthen your daughter' and I declared this and it always will ok? He will come through for you too and you will be so amazed and all the dark clouds will clear, and sometimes it's not just the storm around us which we have to face, but we've got to let God come in and <u>let God</u> be in the place where we don't feel like we can trust God. For you (and many others) with no condemnation in Christ, it's a trust issue.

CLOUDS, GIANTS AND HOUSES

You feel betrayed by God. That's what you feel. You feel let down, you feel let down by the prophetic, you feel let down by the prophets, you feel let down by people, you feel you are to blame and you are letting others down and then you feel let down by God himself! And you don't trust Him!

Right now, that's where you are. And you've got to be real with the Lord and say even in sadness 'Lord, I just don't trust you! I don't feel like you came through for me, when were you here?' Pour out your complaint to the Lord otherwise you will get bitterness in your heart and as a result you will hurt more and then hurt people tend to hurt others and some wounding is really hard and traumatic to heal but God binds up the broken hearted. And there's some anger in you and there's some frustration and there's real sadness and grief and trauma but God is going to help you. (This makes me feel sad for people that have been through a difficult past. I can identify with that pain and torment but I can also testify that God is faithful and He is worthy and able to be trusted no matter how much disappointment or betrayal comes your way.)

Jon: You've got to get real with Jesus in that relationship with Him. It's not just preaching the word or hearing it, that's part of it because for example we have king David and he really got real with God. And I see this David heart you've got, this worship heart, this amazing prophetic heart. You've also got an anointing like Prophetess Marie who can prophecy to everybody! God gave you a powerful anointing and you've got your future political anointing, but you've got a lot of attacks and tests. And you've got background stuff that you need to let God get into and He is wanting to minister to you personally but He can be trusted.

The enemy is a liar!! Don't blame God. I know it's hard but you will get through this in Jesus mighty name. God is a dream maker! He's going to make your dreams come true! Once you get access to that castle, you go and find that sleeping giant and you go and get him right in the third eye, right in the seat of the soul, right in that imagination. Once you stab that giant with the sword of God's word with all those warrior angels around you, you will be amazed!

HIGH WITH THE MOST HIGH

I see you in the spirit with big wings! You don't know how powerful you are in the spirit yet! The reason why you flow over to the Euphrates River is because you had wings and God gave you them! You were with the angels and you were just looking like those angels! Jesus is confirming this word within me.

The kingdom of God suffers violence but the violent (bold, strong, determined, full of faith, fearless warriors in Christ) take it by force (against the enemy and the kingdom of darkness- we fight with the light and we attack back in Jesus!) So make sure that climb keeps happening because God will give you the souls, but it's not about souls right now and it's not about the physical victories, which you need too. You need this emotional spiritual victory now and God gave you it, and He gave you this victory in advance, and he is going to show you. You can trust him!

The prophecy its real it's coming to pass - God will not and cannot forsake you. He will never ever leave you! He doesn't, he can't leave you, it's impossible. He is with you and you'll go through this dark cloud experience and you'll find that in that darkness, he made that darkness light! (In him is no darkness) you'll find him then he will make everything alright, that's when you'll conquer your giant, and that's when all the blessings from Heaven will come! And it will be like an open heaven all the time like you were in before. This is just a test. You've been tested and seen that God is good and then you'll see that He's even greater than goodness itself and that's the glory realm! And the glory realm will come out of you because you are going to prophecy to thousands of people, and you are going to win souls with Christ's wisdom and you are going to heal people and you are going to be a kingdom financier because you love God and God will do all of this for you.

"This then is the message which we have heard of him, and declare unto you, that God is light, and in him is no darkness at all."

—1 John 1:5

CLOUDS, GIANTS AND HOUSES

He is going to show you that you can totally trust Him and He will totally provide, and He will really make your cup overflow. You need us. We need each other! The Body of Christ needs each other! Satan sabotages stuff, he sabotages prophets, but Christ is Lord, and Lord indeed and He has overcome the world. We need each other. This is a revelation awakening for the body of Christ! So I am praying for you, rooting for you and I love you in Jesus name. Amen.

You may be wondering why I have included all this as part of my journal in a book, how to be high with God, well, it's because I want you to see that ministry should be real. I want to go day by day, in God's presence, slowly, and reveal different facets of Christ's ministry that He gives to me and then through me in preaching and teaching and pastoring which is an exciting adventure and when we all help each other more can be revealed.

As prophetess Marie said we are more than teams, we are the family of God. We must learn to be in the valleys and on the mountain tops, taking the highs with the lows each day but not letting the lows affect us, then we will be called ministers and then we will really know our God and do his great exploits which are great supernatural works that He has in store for us, planned in advance.

"He makes the winds His messengers, Flaming fire His ministers."

—Psalms 104:4

"But we have this treasure in earthen vessels, that the excellency of the power may be of God, and not of us."

—2 Corinthians 4:7

As we come more and more into the realisation that Christ lives within us, that if we abide in the Christ Vine, we will be fruitful in Him. We will see Him and know him in all that we do and live in constant high of who he is <u>inside</u> us. We are little jars of clay full of the treasure from Christ, rich, blessed and at peace. <u>We can stay high despite all kinds of troubles,</u> we don't have to be stressed out by anything especially lack, we can know the truth and we will know the truth and the truth will set us free! This year we are coming out of captivity into liberty! World tests or personal tests, Christ is Lord over all, and He absolutely can be trusted as he is in absolute supreme control. We are coming into much higher revelations and experiences in Christ every day! Hallelujah!

Jan: 'It's my desire that God will give me the wealth of the wicked so I can lay it up for his people, that's you and your mum and your sister. You need a new home. You belong to that realm where you have access to church'.

I agreed that we had been deprived from church especially Mum who needs it. I was quite frustrated that we had actually been deliberately prevented from going to church as we live in an isolated place and lifts were not available, or the day or time was attacked, other priorities come in, the Sabbath day was not made holy by all members of the household and important meetings were missed and these disappointments have really got to Mum and made her feel rejected and sad, so I have done my best to pastor and look after 'widows and orphans in their distress' and so has she!

She has been dishonoured and so have I by various persecution and there must be justice seen, as I do not accept seeing her in pain, depressed and frustrated because she can't move forward. As I said earlier we must be real with God!

There has been a lot of family strife and I know this was not right, but that it was all part of tests and long suffering, but that time must come to an end! I have also been mega humiliated, I lost my income which was a benefit, there's no jobs around here, Mum is quite stuck and isolated. I have done my best to be her carer for almost 7 years and I have been blessed with 2 revivals, so all I have got to offer now is the kingdom of heaven! Hallelujah, my life's been sacrificed and I'm on the Altar of surrender daily and I am staying here!

Janet said that our needs would be met, we would get our autonomy first and then we would be able to support the children in Africa and other nations as God would provide for Heaven to Earth Apostolic Ministries International. Amen to that!

'No one is paying for you as you are a minister and that is not right. 'I can't reach those people when I am working all day- I can't, but you can! 'I just can't give up. I could have been evicted and I would end up in the car even though I was ministering while I was living from that vehicle (Part of her awesome testimony) and I was so confused with what to do with my life, but you know what to do with your life, that's to preach and teach. I think I am going to do Ministry where I sit by my computer and tell them what I see. In Samuel 16 David was given a promise.

He was trying to get to the perfect will of God. All the way through to Samuel 24 then it pops up when Saul finally commits suicide and David becomes the official king. But that promise was given to him when he wasn't even 19 years old yet. So, was he not in the perfect will? While he was hiding in caves and he had part of the prophecy but not all of the prophecy was fulfilled, like Bethlehem and Jerusalem. But that wasn't the fulfilled promise, that's not the perfect will either, so all we have to be is in alignment.

Then years can go by, the Lord showed me the years went by, and it still was fulfilled! So I want this life to be not just the first promise in Samuel 16 but the fulfilment of Samuel 24. Those chapters are just like years going by so you have to get out there because you are preaching and teaching to Muslims, to Pakistani's and all kinds of people. You need to spread out to America too, so I see tent revivals like Oral Roberts and these need to be not online but you need to be in person! So we need big ticket items to help begin fund this ministry for God's glory. Many more supporters will help you, Jon!

HIGH WITH THE MOST HIGH

So today a $1.5 million property was handed to me for a sale then all of a sudden this disappeared. I prayed that it would all be doubled and I declared triple sales!' Janet explained that one of the buyers needed a loan but couldn't get it for what she needed and she had to help this lady get her home. We were praying for 4 homes to be sold each month as part of our prophecy this year and Holy Spirit made angels hit me hard in confirmation as a sign and wonder!

Janet spoke to me about her brokerage to be paid off, and we declared the next State for her to take dominion in would be Maryland next to Virginia and then DC. (This was my past prophecy for her) It's important to believe and pray into your prophecies. We must contend for the promises that God has said regardless of tests and time frames! I hope the reader or hearer is feeling encouraged and tapping into your prophetic promises, and NOT giving up! Ministry needs to be more real not just for church, but for every day and accessible in every way – but please – do not burn out your ministers and please support them with finances otherwise it is so difficult and a lot of us feel like quitting the Ministry!

"Surely goodness and love will follow us all the days of our lives and we will dwell with the Lord forever."

—*Psalms 23:6*

Janet explained it's like paying off the mafia for the first 3 months for that brokerage so there's the legal ability to sell houses independently by being not just part of an estate agent, but by becoming one-and she will be a very powerful international agent because God does not lie! She said her current estate agent brokerage took 75% over the last month and a half. I know that we would be coming into breakthrough and that will include better health. This means less stress and great provisions.

CLOUDS, GIANTS AND HOUSES

Ministries are not ran on thin air. Everything we do is from instruction by our Lord, the captain of our salvation and through His faith within. When people realise that all parts of life are gifts and that we shouldn't and dare not take anything for granted, then we are in the daily realm of humility and then 'Let God have all the glory' isn't just a Christian statement. It is absolute fact.

Apart from Christ and his grace, which is His power in us, we can do absolutely nothing. No amount of hard work, help or promises from people will do it, only the grace of God to know, realise and experience this revelation will keep us truly humble before the Lord. The person God will use must be humble and not have any self-reliance within them, they must not and cannot have any pride in them, because it is truly God, our sovereign Lord that does all things!

Knowing these things and experiencing them during all seasons of life has actually released a deeper sense of satisfaction and peace, deeper peace than surface level peace than most people have. Even success can be an idol, and although God wants us to be successful, He must truly get all the glory, we must know that <u>it is Christ in us that ensures success</u>.

So many people are working from their own strength and own resources, no wonder why so many people get burnt out and it is possible to miss God's blessings and God's best simply because we have been working from our own strength. So many people I know are in survival mode and not revival mode, but we are changing season!

Janet must know that with all of life's obstacles, sometimes things slow us down and this is for God's glory, other times God slows us down so we learn to trust him more and therefore God is the one who speeds things up! He makes all things happen whether we realise it or not! Our help comes from the Lord maker of Heaven and Earth.

HIGH WITH THE MOST HIGH

We spoke about moving home in the future and we gave the whole vision and all our past frustrations to the Lord during prayer. A new way of life is coming forth and we are still doing our best in this ministry to help others around the world, providing work and food and other needs that arise especially taking care of others health including orphans. If God puts it upon your heart to support us, you won't regret it and God will reward you, please just get in touch. You will be blessed in getting the gospel around the world. Many evangelistic miracle crusades are being planned, so we look forward to those times! I said to her that we were isolated for too long and needed to find somewhere that was spiritually hot. You can have the anointing and have zero love so the right place and church life community is needed for my Mum in Christ. I want her to feel like she's in a family and that she's got friends, and it will get really hot and it will be a blessing for her because that's what she needs. I really want to see her happy and healthy, because she has really gone through terrible loss and depression. I know I cannot make others happy, only God can do that, but things must change! I do not believe that suffering lasts forever, it may be long but it's not forever! Half the time we can be suffering prophetically for the sake of others in the future so that God will be glorified.

Miracles, signs, salvations and wonders are attached to us and the enemy cannot take us out, he doesn't have the power as we are divinely protected by Christ and he doesn't have the jurisdiction to do what he wants. <u>All of his attacks have failed in advance,</u> so we might as well keep our peace by having the word of God firmly planted in us! Satan has to pay back everything he stole when God gives the orders, so I wouldn't let that bother you either, we just have to continue on, press on, and trust God who absolutely can be trusted. We know that we have an amazing prophecy from God in our life, and as time goes by the anointing breaks the yoke and we all come into a deeper freedom, not just a new location.

Janet said that because Mum is 72, she will be more tired with diabetes, bad eye sight and daily pain and be prone to feel like giving up more

CLOUDS, GIANTS AND HOUSES

especially as she has had many disappointments and losses. I agreed and said in the natural her health was being attacked severely and her mobility was affected daily. I explained that when I took her to Llandudno she struggled with walking. We are praying against mum in a wheelchair!

In my dreams I saw her in one for a short period of time and this turned into such great glory. I still believe she will be an amazing teacher of the Gospel and we are also standing on a prophetic vision which has been repeated to me over the years that Granddad is coming out of the care home, we want to see God's justice especially as he is now 100! I believe these Abrahamic prophecies that seem so crazy, they can still be fulfilled! They might seem to be just for our family but they will be an example to the world that God is real, he fulfils his Word, and that he truly cares about us. When I prophecy I often have to release the 'crazy words' and stand on radical faith in Christ for them.

The Lord spoke to me when we were having our fellowship which I call 'prophetic overlap' saying 'Debs is going to be trusted with the mansions in the future! She's a real estate agent that will have every state in America.' The Lord said 'He will entrust you to Hollywood style mansions if you are faithful with a little you will be faithful with a lot. See God's going to put you in Florida as well, and He is going to entrust you to all different types of properties, because if you can be trusted to handle small rentals, to larger properties, then to mansions, He is going to do that for you! 'So I am going back to what God said at the beginning of the year which was to sell 2 to 4 houses every month and when we are on this target, that is when you'll see the fulfilment of this prophecy as you are one part of Kingdom financier, but the other part is your ministry, which God is saying is sweet.'

I believe I am a preacher and a revelatory teacher, and I am a prophet too, but in this year and season I know where I am being used in the teaching revelations direction, and the revival work in Pakistan online and it is so important to recognise your lane and stay in it, to avoid being in your own strength avoiding any confusion.

HIGH WITH THE MOST HIGH

So I saw Jan to be just like Marie Licciardo in her anointing and that was what God is training her up for in the future as well as being a powerful kingdom financier which was prophesied to her in person by Kim Clement who is now in Heaven. I encouraged her that when that level of anointing was on her she could really see into people's lives to prophecy to them. I explained the different types of oil and how Christ will bring the body into his fullness in time. I saw that her oil wasn't always being used, the liar, the devil was trying to sabotage her.

But we have to forget what he's doing, she will get her sales, she will get her happiness back and in faith we will start meeting together online and in person. (It is all up to God!) We have been to many supernatural meetings, and I am seeing myself conduct interviews like Sid Roth and even Jan's father has raised people from the dead as they flat lined in hospital and he led them to Jesus last minute! We are going to be doing more meetings on zoom and I will preach the gospel, get a worshipper and we will see his remarkable oil coming out for the glory of God.

The attacks have been very intense and who can identify with this? The greatest lovers get the greatest attacks. I see a Zoom church gathering and Marie is like us being at the well, and we need each other I don't know if our meetings will be once a week or once a month, but it's going to start soon as I have already been a Pod bean - podcast minister.

I believe September is sweet and so we are coming into the sweetness of God and Janet has often got sweet words to give out to people and God will give both the finance, ability to make and keep wealth flowing and grow in this prophetic dynamic ministry. God will give you your heart's desires as he makes dreams come true! But be prepared to let all the vision in you DIE!!

Everything is coming to pass that's why it's seen as an attack and I see her getting future real estate leads round California and places like that and I know that's way beyond her wildest dreams but I told her 'I see you and I see these celebrities and rich clients saying 'Hey can you sell my house for me?' You are well known real estate broker and I need you to sell my house for me, because let me tell you something, you

CLOUDS, GIANTS AND HOUSES

have an apostolic kingdom calling for selling people's properties! You have got that!

Janet confirmed that I was prophesying correctly! A Muslim man wanted her to help him sell his town house so he could buy a million dollar house and she was showing him up to 9 million dollar homes. She said 'you didn't even know, I didn't even have a chance to tell you! I got to speak to a Muslim by business man and told him a deal based on referrals so he would get 1 or 2% I gave him advice not to spend 10,000 a month on a mortgage and I would be fully able to find him a pretty home that would suit his needs that was Saturday, the next day he had a big barbecue for his mosque friends to tell all his friends about me!'

(This goes to show that despite major attacks, my prophecies do come to pass! Praise Jesus! I am a prayer winner and I refuse to give up!
Even if the blessing is not for me, I will get my reward in due season.)

Janet said how important it is to mix with different kinds of people and certainly not judge them for a different faith. 'In front of everyone he said you were right! I can trust you!' Because later he explained how he should never buy online for 10k a month mortgage.'

(I appreciate these figures may not mean much to you but I put this story in as a testimony that God answers prayers and that the sums of big money and sales for high ticket items can be given to the righteous and here is a warning they can also be taken away!) He was very impressed because she used wisdom in the Lord and this opens up a new community in the mosque and she prays a blessing on the homes asking that the new resident's will find Jesus there. How wonderful! To conclude it was so good to see Janet built up in the Faith, fully confident and fully able in Christ to sell houses. It is so important to encourage others especially when they feel down as everyone is at different parts of this journey and we all need encouragement at some point in our lives. More and more homes will be sold and this prophecy for her will come to pass and favour has been placed upon her despite all challenges.

HIGH WITH THE MOST HIGH

This is how we have to learn to see things then we will not feel insecure by believing Satan's lies and accusations. We are just being tested by God and God is fully able to keep us in his heavenly peace and provide for us as we continue to work for him faithfully and we know that He will not let us down despite all obstacles, sacrifices and even persecution. God is still with us and bringing that part of his prophetic vision to come to pass. We can fully trust Christ Jesus to help us in every way for his future glory! Amen.

Sadly, since the writing of this book we fell out and Janet did not help me each month to support the ministry and she did not help the orphans and she did not help my Mum. She made us both feel very unwell, worse than before! She wasted a lot of my time, and although I have forgiven her, I have stepped back from that friendship that very badly turned into another betrayal. You have to be very careful with who you make friends with and you have to let the promises you make be in line with God's Spirit otherwise you will hurt a lot of people and this is something that makes me feel very sad but instead of dwelling on it, I forgive, move on and stay in Christ. High with the Most High and God binds up the broken hearted. May God do the same for you if you have ever been through such a terrible ordeal. Christ have mercy and comfort all who grieve and mourn in Zion. We are only fortified in Jesus Christ and not in Man. Amen.

Chapter *Eight*
PRAISE DURING PERSECUTION

(From the 4th September)
REVELATION: REJOICING ALWAYS!

I was in my Sunday Zoom meeting with Pastor Robert Pears who has a fantastic revival YouTube channel and during it I received a powerful vision and deep revelation. Robert said, 'We need to stay in that place of repentance so we stay in that place of blessed assurance, and one lady said how we get this assurance from spending time in the secret place, otherwise we will not understand and we will not get blessed assurance!' Revivalist Robert set me on fire in the spirit during this meeting and I said how I had been listening to Shambach on YouTube about not worrying. That preaching was a bit explosive but he said, 'Rejoice in the Lord ALWAYS' I say it again: Rejoice in the lord always! So I wondered well, how is that possible? How can you rejoice in God always? (At this point the anointing was shaking and heating up my hands!) So I asked the Lord, 'what is going on?! And Robert said 'It's the key to open heaven; It's the key to breakthrough!'

I was thinking about Jan Huss and how he didn't even feel pain during burning, but even before the burning point it was amazing because he was in a prison and he was rejoicing! And again we could think about Paul and Silas rejoicing opening the heavens, the angelic encounters and then I was thinking about Stephen who was stoned and these things gave me fire in spirit and made me feel wow! Oh Lord! Oh goodness! What glory!

Robert Pears was also speaking about seasons and how he didn't like the cold of winters and the Lord said to me 'It's water into wine before it's time! That is exactly what we are going into, we are going into that holy dimension of <u>rejoicing in the Lord always which is a totally supernatural thing</u> when we let go and let God and in the pain we praise God anyway; It will come out of us. We can't help it! This is what I do and I am going to do it even more whether I feel like it or not! Whether I am hurting or not, whether I am in pain or not! Whether I am betrayed or not, I will still give MY GOD ALL MY PRAISE!!

The Rivers of Living water came out of Robs teaching and it's just amazing and I just can't help but feel that awesome energy that comes out of him because he is such an anointed teacher, he really delivers the Word in a powerful way which releases peace to the listener. May the Holy Spirit help us not to forget: that we can actually rejoice in the Lord always! The reason why I am saying about seasons is because <u>we can actually shift the seasons!</u>

Rob doesn't like winter, I don't like winter and yet God is saying to us ' In the winter we can still rejoice, and so we can bring summer - which is the heavenly summer into our winters, into our life, into a different dimension- we can bring this revelation into the middle of winter! So that revelation woke me up and I still find myself astonished! <u>So in pain we can still find his name!</u> We can still encounter God!

PRAISE DURING PERSECUTION

Robert Pears was excited and he also said how the warfare has increased on the earth we need to keep our eyes fixed on Jesus in order to get his perspective on things and not allow our flesh to consume us! He said how we were going into a new season and we are in an exciting time despite the difficult things going on in the earth. 'In my spirit I am very, very disturbed by the politicians and I feel like it's almost like Nazi Germany in the 30's, the Jews knew what was coming, but because we are terrified of the coming persecution, so we are being quiet. And I feel like Christians know what's coming but there's so much pressure being put on us, I find that my messages are being censored and I'm like 'I'm nice!'

I don't get into a lot of controversy but they are censoring me and so I realise what is coming. How much of that we will feel? I don't know, I do believe there is a final move of God Revival coming though and He is really beginning to work on us. He is looking for a church that is pure, holy and we are meant to be a shining light in this hour so if you are going through it, it's God pruning and cleaning, purifying His bride. So we are living in a critical hour.

I look around, the natural eyes get concerned but the spiritual eyes get excited. We get to see that previous generations longed to see! You and I have an opportunity to experience that. I read great literature from the 19th and 20th century all talking about this great revival. They knew something was coming. There's a certain level that we need. You can't stay at the same level you have to receive his grace, you have to have a break to get refreshed because of the times. So you may be stretched and prepared as this new season is coming.

It's like when you are running a marathon there's certain stages where you just have to keep a low pace, and then there's parts where you have to begin to sprint and give it everything you've got, and we are about to enter one of those seasons so get ready Hallelujah!

HIGH WITH THE MOST HIGH

(I absolutely love his teaching which is why I have included it to promote his fantastic work) Also this word confirms what Prophetess Marie says;' you're in the Marathon not a sprint. You are in it for the long haul Jonathan!'

Robert says 'It is challenging. These trials are hard, the pressure is on and it's not like one little attack; It's all these different attacks! One way you know the Devil's behind it all is that he overdoes it! <u>The Devil comes in like a flood but the lord comes in with mightier flood!</u> (His standard of righteousness) The enemy will try to overwhelm you, to persuade you and he always tries to convince you; well clearly you missed it! You stepped out of the grace of God! That's why you've got to rejoice and be glad with a soft heart so that God can easily convict and put things right so you can stand with confidence and continue to run the race!

People will be speaking into your life to condemn you, blame you and convince you to quit and they will produce evidence! This is why you need to have a relationship in the secret place where you remain soft and in a holy fear of the Lord-saying ' God I feel like I'm missing it, put me right!!' Give God the opportunity and time to teach you in the word so you can do the works for God in that relationship of intimacy, love and reverence. The anointing will make it easy and light. He will teach you how to walk right and how to walk strong.' (Please follow Pastor Robert pears on YouTube – Pure Heart Ministries)

Robert pears is an excellent communicator from God's word and his heart, he discerns the evil in our times but he assures us of the safety and peace we get from God in the secret place. Amen.

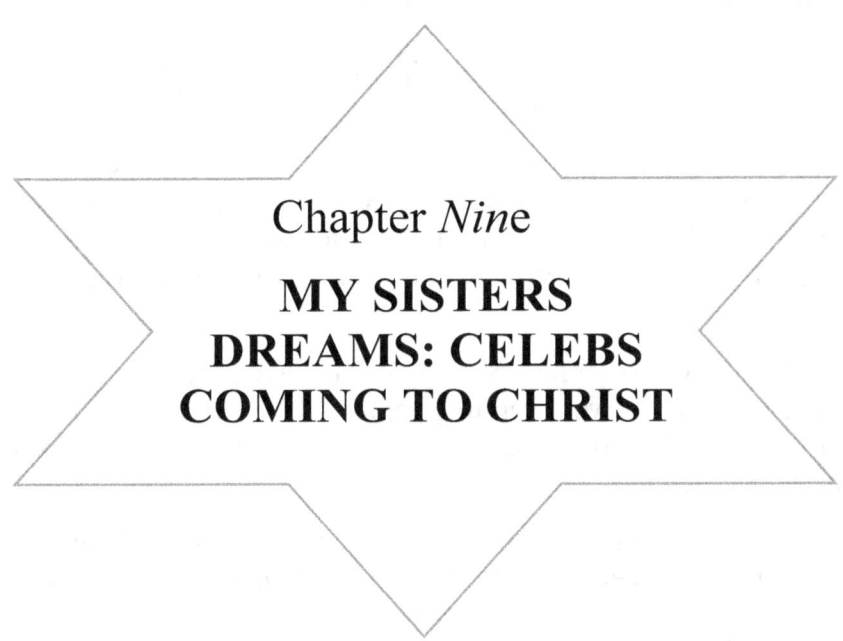

Chapter *Nine*

MY SISTERS DREAMS: CELEBS COMING TO CHRIST

MY SISTERS DREAMS: CELEBS COMING TO CHRIST

My prophetic sister Amy often has very insightful dreams so I have included them as part of the journal part of my book. She was staying with us in Wales at this time. She said this: 'Just the other day I saw online news that rap singer Eminem has been confessing Jesus Christ as his saviour and he has been collaborating with Kanye West (who has started a church) who says now that ' Jesus is the only super star, and he came onto Joel Osteen's show and many celebs are going to his church and it's very musical.

Now from 2001 I dreamt that I saw Eminem's head in a tank of water and at the time I didn't feel that it meant something bad, I felt that it had

HIGH WITH THE MOST HIGH

a good meaning and it came to me that he was going to be saved. It could mean holy water and Mum added that it could mean the pride being cut off him and being given a new head could represent this.

Jon: Yes, I saw pride too! I saw the old identity but that his head will be replaced with the headship of Christ.

My sister also saw herself rapping on the stage with him but she didn't understand this as she is not a rapper! This reminded her of previous musical prophecies and with her BF being able and anointed for prophetic rap and music. Now, you must understand, this was over 20 years ago!

Jon: Yes, we all prayed for him years ago and I have prayed for Marilyn Manson as well. There were certain people and musicians that were in the 90's that seem to have God's hand on them. It is good to secretly pray for others including celebrities.

Amy: Yes and I have prayed for Johnny Depp and Amber Heard and there was a trial between them. He was open and honest saying that he struggled with drugs and drink but that he is not violent to her, he has only kicked objects and things! (Haven't we all) Lots of people did believe him and not her because there were weird spirits around that time. She needs salvation as well so we pray for her as well.

Just before the Ukraine war was announced I dreamt that I saw Putin and Trump and for some strange reason we were working for Trump and we were like friends with him and he was a grandfather figure to us younger ones which was really weird!

And with Putin, I was not sure what it meant, and now he is responsible for so many deaths. But, in this dream I saw Putin in a good light. He was like a different person just like Trump! Then suddenly the war was announced and that was very disturbing.

Jon: I told a man in the Miracle Cafe in Bangor that Aliss Cresswell set up, that I had already had a repeat vision 3 times that Putin will be

MY SISTERS DREAMS: CELEBS COMING TO CHRIST

saved! He was talking about Putin and the current war and I rest assured him that Jesus can do absolutely anything!

One time we went to there and one man asked me 'how do you know you are hearing from God? Especially for big prophecies?' I explained that Prophets do get things wrong and we shouldn't want to stone them to death! And I told that man that I saw 'Putin would be saved by God!' And he said 'well I like your optimism! And he asked again 'but how do you know you are really hearing from God and that it's not your mind?' I said, 'because it's faith and I've been shown 3 times' and he said 'well that's not a confirmation!' and I said well, I still believe what God showed me, and I still believe that Putin can be saved and I think we need to be praying for Putin and others to be saved, so we get compassion for these people that have been used as dictators, because there's something behind them always that makes them the way they are.'

And the man just said, 'well he's just nuts, he causes wars!' and I said well, that's just one way of looking at it but Heaven looks at these people differently. God looks at the heart.' He looked very shocked and was almost disgusted with what I said, which was out of prophetic obedience, so it had to be revealed at that time! My sister said how I was being controversial but then she said ' Let's remember about soul in the Bible' and I added in 'Nebuchadnezzar!'

So God can do it and Mum said 'Oh I wish God had done it before the war!' and then we prayed for everyone affected by the war everywhere, then we went back to the subject about Eminem.

Our 90's rapper slim shady said 'He is my Shepherd. I am armed with Jesus!' It's amazing as his eyes look completely different, he's bearded now and looks at peace. It's really amazing! Eminem is a Grammy award winning celebrity and this is awesome to see celebs coming to Christ. Gods hand is on these people and we've got no idea of the extent of what God's going to do.

HIGH WITH THE MOST HIGH

I heard the Lord say 'I am going to dismantle the new world order in Hollywood!' The Lord also revealed to me there is a fake side of this coming revival. There's a 'cashing in on the gospel move' to make money which God sees very seriously as He can see everyone's motives and He will test all of his people.

My sister found this a very weird thing to say when I revealed this revelation so I said; Well, not really because the kingdom is rich and so if you are rich anyway and you pretend to be saved at a time of when there's going to be a massive move of God - then you'd get even richer! Do you see what I mean? Then we are heading into dangerous territory but I want to clarify, I don't believe that Eminem or Justin Bieber for example, are part of this. Now God reveals that a lot of people will get even more corrupt and perverse and the Lord says ' You've got to watch out for the Golden whale because there's a fake prosperity only rich Jesus which is the Golden whale and He is going to take them out! This was revealed to me in a prophetic dream in 2020 during a revival on podbean with the Ghanaians and others from South Africa and some of those 'Men of God' absolutely loved and worshiped money, mammon and the golden whale! Now with people like Eminem they have already gone to rock bottom, you can tell in his lyrics.

Many celebrities have hit rock bottom and have been very humbled despite their popularity, fame and fortune. We must remember that they are only people! Amy added that Eminem comes from a trailer park background and in America they call some people 'white trash' it's a saying. Mum said rather insightfully, 'They get picked up by the illuminati or cult in operation as soon as they decided to go seriously into the business entertainment industry! 'and even my sister said God wants to rescue people from the illuminati, there's been more than one person that had the courage from God to leave and has revealed the truth about things just like people have come out of Isis, may God protect them in Jesus mighty name.

Some more celebrities were spoken of and we prayed for more of them regardless of satanic cults or not! May there be a complete heavenly Kingdom invasion to the celeb world and especially for a new Azuza

MY SISTERS DREAMS: CELEBS COMING TO CHRIST

street revival in Hollywood—prepare for impact! In Jesus mighty name. Amen.

We as a family continue praying for celebs as much as ordinary people as God is no respecter of persons and God has an Awakening coming!! Never let it leave your heart! Never give up in prayer you don't know what your prayers are doing, so we will continue being prayerful whether satanic forces like it or not. Not even war or the rumours of war can stop us from passionately prayerfully believing in the Lord Jesus Christ and all the nations are His!

> *"Ask of me, and I shall give [thee] the heathen [for] thine inheritance, and the uttermost parts of the earth [for] thy possession."*
>
> —*(Psalms 2:4)*

Chapter *Ten*
FAMILY DREAMS: RESTORATION

Family Dreams. From 4th September 22.
FAMILY RESTORATION.

I will let my dear sister Amy take over here and tell you some more of her dreams. We often have prophetic conversations and I believe this encouragement is sharpening her spiritual sight and prophetic gift that Satan has tried to sabotage but no weapon formed shall prosper! Instead the church is becoming so weaponised that we are morphing into weapons!!

Amy: Mum, Jon and I were travelling around and we were in various cities and there were also parks we went to as well. Now in some previous dreams I have had a lot of things stolen from me and usually it's like bags which I feel is symbolic. It's usually bags being stolen, or getting emptied on the streets or getting lost (Mum also has these

FAMILY DREAMS: RESTORATION

dreams!) So this is the second dream that I can remember of things coming back to me, and I believe it's for all of us! I dreamt of clothes hanging up on clothes hangers at bus stops and me finding different stuff of mine that had been lost or stolen, sort of randomly just around! I think we were walking around prophetically, praying and wanting God to work through us around the areas. This was the general feeling of the dream. Strangely enough there was also this posh kind of underclothes I would say that they used to have in the olden days like corsets, and I don't know why because I have never had those clothes, it's like the kind of clothes the actors wear as part of their costumes like in Downtown Abbey for example. These things were old fashioned out of place in a modern city setting!

But I still feel that the dream represents God restoring things that the Devil stole from us! They are coming back to us and this includes health. We were just talking about how Satan is always targeting our health be it physical, emotional, mental, or accidents and causing as much chaos and trauma as possible, even fibro myalgia— all of it and he thinks he is stopping our destiny but in Jesus name we are going to get greater blessings out of it all. Let's proclaim it and pray:

Thank you Lord that you are going to give back even more that's been stolen like with Job and Joseph and every example there is, so thank you Lord we believe that! We are alive for such a time as this and God's called us and maybe that's why we have been through so much to such an extent and now you can work through us! In Jesus name.

So we keep thinking about this and I feel like God is going to work through us to solve so many various different kinds of situations, problems, circumstances to heal and restore his people and we can now say that we can identify with practically anything and anyone through all kinds of suffering. Even if we haven't been in jail, we can say we know what it feels like to be in jail! A couple of us have even been!!

Jon: Yes and we have been falsely accused and we have all had money stolen from us and had people look down on us for being poor and out of work and people have refused to help us when we have been suffering to the point of complete rejection and abandonment from man including false promises, lies, blame, shame, rejection, accusation, slander leaving us wounded, sad and at great loss but God has never failed us! He has seen the cost! It has been absolutely crazy! A very unprecedented level of strange suffering all prophetic, nothing is wasted, it is all for God's glory. It all works together! Praise Jesus. (You can read more about this in my Tested by God series)

I have had many dreams going back to where I have previously lived (Which is pretty common in dreams, but don't take it for granted, God may be speaking to you and there can often be dreaming patterns that you should try to keep track of or at least notice these. That's why dreams are often the way God speaks to us, but we need to pray and ask God for the meanings and value them even if they seem strange or irrelevant.

And recently in my dreams I have been going back to lots and lots of my old creativity and I had to sift through the things to decide what was needed and what was not. Jesus was giving me very colourful and very creative dreams and just reminding me saying: 'Hey you are actually an artist as well an author and this is still part of your calling. I am still going to use the art and design that you have laid down on my altar. I am still going to use everything!'

In those dreams there was old clothing that I used to wear as a teenager when I was gothic, and hippy quite expressive! I also dreamt about all the old inspiration that I used to collect.

Amy: So old clothing may have actually been more symbolic than what we realised!

Jon: Yes there's lots of stuff about going through my old things. Some of it was mouldy and had to be thrown out which is interesting, there was a whole room of inspiration, there was a whole room full of all my random stuff that I've had over the years since a child, it involved everything I had collected, all things seemed all over the place but

FAMILY DREAMS: RESTORATION

somehow, it was on organised mess. There were different years that had gone by and all the collections of things were from those years. So it was like a collection room, and then after sometime of exploration I had to leave and I was only allowed to take a few things with me and I took some sparkling bright green fabric, a green frog ornament and a book. Very childlike!

Then I had to let go of the whole room with all its old contents and memories but then the Lord spoke to me in the dream saying 'Son, you can come back to this room anytime, so you can take what you need for now, but only a few things can be taken' so it was almost like God gave my authority to take what I needed from the past to get it into my present and get some healing because I took the colour green. That was very important and symbolic for new life-now this introduced me to seeing in the spirit even more and I started to see a Green angel! We had lots of green angels in our garden and that surprised me! But is anything impossible for God? We limit Christ Jesus with our religious consciousness! This is all about RESTORATION! So don't give up! No matter how hard, painful it looks like the enemy has scattered everything; but <u>everything will be restored</u>. God is still in control even if we feel like He is not! That's a revelation of His holy sovereignty that few people are talking about!

Amy: I had another dream of things being stolen. I was on a train, I had two bags and I was on the phone trying to speak to customer services of the rail companies trying to locate them and then I looked behind me and they were there on the seat and I was praising God and this was a testimony to the man beside me and I knew it was a miracle! In real life these types of events can be extremely stressful especially when you are traveling.

Jon: I see that to be symbolic because God wants us to count the small miracles and sometimes we have to open our eyes and look around with the eyes of faith. Even if the bags were missing God can still bring them back. He is fully able to help us in all circumstances and bring angels to protect us, shield us, even hide us or our belongings if necessary, God wants to look after us and let us know that we are safe in his hands, knowing that <u>nothing is impossible for God</u>. The train reveals that we are going somewhere! We are not stagnant.

There was an occurrence of an American lady who wanted her slate tiles that came from her roof to be used in the village for a greater reason and she was spiritual and God used that opportunity for me to witness the gospel to her and she had never heard it the way I put it with revelations- so God knows how to reach each personal differently. This was an answer to prayer because myself and Mum prayed for her to get paving slabs from the village or nearby and the lady was alternative so she asked her house 'where do you want to go?' And do you want to go round the village? Are you needed there?'

This made my sister laugh and I hope it does you too! She wanted parts of her home with cherished memories to go to a new home and she invited us into bless the home which I did wearing sandals which I took off so I walked in there with bare feet! You couldn't make it up!

Amy: that's so bizarre, who does that? You might do that about animals if you were getting them rehomed but not with parts of your house!

Jon: well, she was in tune with the earth energies, but these are all in tune with God and that's what we don't realise!

This is complete confirmation to show that the alternatives are going to come into the kingdom as God will be revealed to all different kinds of people.

Conclusion:

Whether they are celebrities or alternatives, prisoners or ordinary people that don't know Christ they all have the opportunity to know Jesus and can be saved in his holy heavenly Kingdom. Restoration of all things will occur and God may give us somethings that we need from the past but we need to be prepared to sacrifice and leave the rest. Let the past stay in the past and do not go back to it unless God reveals why you need to look at something from it. God can restore dreams, things

FAMILY DREAMS: RESTORATION

you have believed in from the past although you have disregarded them by not seeing their importance or value.

Not all dreams are from God, some are weird and cryptic, so ask Holy Spirit and others, have prayerful fellowship and conversations about them and be aware of God speaking to you through your dreams. God is revealing a lot at this time and we need to be watchful and mindful especially during our night hours. God speaks in unusual ways!

> *"And he answered and told them, Elias verily cometh first, and restoreth all things; and how it is written of the Son of man, that he must suffer many things, and be set at nought. But I say unto you, That Elias is indeed come, and they have done unto him whatsoever they listed, as it is written of him. Verse – the restoration of all things."*
>
> *—Mark 9:12—13*

> *"And I will restore to you the years that the locust hath eaten, the cankerworm, and the caterpiller, and the palmerworm, my great army which I sent among you. And ye shall eat in plenty, and be satisfied, and praise the name of the Lord your God, that hath dealt wondrously with you: and my people shall never be ashamed."*
>
> *—Joel 2:25—26*

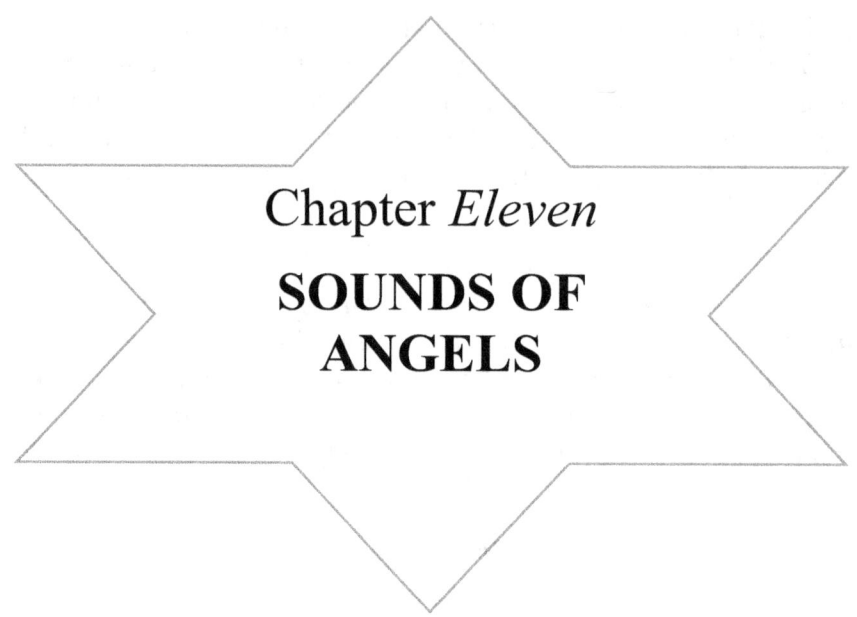

Chapter *Eleven*
SOUNDS OF ANGELS

The next four chapters are based on my past conversations with my old friend Janet. I feel sadness recalling them and I must let go of any pain and any unforgiveness is not an option. I pray for those people who have let me down so badly and caused such bitter stress. May there be a turnaround and repentance. If not, I will continue on with my Jesus.

From 4th September
THE SOUNDS OF ANGELS.

Jon: This is where in the word of God true strength comes from. By abiding in the Word Vine it builds our relationship with God. It shows us that we can trust God no matter what happens. The Word shows us the strategies that God will give us. I saw this for you and the strategy is this:

1. WAIT
2. ALIGN
3. REMAIN

Jan: I just don't want to wake up and have 10 years go by just because I missed the perfect will because I wanted the permissible will!

Jon: Yes we don't want the permissible will and I hear God say, 'You don't want the passive will either!' we don't want to be passive people. The Bible says, 'Be perfect as your father in heaven is perfect'. To be perfect means to be in that supernatural dimension of perfection. 'Holy spirit brings absolute perfection!' to quote Kathryn Kuhlman and we need to nail this quote to our hearts because THE HOLY SPIRIT WILL BRING ABSOLUTE PERFECTION! Amen. We all need the glory realm which brings absolute supernatural perfection including weight loss or weight gain and time redemption! When you go to Heaven, its absolute perfection.

Jan: Yes we are also very busy in heaven!!

Jon: Exactly! I said to Mum the other day, don't go thinking it's all quiet up there, don't go thinking you can just go get a long rest, we need to up our game! I tell you what God will take you to the prayer waterfalls and all you'll hear is this roaring of prayer and you might think well I thought it all supposed to be quiet here! Lol. And God could take you to that part of it and it will be very loud! So don't go thinking you are just going to lay down on some grass and have it easy! Not a chance!

Jan explained that she feels encouraged and rejuvenated by our fellowship and she humbles herself for me to pastor her one to one! I am greatly honoured and I see this as a preparation time before more public ministry. Billy Graham had 9 years to prepare and he said it still wasn't enough! So I need all the time I've got and more before times of more exposure, after all, we just want to glorify Jesus and do ministry well even though God allows for our weak humanity and not our lame religiosity!

Jan told me how she sold her first house in June, then she got three more homes to sell, but even though some fell through, we kept praying for each other despite all the trials. She even had to call a man in Korea who was interested in buying a home. Two buyers were taken away so then we prayed for two more buyers back as God can do anything, in his perfect time: nothing is too difficult for him—we just need to have faith.

Jan: There was a lady who worked for the World Bank and I ended up taking walks with her and she agreed to advertise for me so I will be able to give her 1% of the sale! Isn't that awesome? Jan's sister who is a creative lady and author is into Buddhism and witchcraft and got a tattoo and this really upset Jan, but I explained to her that I was once into wicca/witchcraft and I had to go through it for God's glory, so it was the same for her sister. Jan then began to see that her sister is not giving away her life to the Devil and we re-affirmed her sister's prophetic destiny will be in Christ. She also went to a shrine and said it was the best spiritual experience she's ever known but what a lie!

I saw this as false unity with darkness as words were spoken over her by the new age person and we just interceded and cut curses by the blood of Jesus. I heard the Lord say 'It's dominion over Buddhism and witchcraft that she will get! She will be saved, delivered and then get the Dominion.' I prophesied: 'Because she's got a mark of God on her forehead, not a witches mark, she's going to have complete dominion over witchcraft, Buddhism and the New Age and be able to save many people from that world.' so she's just in the 'story' part of her life where it looks like she's gone away from God, and it looks like she's dedicating herself to other stuff and pagan practises but God is still in this! She will be so astounded by the anointing on your life.

SOUNDS OF ANGELS

Your parents are also supposed to be in security which is not just financial but also emotional security and your father specifically needs spiritual security and he himself also feels that the King of glory has let him down, which God hasn't. Now that's one of the reasons why you go through your battles and there's some subconscious anger towards the Lord but it's alright because Jesus is doing all that, and He took it all on the cross! (I hope and pray those conversations and revelations help someone. This is why I have been called into ministry!)

So our strategy is to wait, to align and remain in the perfect will of God despite storms.

Jesus then revealed another secret to me. REVELATION: ALL OF YOUR DEFEATS WERE REALLY VICTORIES! THEY JUST DONT LOOK LIKE IT YET.

So your defeats are down to your perception and for the grace of God - what is needed? The grace of God to reveal this revelation. They only look like defeats! And we need to tell the Devil that we are going to preach to ourselves and thank God for this revelation! But you see, they only look like defeats from Earth's perspective but in the spirit from Heavens perspective they are victories! For example, when a court case is lost, it really looks and feels like a defeat and politically you didn't win against the system but you did win in the realm of the spirit. Just like Katt Kerr actually won with her Trump prophecy (but not in the natural realm, as controversial as this is!) So all of Janet's so called 'defeats' like her house sales falling through, God tells me they are really secret victories. This is victory! This looks like defeat, and it feels like defeat and it's got the trauma of defeat, but it's actually a Hidden victory! So we must rejoice! (JOIN WITH JOY!)

It is really preparing us to go forward in faith and victory in a realm and with a revelation and authority knowing there is no defeat in Christ. There is only VICTORY and continual victory! It looks like delay and blockage but we don't realise what this is doing for us in the Heavenly places, after all, we are still only in human bodies, with human understanding.

HIGH WITH THE MOST HIGH

Jan: It is preparing us for the real alignment and will of God. The perfect will?

Jon: Yes absolutely! We have to <u>look</u> like we have failed and then God will get all the glory.

"For my thoughts [are] not your thoughts, neither [are] your ways my ways, saith the Lord. For [as] the heavens are higher than the earth, so are my ways higher than your ways, and my thoughts than your thoughts."

—Isaiah 55:8—9

Trust in the Lord with all thine heart; and lean not unto thine own understanding. In all thy ways acknowledge him, and he shall direct thy paths."

—(Proverbs 3:5—6

"Nay, in all these things we are more than conquerors through him that loved us."

—Romans 8:37

I explained to Janet that it was a huge honour to suffer for Christ prophetically and to be left destitute with nothing of this world in the natural because that's when the supernatural can really take over! Kathryn Kuhlman had to live in a car when she couldn't even get a drink of water because no one showed that they cared! She had to die a thousand deaths to self in order to be glorified in Jesus Christ!

This remarkable general lost her man, she had to walk away from the man that she loved, she had people turning against her because she wasn't allowed to preach as a woman. That was religion of course! So she had rejection from her family rejection from everyone around her and no one would even buy her a bottle of water in America! And she questioned in shock, 'What is this Lord?' So Janet has also been through a similar thing - it looked like a defeat but it was a secret 'Kathryn Kuhlman anointing glory'! This is a supernatural calling and I myself identify with Lonnie Frisbee and others, and we are all together in the spirit as no one actually died!! We are all together in Christ, no separation, alive forever more in his huge heavenly family! How glorious!

You see God's got a funny sense of humour where He looks at history and lets it be slightly repeated but in a new way by putting us all together in the Heavenly realms! Even though Satan appears to get the credit for the evil in our planet and atmosphere, all of this will be turned around for good and God can see the final, finished outcome and it's complete victory in Christ! We have our own anointings but God also empowers them by the prayers of the saints on Earth and outside of the earth! I had a dream about Kathryn Kuhlman and I knew without a shadow of a doubt that she and many other saints did not die!! They are literally more alive than ever before, all gathered together as Revivalists and praying for the next great glory awakening!! I feel this revelation burning in me every day regardless of circumstances! To God be the glory!

REVELATION: THE SAINTS NEVER 'DIED' AND THEY NEVER WILL DIE!

"For our light affliction, which is but for a moment, worketh for us a far more exceeding [and] eternal weight of glory; While we look not at the things which are seen, but at the things which are not seen: for the things which are seen [are] temporal; but the things which are not seen [are] eternal."

—**2 Corinthians 4:17—18**

We have got mantles in Heaven as an inheritance from the saints and these actual people are alive in spirit! They are there praying for us to have these amazing revelations and experiences in Christ Jesus. It's the same Holy Spirit in them that is in us! So the same Holy Spirit that was living in Kathryn Kuhlman is the same Holy Spirit that's living within you!! It's not like the person is exactly the same as they were on earth, quite the contrary! Everything they went through on earth, although that's part of it, has worked together for them an eternal weight of glory but we must understand:

- There's a calling for defeat

- There's a calling that makes everything look like it's all gone wrong, it's all ruined, it's all been sabotaged, it's all lost but, which is actually tremendous victory in the spirit!

- And then not only that but we also have these amazing patriarchs and matriarchs in heaven praying for us! They are literally praying or beaming in the revelations to us, full of Holy Spirit joy that really all of our defeats were secret victories all for God's glory! Thank you Jesus.

So if you are being 'attacked' and all of these strange trials just keep on increasing—it's time to rejoice in the Lord always— not just when you feel like it because of your high calling, this is the reason why and God has created you to do good works in Him in advance!

"For we are his workmanship, created in Christ Jesus unto good works, which God hath before ordained that we should walk in them."

—**Ephesians 2:10**

"Before I formed thee in the belly I knew thee; and before thou camest forth out of the womb I sanctified thee, [and] I ordained thee a prophet unto the nations."

—*Jeremiah 1:5*

Chapter *Twelve*
PRAYERS FROM HEAVEN: REVELATION

PRAYERS FROM HEAVEN RELEASE REVELATION!

I am really into the heart of God and I really want to know what he thinks about things on a day to day basis and what he sees and sometimes He shows me more in the Spirit, but I have to humble myself, pray, believe and wait patiently for Him. I feel this is a key to learning how to be in the Spirit. By God's grace I even begin to understand things that are outside of the Bible because God is in the Bible yes, but he is also bigger than the Bible!

This chapter is based on my conversation with Janet.

HIGH WITH THE MOST HIGH

Janet said to me 'His word can't return to Him ....And I said in response, 'God will give you the desires of your heart, which is written in the WORD and God knows what's in our heart and the 'impossible' is His domain. It's not our domain yet, but we going to come into that domain and we must realise that in Christ, we are going to resurrect the dead! But half the time we are the ones that need the resurrection!

Jan: So we have to trust in God completely! Jon: Yes it must be daily trust, and we really can trust God because he never fails and he always wins triumphantly. So this supernatural realm of VICTORY is ours as part of our inheritance.

I always call it the forsaking of feelings. It's not like I'm just a hard stone, the thing is, I just refuse to acknowledge all of those feelings that breed mistrust of God and in Christs strength I refuse to let them dominate me, because half the time Satan takes advantage of that and twists feelings trying to make me feel a lot of random stuff, believing any lie he can try to sell to me so I am not giving the Devil the glory!

At the end of the day it's my stuff that I am working through with God and I am learning to trust Jesus more and more every day for the impossible. And then I have to be as a prophet prophesying the impossible things and even that stretches me further because when people come back to me and say ' Oh it's not happening and it's terrible man of God!' So my response is it might be, 'Oh, but God is wonderful! Just wait patiently please!'

So I will do what I can do, which is to praise and worship Jesus every day and then Heaven will come down, because I praise God in the pain every day! I sometimes spend so much time with God in praise and this opens up the praise realm and then the worship realm and then the glory realm and this awesome revelation comes from Ruth ward Heflin, who is alive forever more in glory and I am living proof that it works! Now the pain and suffering is still there but the thing is, I don't make it my focus, even though it tries to take my focus, my focus is always the Lord Jesus Christ in all circumstances. I have learned to be content, His goodness and His glory comes in, his wonderful heavenly reality floods my atmosphere and then when I am filled with Holy Spirit or even are very weak I will then prophecy to someone. I want to be in tune with Gods heart. God has us on His heart and I want to be joined to His heart despite the difficulties of this current life. I just want to be in tune with Christ's beating singing heart of: LOVE ETERNAL!

People say to me 'This has happened yet and I say 'we have to wait' so this period of time by waiting on God is all part of trusting Christ which includes the perfect will of God, so when we keep looking at Jesus: Jesus is completely perfect and He is all we need. This way we are able to keep our focus on God daily and the miracles will then flow! The Lord God waited on His father, he got away from the crowd and he is was human too much like 'I can't handle this today! I need to be with my daddy! I'm going to wait and pray I am going to align myself with Heaven and I am going to remain here until God's perfection comes out of me!' and He knew it! He was totally dependent on his Heavenly Father. He knew that's what he had to do and this is the same for us as ministers of the Gospel or business men, we need to wait on God and let Him work his perfection in us through dependent, humble prayer.

It's very easy to believe a lie but we need these rooted out of us in Jesus mighty name. Angels are being sent to help us to believe and receive these heavenly revelations, but these so called 'defeats' are not manifesting yet as victories, but God sees them all and his eyesight is very different to ours, so we need to humble ourselves to see in the Spirit and we have been severely tested on this!

If you write the word DEFEAT and you turn it on its head it will just be an upside down mess. But Jesus says ' I have flipped defeat on its head and turned it into complete VICTORY!' That's God!

I hope you begin to see that God takes something that we did wrong and then He turns it all around. You can be so easily aware of all the past defeats and all the shame that went with them and then suddenly God fixes it all. But you see child of God it's not just fixed and able to be broken again -He makes it completely perfect! God doesn't just do a patch up job, He does a perfect job. I remember these words from my home group in Cornwall where I lived for 7 years. When I was speaking with Janet, she was amazed because she had never seen that before. Praise Jesus!

All of your defeats- dear reader or listener: these defeats are collecting glory! We may have no idea what we are going through but we are collecting glory! DEFEAT (when in Christ) is really VICTORY! This is a revelation that removes religion and transforms nations! It all gets turned around! (See Romans 8:28)

So when we are going through all these terrible things and it looks like defeats and it feels like defeats and it feels like you are beyond worn out from all the stress and strain of life and we fail in battles and we think 'Oh that didn't work out! Where were you in this thing or that thing LORD? We exclaim in vain! God said to me that 'If you can look at that word defeat and see that I have already flipped it upside down, even though it may not make sense to you now, you'll see that I am standing on top of that WORD and it says VICTORY and then you'll see complete victory in every area of your life because of the defeats!'

"Fret not thyself because of evildoers, neither be thou envious against the workers of iniquity. For they shall soon be cut down like the grass, and wither as the green herb. Trust in the Lord, and do good; [so] shalt thou dwell in the land, and verily thou shalt be fed"

—Psalm 37:1—3

So these wicked people have already got all they need while the poor, needy and righteous have suffered and it hardly seems fair and they appear to have everything they need now, from a natural perspective and Jesus said the wicked are living for the things of this world, they have had their inheritance, where as we are not just waiting for an inheritance, but we are God's inheritance! God gets to INHERIT US! (See Ephesians 1: 1—12) so how can he inherit us? Here is the WORD.

PRAYERS FROM HEAVEN

Everything is happening to us because we are the living sacrifices of Christ! We are going through the defeat and that's turning into Christ's victory which he has already won for us in advance! The victory is assured to us in the spirit. I hope you can catch the revelation and then soon the waves of revelation waves will flood over you! Joy and fresh strength and health is being restored to someone reading this right now. Our glorious King of kings is watching us and He can see everything and He is excited. He says 'I know you and I will sell the houses for you prophetess Janet and you'll be united in my Body!' He sees every travel ticket that will ever be bought by us in advance!

He says 'He has defeated death and that we are his royal children and nothing is impossible for him and to those who believe and that all of this has been planned in advance and the truth is from Heavens perspective: The Body of Christ shall know no defeat -only victory!' Prophetess Marie always helps us to see this and she has travelled extensively praying for 27 barren ladies in India and they all had been sterilised by the government and they all were pregnant the next year!

So we really need to catch this revelation both individually and corporately 'that all the defeats you've ever been through, throughout your whole life were actually secret victories for Christ and God says 'I am going to show you my total triumph and you'll be brought into complete perfection of this revelation by the power of my Holy Spirit dwelling within you all!' This is a wakeup call to the church! So let's praise Jesus and keep it up!!

WE KNOW NO DEFEAT ONLY VICTORY!

God is excited about you! He's so in love with you, he's so obsessed with you! He so wants to spend time with you! He loves you so much and he wants us to understand that these defeats were really secret victories! It's such a wonder! And you don't even have to understand it all! That's the relief of accepting, aligning and believing in faith. Then peace flows like a river! We don't have to understand it all but by being like a little child we just believe by faith.

"And said, Verily I say unto you, Except ye be converted, and become as little children, ye shall not enter into the kingdom of heaven. Whosoever therefore shall humble himself as this little child, the same is greatest in the kingdom of heaven. Verse-Kingdom of heaven -little child."

—Mathew 18:3—4

"For therein is the righteousness of God revealed from faith to faith: as it is written, The just shall live by faith."

—Romans 1:17

You can see very clearly these things are in the Word of God but I have just heard from the Lord and paraphrased it. You see in the natural, my life really does look like a complete and utter defeat, but really it's just absolutely glorious! We are a living sacrifice so we are totally OK with it!

Jan: OK, so we are fighting back with the Word and revelations and we are asking God in humility to position war angels?

Jon: Yes war angels are everywhere! My hand is shaking in the anointing right now. God has given me so many revelations, this is why I am always attacked and this is why I look defeated, but I don't care about that stuff! It does not matter! It doesn't matter if I am in pain; I am still going to praise His name. Oh Jesus, Nobody knows how much I love him. No one knows! And God just pours in more and more love, more oil and more grace every single day and I can be as weak as possible as a man, but God is so beautiful to me! He is so wonderful!

Dear reader, do not feel anxiety and let go of religious strife. You are already there! It's all in Heaven! So you have already got it! We have already got it in the WORD. We have got in the revelation and who is Revelation? JESUS CHRIST IS REVELATION. YOU'VE GOT IT ALREADY!

So what happens is the devil comes along and he tries to twist the word of God to say, 'Hey, this isn't working out for you! You've done something wrong! You are responsible for this or that and you are to blame!' Satan always does the same old stuff: blame, shame, defeat tactics but we are not ignorant of the devil's devices! Every single defeat is a VICTORY in Christ! And I am just going to preach to the Devil until he has his ears burnt off because we need to preach to the devils because our defeats are Christ's victories! Lol! So rejoice! Christ has won and He will not just fix it for us, but vindicate it for us. He intercedes for us, so we will see complete justice! We are that special royal generation and the Body of Christ is awakening daily to who God really is and what He has really done!

Someone praise Jesus! At times you'll see complete injustice, that's what it feels like and you will feel like God has let you down and other people have let you down, and then you've let yourself down and then the boring old Devil comes along and he has a field day trying to manipulate your emotions and then you'll likely have a little pity party together, and meanwhile: Jesus remains LORD over all. Laughing from the Heavens! Lol. No! We are not having no pity party. We are powerful in Christ, in the Word, in the revelation which is the Word and Spirit together! And we are more powerful together than you can ever imagine if only we would stop all our petit religious divisions and lame arguments and rotten poisonous pride. Worship God daily, make too much time for Him and it will all melt away and you'll flow in the rivers of revelation grace!

HIGH WITH THE MOST HIGH

Jan: When I was in my 30's like you I had so much hope but then 20 something years went by and things got worse!

Jon: So those 20 years were under the blood of the Lamb! I didn't know you then, if I had known you, I would have been standing with you all the time, but God knows you and He has planned the very best for you. Those 20 years that you thought were wasted: this is your alabaster box! You are an offering! You are sweet to God. It might have felt bitter to you but you were sweet to Christ because you love him.

Jan: I had such hope living in that car' (she had to live in a car for 6 years and sleep at other people's homes because she was made homeless in America and her family did not help her so as a result, this was very traumatic. This is why I am still praying for her and I forgive her as we should always forgive each other)…she continues, 'But I had an idol, the man I loved, and I had to ask God to forgive me, just like you had an idol (I confirmed that my previous relationship became an idol. I loved him, there's no doubt about it) But having any idol is a sin.

Jon: Yes and I didn't know he was an idol, but I had to lose everything! I gave up everything to follow God and it cost me great heartache. God loves us so much; He burns in love for us every day! He sings love songs over us and He is like 'why aren't you hearing them?' 'You are my Beloved!' But, you must see He doesn't want us to have idols as He is saying 'you guys are going to miss the point! I've got to be your everything and you're going to understand that when I'm your everything. I will give you everything! And you are my everything, Father!

You see this is how life is with Jesus and we just lay all our life down daily and the Devil is there to remind us, trying to send his demons out to remind us of defeats, or shaming, blaming or name calling or making things feel bitter for us when actually God is saying 'Hey all this bitterness is sweet! I have turned all your defeats into victories. I have won this battle! And I have won this in you and you overcome!', Father.

So, the defeats and perceived defeats are over! Thank you, Jesus. They are over and they are turned into victories. So that means all house sales, all the things that didn't work out everything! The whole lot everything! Janet was saying how when she wakes up in pain and her legs are hurting and her feet are aching and I told her that is a spirit of heaviness and we have to do our best to look after our physical bodies as well. I often wake in pain and have pain intermittently all day but God is still the healer and He even heals through me! We should be flowing in deep revelation and not feeling like just because bad and traumatic things have happened to us that God has left us! The reality is God wants us to feel empowered and victorious equipped in revelation and overflowing with praise but He won't force this upon us.

Janet wondered why she was once in love with such a mean man, a narcissist whom she had prayed for over the years all to no effect, an abusive spirit had tried to sabotage her destiny and it can be very hard to see the light at the end of the tunnel especially as the tests and long suffering continues and you end up feeling tired, exhausted and humiliated daily but God still has a plan and He still turns around all evil plans and He always wins triumphantly! She felt responsible and to blame for taking the 'wrong path' and more clarity was needed to understand past decisions in order to make better ones in the light and revelation of God's Holy Word. We can all fall in love with the wrong person and at the wrong time, some things do not last. They are for times and seasons and that doesn't mean that we have missed God or worse, that He does not love us and want the best for us. Man, I am winding up some religious spirits every single day! As Joyce Meyer says 'I am going to do my absolute best to everyday make the Devil mad!' Now, that is an attitude for altitude! Go Joyce!

Janet said 'This time God didn't intervene and I was just left alone and I feel like I did this!'

I explained to her, and I explain to you, that no matter what choice, no matter what consequences there is no path, no decision that God cannot turn around, so we do not have to be afraid, only that we should not be ignorant of God's love. It's a shame that we didn't know it once as the love of Christ and His holy angels protect us from lots of harm, but even with making mistakes God can turn it around.

Even with molestation and manipulation one can get an abusive mindset, and abusive spirits can try to attach to the soul. So yes, deliverance is needed, and God can do that! We just have to trust Christ with every area of our lives because He will not let us down, our lives here are temporary compared to eternity. Jesus can turn any situation around! Janet explained a story of how she saw a man once who manifested demons to her father, and yet her father didn't warn her and this led to her being molested and several other evil things that occurred and sadly she did blame herself but all of this is not true. We are only partly responsible for our lives why? Because there is a whole evil spiritual realm plotting against us and we can't see all the unseen things so God does despite consequences, He still loves us and He still turns around all evil for the good of those who love Him. Love is the key to understanding God, not religion, not concepts of spirituality but love and when you let go, let God's love to love you and you will feel loved and be the love for others.

Amen.

Chapter *Thirteen*
CLOSE TO THE BROKENHEARTED: REVELATION

CLOSE TO THE BROKEN HEARTED REVELATION

Prophetess Janet and many other people all feel the same way that each of our decisions all have a knock-on effect which they do have but they can really upset us deeply and chip away at our trust of God, but it doesn't have to be this way. We have to be very careful of how we think because by believing different lies subconsciously and consciously this is going to affect us and our decision-making process. Our view of God can easily be distorted because bad things have happened, are currently happening and do happen in the future, all of this can feel overwhelming and bewildering leaving us with a warped, distant, uncaring vision of God and a distorted sense of self with a fractured self-esteem. These difficult feelings and emotions don't go anywhere there are stored up subconsciously and they are used against us in the form of 'psychological protection' this is why we react and not respond from a place of peace from past pain as a sense of 'security'. The enemy wants us to feel insecurity, and God wants us to feel completely secure and safe. God is our safe tower and the righteous run to Him and are safe, so we are secure and well aware! <u>We need to let God bring light to our past</u> and how He does this is up to Him, but if we don't, we will have a distorted view of God, ourselves and others and we will blame others and ourselves and our relationships, but it doesn't have to be this way Jesus saves!

It's very easy to blame ourselves, others or God, but sometimes we have to just let life happen to us, meaning: do not fight what is happening, there is a bliss in surrender, <u>there is sometimes wisdom hidden in the silence</u>. We need to be aware of what season we are in and we can trust God in every season.

If God wants us to face the past, let's do it with Jesus, not being worrisome and burdensome full of anxiety and fear! No way! Let Christ have the final say! Choose to win in Christ today! Receive the anointing from the Word and the Spirit to overcome all obstacles in the present, and all pain of the past. You can't be held back by abiding in the Supernatural Vine. You'll soon start to produce supernatural fruits. This ends striving and fighting, and wrestling blaming and shaming deep within. Amen!

Christ sees all our thoughts, and out of all the chaos, and frustration, He brings His divine order! We don't have to feel held back, being secretly angry with ourselves, others or God – just because life hasn't gone the way we expected! Let's learn to roll with the punches, take each day at a time and be thankful for daily grace. We are so blessed. There's two ways to look at life!
1. The cup is half empty!
2. The cup is half full!

CLOSE TO THE BROKENHEARTERED

Your attitude is your paintbrush, it colours everything we do, say and think! Myself and Janet were having this conversation about long suffering and waiting on God's promises:

Jan: I don't know what happened and I feel like I screwed up. I would go looking for my future husband in the grocery store and I would question if he was in church and I would go and look but he was never around! Why did he never show up? I don't know!

Jon: I can see why that would torment you, and I can see how the enemy would use that against you, which gives him a legal 'foot hold' because at the end of day Satan is trying to rob you of a revelation of the sovereignty of God! God lives inside you and the truth of the matter is it looks like we make mistakes but Gods Holy Spirit is inside us and Christ turns around the mistakes into total victories! He turns them around. And for some awesome reason Christ died for sinners, not Saints, and not perfect people. He resists the self-righteous or proud. So, he died for people that make mistakes! And this is only for them to be turned into complete victory, can you believe that?

Jan: Does that cover losing the one you love, having a broken heart, and trying to cope with the pain and loss of someone not loving you?

Jon: That's right! Absolutely of course, so here's another revelation:

REVELATION: THE LORD IS CLOSE TO THE BROKEN HEARTED

Do you know what close means in this context? It means He is stuck to you! So when I had my heart broken over my relationship, and people easily criticize saying 'well that's sin anyway!' But I tell you, sin or no sin, I don't even care what people call it, I don't care what people brand me as, I know what love is and I know what heartache is and I was so heart broken, but God came over to me when I was so broken, and so suicidal and even though I was rebuking that spirit of suicide it was very persistent that it tried to cause me to think that I had lost all hope and reason to live!

So, I rebuked despair and all of Hell but it didn't go anywhere I was in a dark cloud experience and that's where I met the Lord Jesus Christ all over again! One particular night I remember, I phoned up the Samaritans for the anti-suicide help line and they didn't have any hope they had no answers for me—I mean nothing! They didn't want to hear about my faith and I was very shocked. I know suicide is a spirit because I had it when I was a child on and off, and I've had it at different times in my life, but that evil spirit came back with a vengeance! When that spirit manifests and invades your thoughts all you feel is 'I want to die! I don't want to be here! I can't cope with this, I don't want to breathe, I can't breathe. I need that person in my life!

Now, this guy had Jesus in them at that point, but I didn't realize he was an idol, I didn't realize any of it, and I gave him everything I had which was God, and then I saw the change in that person. It was so dramatic; I've never seen anything like it. I was amazed because they received God as a Saviour and then they rejected me! Does that make sense? It was some sort of subconscious thing and I couldn't handle that level of pain and trauma, so I went into this complete depressive state of mind, and I don't know how to describe just how deep the darkness was and how bad I felt, and I was tormented because the clocks couldn't turn back, the clocks went forward, but I was stuck in the past, in the trauma repeating itself over and over and over again, tormenting me all light, all energy, and all hope was annihilated! I just couldn't see a way out, I couldn't see a way forward, all I could see and feel was crushing deep darkness, getting darker and darker every moment with no sense of any reason to live at all.

CLOSE TO THE BROKENHEARTERED

Jan: So, did you go to a psychic or counsellor?

Jon: No! I didn't go anywhere! Can you imagine? I was stuck here and my family just left me in the room, in the dark, so I tried to pray, feeling only despair, gloom and blame.

"You have taken from me friend and neighbour – darkness is my closest friend." **Psalm 88.18 (NIV)**

Psalm 88, 3—9, 16.17 / Psalm 89.38

So, I prayed 'Lord, the only way I can get over this death and despair and suicidal spirit is if you come in, and you put all of your fullness of who you are in my heart. You have to be everything!'

So, I repented of having anything and anyone as an idol in my heart ever! I cannot ever have it there and I said 'Come into me Lord God of Abraham in greater fullness, just please take over my life' At that point I was so weak and I couldn't cope anymore and I was going to sleep and it was in the middle of the night that Jesus Christ appeared to me above my head, He flew through the ceiling, it was amazing and He came and kissed me on my lips as I was going to sleep and He said 'I am your lover and I am never ever going to let you go!' and then I fell asleep. From that moment on, I knew He had done it all, Christ has overcome the world – I got a greater realization of the Cross and the authority Jesus has over broken hearts and that if I stay contrite, I would be blessed.

There is a difference between being broken hearted and being contrite.

God told me: 'If you are contrite, it's like you are consistently broken before God, but you are not damaged! Being broken and damaged is not the same even if its feels like it is! So, God wants something in the middle between broken and damaged and that happy holy medium that goes in the middle is called 'contrite before the Lord' which is actually a dimension half the time I don't even know what I am saying until I say it: God has given me the grace to speak out mysteries and it surprises me and my listener! Being contrite is a dimension of living. For example, when there is humility, then there's being contrite which lets you see 'I have nothing in this world to offer anyone, absolutely nothing! I lost the one person that I loved, that was the one person that I loved of my own kind, in the sexuality that I understood the most – at the time. It was as true as I could be within myself and my journey and I don't care if people say it's a lie or not!

Previously before this relationship I did marry a lady but it was not the same, but it wasn't the same love or same energy, it was different, and then when God came into my past relationship and saved that man, the whole dynamic was changed, so the loss was just horrendous! That person was him, and I saw the change. I saw Jesus Christ leap into his heart and change him! And I saw all the miracles including no more dyslexia and he became a powerful runner which were phenomenal things to witness, so God did all of that, but I was left beyond broken. It is one thing losing someone you love and are so attracted too and there is another thing losing your best friend. But not everything lasts forever.

Janet asked me about soul ties and yes, I had to ask God to break the soul tie completely and God said to me 'If I break the soul tie for you, I am always going to need you to be contrite so you can be used for my higher calling son'. He continued and spoke this comforting revelation to my soul:

'I need you to be contrite. I need you to still be broken so that I can work with you, so you will never ever have any idols and you won't be proud, then you'll be my Minister!' The anointing was shaking my hands as I spoke out this message.

So, I ask myself this question everyday: Am I broken hearted? Maybe, but what I am is contrite, and if there are any broken parts of my life, God pours in liquid love gold to the broken hearted and contrite. So, He

CLOSE TO THE BROKENHEARTERED

keeps me humble by allowing me to look defeated by these mistakes, all the waters look to others like they are bitter in my life, well, they are clearly not and God stays 'Those bitter waters are turning sweet' and that's a revelation too. We are therefore not damaged; we are not too broken that God doesn't care and that He hasn't already taken that pain and damage of a broken heart– when He has! He has taken the true broken heart, He was the broken heart, He was the image of the broken heart on the cross! Look at an image of Jesus on the Cross that was the broken heart! That was the defeat, that was the time that you felt you went the wrong way, that was the time that we sinned against God – that was the time! He did everything! That's my only Passion! My passion is his passion!

My idol was my Ex and that was the one that I loved because God gave me a love for him and then I fell for someone else which did not work out! What a nightmare, and now I have the Lord Jesus Christ even closer than ever! I will not be labelled or dictated too by the church either if that makes me unpopular, then so be it. I must follow Jesus and I have made Him my absolute number one. I have married the Lamb of God!

I am praying for a special public figure that I may not ever get to meet, yet my intercessions are registered in heaven and all my sacrifices and the sacrifices of my family are known by God. So without being too personal here, I may have been foolish, I may have crazy Faith, but yet it looks like a defeat and the Devil keeps going on and on and on at me every single day 'Well, Satan-change the record!'

You see, I know the revelation, if I stay humble and I stay contrite, and I stay completely broken before the Lord Jesus Christ. My God has turned around all these defeats into his sweet victory and this is what we can see in our lives sweet victories! (With the September theme of sweetness being released!) These sweet victories will come out of all our prophecies. It will come out as sweet success, at the right time and we are praying for sales because we have laid down our lives like living sacrifices for what I am so passionate about because I've got my Jesus and no one and nothing can take Him away! So, it's pure joy every day! My adopted family can't give that to me, they give me a space and I am so very grateful for the time and space to' be built up in the Lord to prepare for ministry- they have given me so much, but they can't give me Jesus! I've got to access my Jesus every day through my relationship with God-He has to be my everything otherwise I don't want to speak! I don't want to breathe, I don't want to be here unless I've got my Jesus! I'm desperate! I am a desperate man.

Jan: After hearing that level of brokenness, I understand what happened to you now. You have let God connect that broken heart, and that soul to be transferred back to Jesus right?

Jon: Everything and all my love shifted to Jesus Christ!

Janet and I were praying for her soul to be fully connected and engaged with Jesus and flooded with fresh hope again. She explained how her father is in pain and has known such defeat and yet once he was raising people from the dead in hospital after they had flat lined! She saw that there was a very deep root that needs to heal and for years she has been desperately trying to find the answers. We prayed for the Lords perfect will!

I see it like this:
1. All our defeats are secret victories.
2. The Lord is close to the broken hearted and he turns evil around for good (Romans 8:28)
3. We want the perfect will of God not the permissible.
4. There are different levels of brokenness
5. We can release thankfulness and praise despite pain and trauma, inwardly and outwardly!

Jan: Is a contrite heart like a spirit that's lost its way? I feel like I have lost my way.

Me. Yes, in some ways, but you haven't lost your way. These are all accusations, not feeling loved is an accusation, blame, shame and condemnation is all the Devil's realm and he tries all that on! Satan blames, shames, condemns making us feel guilty saying, 'you've missed it! And you are to blame! You're this, you're the other...'e.t.c. all that is the condemnation realm. There's a huge difference between being in the condemnation realm and the being in Christ realm.

"[There is] therefore now no condemnation to them which are in Christ Jesus, who walk not after the flesh, but after the Spirit. For the law of the Spirit of life in Christ Jesus hath made me free from the law of sin and death."

—(Romans 8:1—2)

When you are in Christ, you can begin to see from the secret place that all of your defeats are complete victories and this gives you joy, peace and thankfulness despite trials. All of our sense of purity and holy living, it isn't anything that we can really do ourselves we are not holy in our own efforts—that is considered self-righteousness (filthy rags), but we are seen as holy in God's sight because Christ is perfect in us!

I did a video series on YouTube years ago when I was still in that relationship with that man and it was about learning to accept, like and then love yourself in Christ. I have found these to be levels and therefore realms in Christ that lead to REVIVAL! In those videos about 'Learning to Love Yourself' I spoke about how God sees us RIGHT IN HIS SIGHT! Big shock for the religious— that little collection!

"Blessed are those that are pure in heart, they will see God."

—Mathew 5:8

How do you stay pure in heart? Well you must stay in a state called being contrite. When you are contrite, you know you are broken and you know that God's Love has come in and touched you, and you know that God's changed you from within, and you know it's this inner working of the Holy Spirit. A lot of people are all about the gifts of God but I am not all about that. I pray 'Lord God, please sort out my character so you can make me a minister and God says: 'Ok son, you're my living sacrifice, I need you to have a contrite, humble, holy heart from you every day and I will give you that!'

This makes me very humbled before my Almighty God. So I asked the Lord 'Does this mean that I won't have anyone to love in a relationship physically in my life?' and He said 'So be it for now son.' But I know that from GOD personally that I am loved!! My response was 'Wow! You really are the lover of my soul. You are my counsellor, you're my helper, you're my VIP person that I can go to about anything, anytime and you've turned it all around for me: you've rigged it in my favour already!' (I am trying not to get OTT too happy!) 'And God, you've made me contrite and broken before you. So you can pour out your glory in this vessel. This is your whole plan!' Thank you, Jesus!

So let's speak of the next revelation:

'PRAISE GOD DESPITE THE PAIN AND THEN PRAISE HIM AGAIN AND AGAIN!'

So I have the pain daily but I still will praise Him! Man, I feel high! I feel so electrified! I will be sanctified and God will be glorified! And he will be seen and magnified in a brand new way! Yes JESUS! I WILL PRAISE YOU TODAY!!

And when I do this, oh goodness, Heaven comes down! I just give God _all_ the glory and I say 'Wow! Thank you, Jesus. You are in everything. You are my everything!!'

I AM GETTING LOVE DRUNK ON REVELATION! You are blessed to handle this costly book in your hands or hear it somewhere and I feel absolutely love drunk and love whacked! He accepted me as

CLOSE TO THE BROKENHEARTERED

I am! I smashed the system of religion on its head and God stuck around to be FOUND by me!

"DELIGHT yourself in the Lord; and He will give you the DESIRES of YOUR HEART."

—Psalms 37:4

Then I asked God 'Do you mean you were in all bad memories of my childhood? Do you mean you were in all my relationships? Do you mean you were in all of this? And You were in all that? You're in it all, you are in today! You are in the stress of that!- you are in everything!! This is really the next revelation:

REVELATION:

JESUS IS IN EVERYTHING AND HE WILL FILL EVERYTHING IN EVERY WAY AND HE WILL TURN AROUND ABSOLUTELY EVERYTHING!

"He that descended is the same also that ascended up far above all heavens, that he might fill all things.)"

—Ephesians 4:10

Jan: That's a lot of revelation. Praise Jesus! Lord I need to receive your healing. I need healing from all the years gone by. (Who can identify with this conversation?) I am going to ask for forgiveness. I am not going to take the fear, I am going to rebuke the fear in Jesus name.

HIGH WITH THE MOST HIGH

Lord, you are my first thought when I wake up and I'm sorry for not always keeping you first (me too). It's hard for me to be still sometimes and I have been listening to audio Bible and I feel so exhausted and I need victory now and so it can't hurt to believe one more time.

Jon: No! Not one more time! We keep on believing every single day no matter what pain we go through! We will never stop believing and Satan is getting really mad with us because he thinks they really are BELIEVER'S! We better do everything we can to stop them! Satan is desperately trying to motivate his troops, putting pressure on them every day and threatening them with hell fire and no inhabitable bodies to dwell in on the earth realm. But even though he still thinks he is in control, God laughs at him from HOLY HEAVEN!!

Satan angrily snaps at his lesser minions the fallen angels 'Come on devils let's do everything possible so we can distract them from who and what they really believe in the name above all names the Lord Jesus Christ, the one we fear the most, the one that's living inside them! He's the one that's being humiliated and not them. Let's make them think that it's all their fault and let's blame them and shame them and put things in their life that try to upset them even though we can't do it-because we haven't got permission!'

Ha ha. Learn to laugh from Heaven at the demons and praise Jesus for the devil's defeat.

Revelation 7:

THE DEVIL DOESN'T HAVE AS MUCH POWER AS WE HAVE GIVEN HIM AND WE CAN TAKE BACK HIS POWER THROUGH JESUS AND BY ABIDING IN THE SUPERNATURAL VINE OVERCOMING ALL THINGS THROUGH CHRIST WHO GIVES US VICTORY!

The Church has given him way too much power and we do it through our thoughts and our words and we are coming into full agreement with

CLOSE TO THE BROKENHEARTERED

what God's done already! So if you can say to God 'Lord I am in so much pain (any type) and I can't cope, and I desperately need you. I need you! I need you every day! That's about as holy as it needs to get! Every single day do this confess how much you need Jesus and that you don't want a religious self-righteous, proud mindset and then Heaven will break out! We prayed for immediate miracles, and thanked God for sweet victories in advance and I asked God to translate these revelations into Janet so she was comforted and clothed from above in Jesus mighty name. I also pray the same for you dear reader or listener.

These revelations are like weapons, so every time fear, intimidation, doubt or anything evil comes along, with shame, blame, guilt, torment and the feeling like you missed it well we are going to pray! Spirit of condemnation I cast you out! Out of me, out of my friends, out of the body of Christ -get out of our lives! Thank you Father in Jesus name.

There is no fear in love; but perfect love casteth out fear: because fear hath torment. He that feareth is not made perfect in love."

—*1 John 4:18*

Now I am trying not to get too happy just in case souls are saved by just laughing in the presence of Jesus! That would be a pretty wacky sign and wonder- now wouldn't it? I wouldn't be surprised that God did that in this ministry. Jesus Christ is my Prince of Peace and my provision and my shield against the devils attacks and accusations. I am always safe in Jesus.

In summary here are the 7 Revelation weapons:

1. ALL OUR DEFEATS ARE SECRET VICTORIES!
2. THE LORD IS CLOSE TO THE BROKEN HEARTED
3. WE WANT THE PERFECT WILL OF GOD NOT PERMISSIVE.

HIGH WITH THE MOST HIGH

4. BEING CONTRITE AND HUMBLE BEFORE GOD = ENCOUNTERS
5. BE THANKFUL AND PRAISE GOD THROUGH PAIN!
6. CHRIST IS SECRETLY HIDDEN BEHIND ALL + ROMANS 8:28
7. THE DEVIL AND DEMONS I HAVE AS MUCH POWER AS WE GAVE THEM AND WE CAN TAKE BACK THAT POWER!

I pray that you feel included and comforted in our conversations as this is often where a lot of revelations are released, when we are helping others- Christ's power flows. Remember, He rests on us when we are persecuted or tormented or weakened or feeling stressed out! These things don't really make sense to our natural mind but praise God when applied they bring God glory! Be blessed in Jesus Christ's almighty name.

With Love,

Heaven to Earth Apostolic Ministries International.

Chapter *Fourteen*
YOU DIDN'T MISS IT: REVELATION

I pray that you are starting to see the true source of my joy which is always hidden in Christ. Of course, I get bad days but I don't let these days win over my emotions, prayerfully and in humility I present my body, soul and mind to Christ Jesus every day. He is always full of surprises and each time with Him and His people in His presence I can feel deep changes within me equipping me not just for the next battle but to have a better more hidden life in Him. There is a time to be seen and there is a time to be hidden. I just want God to be glorified, magnified and exalted above all else and I am willing to wait even with nothing, no money at times, just in complete surrender, that Christ will meet my needs. If those needs are emotional. I just look to Jesus' trust, not to man. In Him is all I need. Even if you don't understand how I got high and why I got so high in Christ that's ok too. Let it go. You don't have to understand everything now.

HIGH WITH THE MOST HIGH

"Trust in the Lord with all thine heart; and lean not unto thine own understanding. In all thy ways acknowledge him, and He shall direct thy paths."

—Proverbs 3:5—6

Our pathways are hidden with gold and treasures yet half the time we can't see them. I know that God is preparing me to have more and more encounters this year as His Prophetic promise of coming out of captivity into perfect liberty has been coming to fruition, and I am forever grateful, forever full of joy despite all of the misery and suffering it will all be worth it all!

This is what I said to Janet: 'The Truth is you never missed it! You never ever missed it because chose you as His own daughter before the foundation of the world to do His perfect will, and from God's perspective they never missed it! We become Sons and daughters of the Highest God by revelation by Gods sovereign plan.

Jan: Oh, I get it! God is the Alpha and Omega! That means He works from the beginning to the end, so He knew about King David and how he fell with Bathsheba (in advance) and He knew about the Devil and how he would fall and I am just done with falling. So, I think I am starting to catch up! So, when you said 'you don't miss it' what you mean is, it's not that I didn't do wrong, it's just the Lord already know!

Jon: Exactly that is freedom! When I got saved, the Lord spoke to me about all the different things around me, all the objects in our lives and He said 'I know where this is, where that is, where that came from, how it was made, when it was made and for what reason! I know where this object on your desk was manufactured and I know absolutely every single detail all around you. I know all about you, I know your bloodline, I know everything about you've ever done, said or thought and I have forgiven you!' That blew my mind and left me in awe of my Holy Creator.

So, in bewilderment I questioned "Is that really the Gospel?' and God said' Yes, it's the Gospel and what's going to happen is, you are going to forget it!'

Lol, you see, that's what the Devils job is to tire us out, to make us forget what God has already done. It's the good news, it's so glorious we are going to be drunk in the Holy Spirit when we get the revelation of its power and it's already happening and I am trying to hold myself back! The thing that has changed my life and my outlook on life especially when you feel that things are so unfair is that <u>praising God through the pain brings the latter day rain!</u> With all our mistakes, they might be a problem to others or to you or both, but God has already turned them all around! He has turned them into total victories! He saw them all in advance and He forgave you and me for everything! No wonder I have got fire in the Spirit! I am trying to keep calm. This is the good excellent and awesome news of our salvation! This is what it means to be saved!

> *"And I heard a loud voice saying in heaven, Now is come salvation, and strength, and the kingdom of our God, and the power of his Christ: for the accuser of our brethren is cast down, which accused them before our God day and night."*
>
> *—Revelation 12:10*

YOU ARE FORGIVEN! Can you imagine? I heard the Lord say: 'Alpha-Omega and now put yourself in the middle! I am hugging you in the middle of Alpha and Omega.

I have loved you, chosen you and anointed you by the Holy Spirit before the foundations of the actual world began and I will love you and be with you until the end of time!'

There's a song on the movie Moulin Rouge 'I will love you till the end of time' and it always speaks to me 'I will love you until your dying day!' Well, we don't die! We only get upgraded! And another sung that is in my heart by Whitney Houston 'I will always love you'. That's God! He can't help it, He's overflowing with love all the time and we don't realize it, the only reason why we feel 'we have missed it' is because we are listening to the Devil's crap! That's the truth of it! And people are perishing for lack of knowledge which is Gnosis: Revelation knowledge of the scriptures, which means experiencing the power of them daily, which is the foundation of the Word of God inside us. He is the foundation, but He gives us revelation by His Spirit everyday but we must be alert, awake and listening.

Jan: So, you truly believe Jon, that God is in business of making it all right again?

Jon: Of course, His into total restoration!

Jan: My Dad is 80 years old, but could it be that he was not in the perfect will of God?

Jon: Well, to answer that question, I believe your dad listened to the wrong voices that were around him at the time (as we all can), I believe he was put into some bad company and there was a religious spirit and he believed the lie that the Devil was more powerful! Unfortunately, the Devil used people specifically the Spirit of religion got hold of him (and countless others) but its ok, because Jesus has forgiven that.

Jan: Do you mean that God never delivered him from that? Is that what you mean?

Jon: Yes, definitely and I see that in the Spirit, he feels that God let him down, he feels this subconsciously (who can relate?) I know he also feels that God let him down with his business too.

YOU DIDN'T MISS IT

Jan: Yes, that's how he feels, but could it be that God is not a part of that covenant because God is a covenant keeping God? Meaning my father's old company hurt so many people?

Jon: Yes, God keeps the covenants which are His promises that He cannot break, where as we make promises and break them; we even call these contracts but a promise, a contract and a covenant is not the same. Only God can make a true covenant, which He has done with His people for all of creation through the blood of Jesus.

Jan: My brother still works for that company and it's crushed our family. My father had much fear that he has got too old and he thinks he's missed it! The family fell out with each other and he was left wondering how to start over without my brother. It was very scary so! Thank God has grace on that. The company was destroyed, every dream he had and it's not funny! So, what is that? Could it be that you're not believing in God anymore to do your work for you or with you because there's something bad that's stopped you from making money?

Jon: It might be that, but we have got to remember we can't see people's hearts but God can. God might reveal to your Dad that the company may have been an idol. If you love things of this world more than God, the Lord is going to test you on that. This is what the Lord does, He is going to eventually pull those things away from people there's a few reasons why we can't have idols:

- They reveal our attention, focus, time, energy and devotion to someone else.
- They reveal where our heart is where our heart is, their treasure is also.
- They keep us carnally minded.
- They block blessings and make us selfish.

HIGH WITH THE MOST HIGH

When exposed by the Lord, we fight and resist not wanting to get rid of them, thus resisting change by God in our lives. If we have a big calling, we must love God first even above ministry or any kind of church related service. By having idols, we are blinded and we can stop giving but most of all we worship them as Gods first. I also call idols 'props' because people rely on them. We rely on props in life for our security because we think our security is where our value comes from which is a lie from Hell!

Jan: Yes, and my father never had anything after that, he was removed from his one 'empire' and they accused him of something and that company sold for $400 million and he didn't get anything! He lost his job, the attorney lawyers of New York State investigated him for a crime he never committed, they said he was guilty and he could no longer work in medical care and all he needed to do was go back to school for a different degree, start all over again at 50years old in Miami, Florida. He was a fighter building prosthetic arms and legs trying to help people, he was a blessing, but he's never gotten over that. There was no restitution there was no recompense so I don't understand the perfect will? I don't know Lord, what happened to my father? I can't figure it out and I don't like the pattern of it and it seems like that company hurt me too!

Jon: We have to seek first the Kingdom and then all is added to us! Your father had to do the same, that includes an anointed company if he was supposed to have a company and not a ministry, you see, we can't see his heart. We can't see what went on behind his decision-making processes with the company, but clearly the fruit of it all has been a rob job! And that devil has taken advantage and left your Dad with nothing and basically hardened his heart and you shouldn't have been living in a car for those years, and your brother turning against you and even your sister by turning towards witchcraft – all of that is the rob job of the Devil, but with the whole thing, the buck stops at the Cross because Christ took it all and God says 'I've put a Prophetess in the family and everything will be turned around, so even though it looks like things in

YOU DIDN'T MISS IT

her life are a defeat, even though it looks like a complete loss, a misery and a great shame and a waste: I don't condemn anyone but I've put my Word in this Prophetess!'

And God will make that word come to pass because that's who God is! So, God will show you, and your father and your whole family just how glorious He is through all of the trials and all of the persecutions and all of the defeats, it is going to be turned around to produce a phenomenal victory in Christ. Even as your Dad is in his 80's I don't believe he is supposed to die a broken-hearted man. I believe he is supposed to see the glory of God in the land of the living this is what we are praying for him and your family and so we have made the vision crystal clear on modern day tablets, iPad and kindle! We want him to see justice and you should see the justice of God! I am a man; I believe that speaks a word of God that might look impossible but the justice of Christ will come out of it because of the injustices that we have suffered.

And our lives are living sacrifices. The sooner we realize that as the Church, the better! Because yes, your Dad had a company, and yes it all went wrong and just because the Devil did a rob job, that doesn't mean that God cannot do a complete restoration and make your cups overflow for you and your entire family. That's what we are praying for and believing for your story to turn around for God's glory!

Jan: In Jesus name, yes and 3 months ago, Prophetess Marie said to my Father that his restoration was going to come through my real estate!

Jon: Praise Jesus! So, it's all there!

Jan: How does she see that?

Jon: It is done in Jesus loving holy name.

Jan: What you just said about everything being restored is absolutely right! That was the confirmation because he is not in real estate, but do you think he needs to be in real estate?

Jon: NO! of course not, you'll support him, you'll be living from the overflow that it will overflow to him. It will bring him so much joy

HIGH WITH THE MOST HIGH

'He will say wow! My wonderful daughter!' Janet, you are a Joseph prophet!

Jan: Oh my gosh. Yes, all the family rejection!

Jon: You see now why we have so much in common. I too am a Joseph prophet: we are the message!

Jan: Yes! They took my home and they financially touched me badly. They ruined me there, and so here we go right?

Jon: These were evil powers not your parents at all! Your parents and family had a dark veil over them, God bless their souls, but they have had darkness over them (as we all do from time to time -all for God's future glory!) only, they just haven't seen it and these veils are over all of us so that we don't see it, but God is saying:

'Look, I will bring you into all truth' That's what the Holy Spirits job is and God shines His light into that situation and says 'This is not a defeat; this is your victory and you are the prophetess of the family, you are in Christ, not in condemnation. You are a Joseph with a political calling and you will have a real estate business that will be so well known, so successful, so famous you will be blessed like Abraham and Joseph was for trusting me all over America. You will be fully able to support your family. Your cup will overflow and you will get your dreams to come true, all through my perfect love which is the glue!'

God wants to give you're the desires of your heart and I don't know what they are and were, I don't know what Kataleena's were. I didn't know anything but God tells me what peoples desires of their hearts are because I am a heart man! That's what I am by Grace. I have been created from a heavenly dimension to be a heart person. I am not a head person, I'm a heart person.

YOU DIDN'T MISS IT

God made this way by His grace, and He has done it as a special gift for the Church. He is making us all heart people and He says the pure in heart, the contrite in heart, the meek in heart, these one the ones that are going to see the kingdom. These are the ones that have had their lives completely defeated, and broken down, cramped and clamped down, squashed and taken away! When things have been squandered and wasted all of that, Christ is in it all! The victory and the revelation is that God is in all of it! And we are going to see a turnaround in Jesus' name -I don't care if they are in their 80's, 90's or 100's – they are going to see a turnaround our God does not fail us, He will never forsake us ever! He will always love us and it doesn't matter how bad the devil's defeat jobs were, all the rob jobs. Christ is coming through for you! And <u>we will see absolute perfection</u>, so all we do is wait on God, renew our minds, renew our strength, align ourselves, be in the Vine, abiding, remain in Him and then Holy Spirit brings absolute perfection we will be in the glory realm of complete absolute perfection and in Christ there is no condemnation! There is no blame, no shame, no guilt and all our sins got forgiven – before the foundation of the world!

Christ took us on the cross and He loved us and He took all the evil stuff to Hell and that's where it belongs and He says:

'You are my sons and daughters of the Highest El Shaddai: And you've got authority to cast out those evil things and take them out of your life and out of lives of other people and I am going to show you how victorious you are in my love and even though it looks like a complete mess, I am the Messiah who brings a complete message out of it!'

Christ Jesus is going to anoint us every day because God isn't in the business of just giving out one anointing. He gives us fresh oil every day! Amen praise Jesus, so we are not lacking anything. Every day, we ask for fresh oil and we ask for ability for the grace to have a broken humble and contrite heart and be pure in God because it is God doing this – not us! After this time of fellowship, we prayed for our families and left the rest with God, He is the Lover of our souls. He made Love His Goal and **He overcome all so in Christ we win!**

As a Prophet sometimes it can be tiring to explain sometimes to others why I don't just prophesy to everyone, after all, it's God's prophecies, yes I have in part responsibility, but prophecy is only known in part. I think God does conceal things to keep His elect concealed too! He will not be glorified until the time is right and we cannot make it happen, we cannot bring prophecies about, we must do our part by waiting on God and only prophesying as Gods Holy Spirit leads us, otherwise we prophesy in vain and that can do a lot more damage.

I don't keep covenants. That is for Christ, I am just a weak dependent on God man, I hate to admit that but it's the truth, I need Jesus because He has created me to become His message, His messenger and His sign and wonder but He does all things in His time, His perfect time, He is never early but He is never late. The God Head and the 7 spirits around the throne will be glorified in the name of perfect Love. Amen.

"And out of the throne proceeded lightnings and thunderings and voices: and [there were] seven lamps of fire burning before the throne, which are the seven Spirits of God."

—Revelation 4:5

Chapter *Fifteen*
DREAMS AND PORTALS

Dreams and Portals (With My Sister)

During a time of fellowship this September 2022 we were just speaking and praying into some of our past dreams and whether there was any fresh interpretation that we could add. It's a nice thing to do when you are all together as everyone is going to see something different, and because God speaks in lots of different ways it can be liberating hearing others' views, interpretations about our past dreams. We shouldn't be scared of being deceived or confused because Holy Spirit will always lead us into all truth. Somethings we are supposed to know things and recognize what is needed in our dreams, but, the other things we should let go of. Not everything will be needed when looking at the subconscious elements of dreaming. Yes, God speaks though dreams, He puts strange patterns together and we should be attentive to what the Holy Spirit is saying and when.

It should never cause conflict if someone doesn't agree, do not seek control or dominance, there is no need to in our fellowship, we are not in competition, but in Christs harmony with each other. I do believe that one day we will be dreaming similar or the same dreams because of the Holy outpouring that is coming! Remember if you do this in a group, respect for each other is key. No one is saying you have to agree. In fact diversity can bring unity! Opposites do attract just like a magnet. So, you must get rid of the legalism attitude of being 'right and wrong' when interpreting each other's dreams. Have fun! You will see things that others might not have!

Conversation about dreams

We were just talking about a dream I had about my old friend and lover and I was in his mother's attic and we were sorting out stuff, but then the dream shifted into lots of different attics. The meaning of attic is basically the subconsciousness as is water or caves for example. This reminded us of Mum's strange/ demonic birds found in Grandad's attic which was rather profound. So now my sister Amy is going to tell us about hers in relation to North London where her grandparents lived.

Amy: My sister and I were in their home and my aunt and uncle had gone, I didn't think Grandad was living there at the time, but I have had dreams about him coming back!

(This matches up with our family prophecy that I have seen many times as an injustice has been done to Grandad so we are praying for him; he was tricked, losing power of attorney, therefore the wealth of the family was compromised and stolen! He was branded with early dementia and yet he is a very prayerful man who can see that he has been very wronged. This has blocked a lot blessings for the whole family but we

are still believing that God has a greater plan). I just wanted to explain some of the background story as I believe God can still answer the prayers of an older gentleman even from a care home! Praise Jesus in advance!

DREAMS AND PORTALS

Amy: We were worried that our aunt and uncle were going to be angry because we had broken a saucepan or something because they sometimes can be upset over small things and we know this is not really them it is an evil spirit affecting them. Then the next thing is there was oil coming through the ceiling and dripping down the walls and suddenly at first my reaction was oh no! What are we going to do? I felt like, Oh No! There's more damage happening to the house! It felt as if we were responsible, but then I realized it was oil which I see to be really symbolic of good things, Holy Spirit, anointing and then I saw Jesus standing there in the office part next to the kitchen which was all open plan. We were looking at Him from the angle of the kitchen and there was something strange. I didn't see what was usually there like the table and chairs and the boiler cupboard but I did see there was writing on the wall in rainbow colours. The overall feeling that I got from the letters was comforting to me that things were going to be alright!

Jon: Yes Amy, that rainbow means the Covenant with God and your grandparents and God cannot break a covenant with us which beyond amazing because of Jesus and what He has done for all of us.

Amy: Great! In another dream we were looking after the house and there were things that were stolen, somehow burglars got in and took things. I was like 'oh no these important things have been stolen!' In particular it was including albums of old records (memories).

So, I woke up with the feeling that the Devils tried to steal music from us all but that we were meant to be in music before now for God and lots of different things have been stolen from our family. But the overall feeling despite all the attacks is that the whole family is going to be really delivered, rescued completely and brought into good things for God.

Another dream was my boyfriend Hans and myself were engaged to get married and I have had a series of these kind of dreams close to each other and my Uncle seemed really different, there was no hostility and he said that I could have my reception in the garden which also appeared very different with lots of tables and chains all up a slope which ran along the house, where there was an outhouse which isn't normally there, it's quite bizarre because at the moment there is a neighbour's house there and not a green slope! There was also window that I looked out of that's not even there, it was as if all those tables and chairs were for functions and we were considering having a wedding reception there. Part of that dream revealed a young lad that we had fostered or adopted or we were about to, and he was around 14 and he loved football and my uncle really welcomed him into the family, everything seemed very different! It felt so real, like we were all big happy family.

Jon: Yes, that reminds me of that Trump dream you had Amy, where he was like a grandfather figure, everyone was completely different! It's almost like a parallel world, hidden but revealed in dreams, an alternate reality!

Amy: Maybe, it was symbolic from Grandads home to get deliverance from, and there was these metal doors, almost like a crypt and a very, very big safe which was walk in, and there was a person in there, but it was almost like a hologram or AI type of person who would come through a portal like in Star Trek. So right in the middle of North London there was this weird portal and if you stepped in it, you could get zapped to another place.

Jon: Anywhere people have been gathering in the name of Jesus Christ and are praying is still a portal! Some are weaker than others. What happens is the Devil is very attracted to portals, that's why he attacks this house! He's attacked Grandads home with everything he's got because he's deliberately attacked the family unity. But guess what? There will be a portal in Grandads care home! You see, I have seen visions of this, I have seen the Angels come.

Amy: Ah! This leads on to the other dreams I had, another one was where Grandad had come back and he was sitting at the head of the table and he was very youthful again, like all things were being renewed and then we were getting ready for loads of people who were going to come to the house and we wondered 'how on earth are we going to cook for all these people?' and it was evening and I was tired and I wondered how we were going to do it, but anxiously I felt it was too much.

Suddenly the atmosphere changed and then everything was possible. There were lots of different people all coming in, I don't know who they were and it was like they were all becoming part of the family it was absolutely loads of people – huge crowds as if they had been strangers but there weren't strangers anymore!

Jon: Wow! God can do it. The Lord has this thing, I have noticed about houses. If the house or building has had a lot of prayer in, then it's not like a normal house; it turns into a portal! So, all hell reigns down to try and upset the inhabitants of the house to cause to problems to the household and make the house mourn and weep because of the onslaught of attacks making it feel like it's been rejected and then the owners start rejecting the house. God showed me all this in a wounded house vision once (you can find this in my book series 'Revelations, and Meditations')
So, you need to understand the enemy targets prayerful places because they become a great threat to him. Prayerful houses still remain a prayerful portal even if the unseen enemies can come in and out, as part of our tests, or through sin; barriers of protection are lowered. This is a bit like the Midianite Spirits which used to camp all around Israel and they used to take territory of where ever Israel was and this is also like the Philistines and the Ark of Covenant. The enemy is always attracted to what we've got and he not only wants that but he wants to know our future too, and because he does **not** know all things, he is a very frustrated loser, having <u>lost in advance</u> and this in itself is a revelation that we can look at another time.

Of course, the enemy will do everything in his power (which is very limited compared to Christs!) to steal from the Saints including their energy, health, wealth, joy, revelations and oil. Satan is always out to sabotage everything but we must know that Love always wins, and all evil will be turned around. This is the Gospel and I can never get over it! Praise Jesus!

The enemy is well aware of what we are doing in the spirit and is jealous of the effects of our prayers and although we can't see this, but Satan is granted certain permission by God's sovereignty to see elements of our lives, but one thing for sure is that we are hidden in Christ (see verse) in the secret place.

"He that dwelleth in the secret place of the most High shall abide under the shadow of the Almighty."

– Psalm 91:1

REVELATION: WHEN WE PRAY IT OPENS A PORTAL

The more we pray in a place or home, it can all be completely covered by a portal! This I what God's plan is! I have even seen them over our home and in some rooms at times. This is the reason why we are quite attached to this home but this family home is going under so many different attacks.

Amy: It's really weird things that most houses don't go through!

Jon: That's what I mean! It's so very strange! That's a good example of a portal, but what about a bad example? A portal to the occult (and by this I don't just mean the unseen realm) Now if you were to God forbid, open a portal to the occult and you dedicated the place to demons, you'd get the whole place haunted which can stay haunted for a long period of time.

DREAMS AND PORTALS

Amy: We have lived in buildings like that as well!

Jon: Some people after having had the estate agent show them the house can get a really every feeling about the property and sometimes it can be very dramatic. It's not just one couple, its lots of them, one after the other. Even I can sometimes be sensitive to ESP (Extra sensory perception). This tells us the paranormal is real and people can feel its effects!

Amy: Half the time they aren't even believers too! So basically, we see that houses are very significant in general and if we dream about them there's a lot of meaning behind them in these past dreams we've had and we have all lived in some strange places with some strange things happening. This is crystal clear that we want what God wants, that He is more powerful and He turns the darkest things around, the worst kind of problems and the worst strange situations, the most painful, confusing things and the scariest things that try to be scary into the most Glory!

Jon: You've got the revelation sis! (I hope you are able to catch it too my reader or listener)

Amy: Where I live currently in Derby is called one of the most haunted cities in England so therefore God told me to go there and therefore its connected to all of us and we believe it's one of the places that God really wants to do something in we believe. The churches are strategically placed there, a lot of them are helping the homeless. When I first arrived at Derby they told me that I should go on the ghost walk, the driver said to me on the 17th September 2017, it was the day St Werb's Church reopened after having a complete overhaul and its now a church of Holy Trinity Brompton, making it a completely different kind of church then it used to be and we like history, but if there's any evil spirits in Derby doing a horrible work there, which I have experienced weird things there then it's important to recognize the importance of these portals.

I've seen people act very weird and being high on that strange new Zombie drug where they lay around in the streets or stand around like statutes for hours, but they get violent if you get to close, it's very strange! There's something going on there with gangs, murders, people being stabbed, prostitution, it's not an easy place to live at all! (Just to give you the picture!) Sometimes it tries to make me feel on edge and stressed but I want God to turn it all around, and I believe that He wants to do that. The whole spiritual atmosphere, the climate and the effects on the people, the poverty spirit, the murder spirit. God wants to stop all of that and I believe He wants to use Derby and some of the places that have got the worst reputation and this includes the very street that I am still in!

It's so bad there that you can't even have a post box because someone put an infected needle inside and this infected the postman and he lost his job and he's now forever got this horrible illness! That's how to the shocking extent they had to even lock that post box and you can't even use it!

Jon: I can testify I have seen this post-box. Disgusting behaviour. This so reminds me of the Bronx in NYC and there is this ex-Satanist called John Ramirez which lots of people may have heard of from his ministry and great book 'Inside the Devils Cauldron' and my friend from Pakistan knows him which is rather amazing and this is where God wants me to do a future crusade in Karachi and lots of people have gone to that same area and done crusades like Todd Bentley, the Shamp's and others, also another man of God is coming in October. This is a portal!

Here's another example, Whitney Houston's first church where she was first singing Gospel in New Jersey, well I dreamt about that very church and I heard Whitney's voice and I woke up hearing her speaking to me about faith, about Jesus, about music and about my calling – it was an amazing night visitation style dream, so I feel like I have met her in the Spirit and God said to me 'That church is so important for my future revival in America – I find this really amazing!

Amy: Wow, they are in Heaven praying for people! Whitney Houston and her daughter and the good people surrounding them – aww.

Jon: Yes, she's going to be singing at the Wedding Feast of the Lamb, someone had a prophecy about it after she died and knew she would be murdered in advance!

Amy: Yes, and Michael Jackson too, and you had a vision the other day where he was dancing?

Jon: Michael Jackson was dancing in the flames of God doing the moonwalk yes, and today I read in the scriptures 'when you go through the fire you will not burn!' and this made me laugh at God's victory which always or often looks like a terrible defeat from the terrestrial perspective down here, but is really a great awesome victory from the Celestial perspective! They are both in the glory realms, so God has already turned it around for them, while we are still waiting! Lol. So, when I kept hearing Billy Jean very loudly in my mind for no reason, then I saw this vision! Well, that did make me laugh, but it was so prophetic because God was saying 'You should dance in the flames!' So, when they persecute you, you should be dancing!' This leads me onto my next revelation. We really can rejoice in all circumstances 'I say it again: REJOICE!'

"Rejoice in the Lord alway: [and] again I say, Rejoice. Let your moderation be known unto all men. The Lord [is] at hand. Be careful for nothing; but in every thing by prayer and supplication with thanksgiving let your requests be made known unto God. And the peace of God, which passeth all understanding, shall keep your hearts and minds through Christ Jesus."

HIGH WITH THE MOST HIGH

—Philippians 4:4—7

REVELATION: WE CAN REJOICE IN THE LORD ALWAYS!

Revivalist historian, Pastor Robert Pears said it's the key to breakthrough, because many people are praying for breakthrough and they don't know how to get it!'

Luke 6.22 'Blessed are you when people hate you, when they exclude you and insult you and reject your name as evil because of the Son of Man (it's not because of you, it's because of the Son of Man every time)' and then it's saying 'Rejoice in that day and leap for joy because Great is your reward in Heaven!'

So, he gave this example of Marie Woodworth Etta and he was reading a copy of her diary and basically the natural rain came down and no one came to her meeting but she said 'well come on! 'Let's just rejoice anyway!' so she did and she clapped her hands and as she really prophetically rejoiced, it was in that action of doing that, and every day she kept doing that and before you knew it, it was like a clap that had opened up the Heavens and do you know what was the result? One thousand people turned up to hear her preach the next day, so when she had about two or three thousand people at meeting in the local vicinity, all around the area in the shopping malls and even in the woods, they started getting encounters with God all over the place.

This also happened with Andrew Murray in South Africa and Charles Finney in America! Real revival was breaking out everywhere! Andrew Murray used to go back and forth on horseback or on his feet for years and years to witness the Gospel and intercede for and then one time Revival broke out in one of the house groups that he was visiting and he was really surprised by this and there was this little black teenager and she first heard the winds of angels all the way through the place where people were assembled, but the amazing thing is, she heard the wind of God and no one else heard it! She exclaimed 'Can't everyone hear the wind?' so Revival broke out, and then what happened is a stranger turned up with an American accent and he said to Andrew Murray 'This is of God' and Andrew repented by this rebuke because at first Andrew didn't like the messy outburst of revival even though he had been praying all those years all that intercession over the years and can you imagine? When revival broke out, he didn't like it! So, this American turned up out of the blue and then he went, and the thing is there were no Americans around that area at all! So, he could have been an angel, it's very possible, the people came outside and they were so convicted by the power of the Holy Spirit that it spread all over the town and people were falling in bushes and they were just crying!

They just kept crying out for mercy and to be saved from their sins and these were just ordinary people that weren't anywhere near the meeting, it just continued like that, really outstanding! So, this is the secret of revival!

'When my people pray, I will hear from Heaven and I will save them from their sins and I will heal them and their land!' 2 Chronicles 7:14. He heals us and He heals our land.

So, Luke 6.22 says 'Rejoice in that day' and Pastor Robert Pears had a revelation while reading Woodworth Etta's diary, so even though nothing looks like it's happening, rejoice! Do something! So here is the Action: Leap for joy! Robert Pears realized when you get an attack, you can fight back: Rejoice! You should think not that the counter attack of the Devil is hurting you but you should hurt it back with the counterattack of the Holy Spirit to rejoice because your name is written in Heaven, and your name was crucified with the Son of Man. The revelation is, it's the Son of Man and you Being Persecuted and you are actually blessed.

So therefore, the key to your breakthrough is to REJOICE IN THE

HIGH WITH THE MOST HIGH

ATTACK! Isn't that amazing? And you <u>do it in that day</u> and this 'now' and 'in that day' word in is an impartation word because:

'If any man be in Christ: He is a creation'
'There's no condemnation in Christ'

REVELATION: BEING IN CHRIST IS A HIGHER DIMENSION!

I am also reminded of the amazing Martyr Jan Huss from Bohemia (Czech Republic) a reformer who was burnt at the stake, but before they did that, he was just so full of joy in the prison and they could hear his singing for a long way and they wondered 'what's that? What's that man singing about? Why is he so happy?' Well, he was rejoicing so much that when he was being burnt alive, he was singing praises!

The point is it had opened Heaven, I am sure that he didn't feel pain because he was in a different dimension! The same is true for when St. Stephen was stoned, so a different dimension opens up in the middle of an attack if you rejoice! And I find this revelation absolutely phenomenal! Praise God! That's the key to Breakthrough so when you get an anxiety attack, rejoice and thank God. This is how you must fight back! Why? Because it's a weapon. Praise and worship is a weapon and I really use it! But it does even more than we can ever imagine because it opens up higher dimensions of Heaven. This can happen to us not just because we are having a good day, but in the bad, ugly and painful days – we can praise!

Rejoice in that day and leap for joy – so there needs to be an action that proves you really are supernaturally happy when you aren't feeling it too, praise God! Because 'Great is our reward in Heaven'

So, to amplify this prophetic revelation further it could read:

DREAMS AND PORTALS

'Great is your reward in Heaven that will come out of Heaven through you!'

This will then spread to other people, so that's what Woodworth Etta did, it was raining and pouring, nothing was happening, but she was praising and clapping!

Another example is a modern Revivalist called Jessie Green, well, during Covid she went to where she had been praying for years with little to no effect she felt, but during 2020 coronavirus she went to Huntington Beach California and then revival suddenly broke out! This was featured on Sid Roth this year and even police couldn't stop it! So sometimes it's when you not expecting it like today before the zoom meeting with Robert Pears, I started to see in the Spirit an outline briefly of the Throne of Grace and I was like whoa! What's that? 'I had an impartation, I was crying before the meeting and I thought' that's embarrassing!' because I was not expecting it, because I didn't really feel I was that engaged in my worship, I was just sitting in God's Presence, just waiting on Him!

"But they that wait upon the Lord shall renew [their] strength; they shall mount up with wings as eagles; they shall run, and not be weary; [and] they shall walk, and not faint."

—Isaiah 40:31

So, we are going to be soaring over our problems and soaring over our pain. When people are hating us and taking us wrongly, misunderstanding us, or if they are hating among themselves or having their own misunderstandings, we've got to understand that's got nothing to do with us, we will pray for them, and we will do something rather unique and special. Rejoicing! We will secretly jump around with God in our mind if we cannot express this outwardly and we will jump around with God in our heart and that will release an open Heaven over the whole situation and that's what God was always doing! He must have been supernaturally rejoicing, releasing the Heavens in His miracles and even prior to them happening. Maybe in His prayer time alone at night He saw these things in advance? Jesus could certainly see in the Spirit, but I bet there were times when he had spiritual warfare and had to contend to see in the spirit and He had to trust anyway, thus fulfilling the prophecy and the fact that He was co-divine God and a Man in one! Well, that's how it is for us today. We get different times and seasons, some more painful and isolating than others wouldn't you say?

"Believest thou not that I am in the Father, and the Father in me? the words that I speak unto you I speak not of myself: but the Father that dwelleth in me, he doeth the works."

—*John 14:10*

There was different things that He did:

- He wept and it opened a portal!
- He had compassion – it opened a portal!
- He prayed – it opened a portal!
- He rejoiced – it opened portals!

So, I hope you are seeing that we have authority to open portals of Heaven and we have the same awesome responsibility in Christ and authority to close demonic portals! There are gates of Heaven and we actually are a gateway of righteousness. Praise Jesus. I learnt this from the Holy Bible through revelations and then I started seeing it being mentioned more in the Body of Christ by preachers like Ian Clayton, Justin Abraham, Nancy Cowen, and Jerome Nelson, I was so happy as we are in sync, speaking the same language! Do you want the 'Wow! Anointing?'

DREAMS AND PORTALS

Amy: So, if the demons are in any way talking in our heads and people need deliverance from demons or whatever it is – we can just rejoice anyway and it all gets turned around!

Jon: Yes, we can rejoice IN THE LORD ALWAYS!

I recommend listening to the message on YouTube called 'Do not worry' by R. W Schambach and he also has done ministry with Benny Hinn previously, who I am absolutely convinced that I will meet. It's a very fiery message but it's very good, and I've listened to it twice now because at one point. I had my trance music on in the background with that on because sometimes preaching's a bit too intense, sometimes we need to mute it so I needed something to calm it a bit. So, I was just listening mostly to my trance to relax and I had this on in the background but then I caught a revelation, **we should rejoice in the Lord always! – not just when we feel like it! I say it again rejoice!**

That's what releases the blessing and angelic glory!! I got to see the brief visionary of the Throne of Grace before the Sunday meeting and its quite something because Roberts Pears message ended on **'Grace will be given to you in that day – so let us draw near to the Throne of Grace where you will find help in time of need.**

The Grace is released to you through Holy Spirit is the revelation glory because supernaturally God wants to take over your natural. So, the point is it's not nice when people say horrible things to us or about us, or we are under fire or facing spiritual oppositions and attacks and counterattacks. But it's not about me or my comfort. It's about God and God is happy about it because He has already overcome so we might as well overcome too!

Amy: Because He sees the future of deliverance, He can see the future already!

(My sister was still listening to me preach!)

Jon: Yes, He can see the fact that Eminem was writing horrible lyrics about drugs and sex influencing the youth but know but now that that he's saved what about all those people who have listened to his material?

Amy: They will get saved!

Jon: Yes exactly! They are going to say 'Excuse me, I want to be saved too!' We used to listen to Eminem and we used to get high, steal things and do this or that but now look at us!!

Amy: And yet he was once so angry and proud and rebellious. Glory to God!
So how do we know who will be used by God for his awesome Kingdom plan? Everything is leading up to his remarkable great and glorious time in history again!

We both agreed in unison 'They are about to be used!' Hollywood's revival is about to break out and be much bigger than Azuza street and it will be Gods Holy-wood.

Amy: Eminem had a lot of anger at from the past, I am sure he will say this as part of his testimony and all the pride and refutation he had to make up for feeling inadequate and for feeling insecure and scared it can come out as pride in people. But thou he's realized now that Jesus is all he needs and people who have liked him are going to realize that too. Amen.

I praise God for my prophetic sister! The Glory of God is whirling around her in the Spirit!

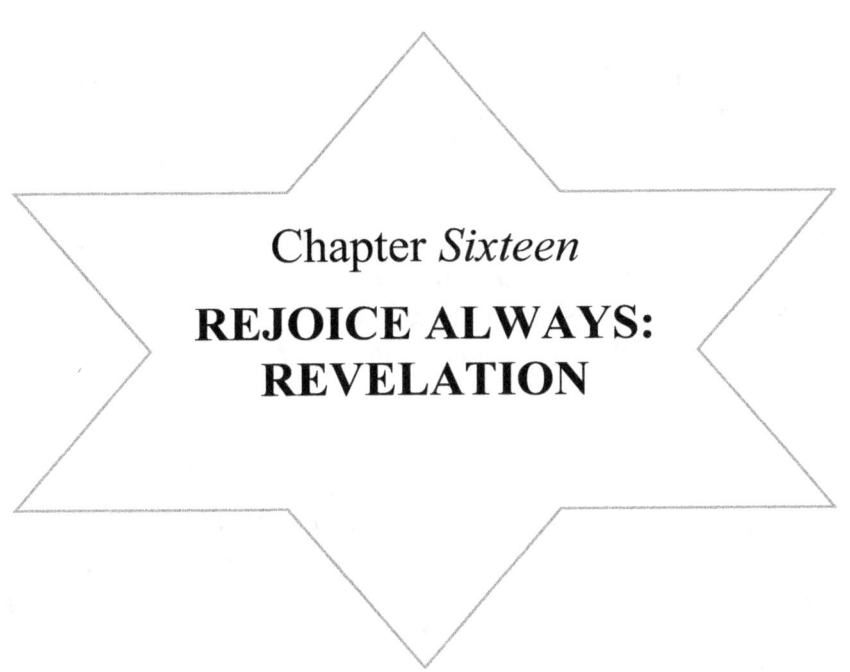

Chapter *Sixteen*
REJOICE ALWAYS: REVELATION

REJOICE ALWAYS REVELATION:

To understand realms of supernatural joy we must start with:

THANKSGIVING realms
GRATITUDE realm
PRAISE realm
WORSHIP realm
GLORY realms

The result is an open Heaven, so why rejoice and what does it really mean? Well, you are re-joining with a spirit called Joy!

So <u>we can make the choice to rejoice</u> in or thanksgiving, and then we <u>join with Joy</u>.

HIGH WITH THE MOST HIGH

ASK THAT YOUR JOY BE COMPLETE! ASK THAT YOU BE STRENGTHENED AND EMPOWERED BY JOY!

"And in that day ye shall ask me nothing. Verily, verily, I say unto you, Whatsoever ye shall ask the Father in my name, he will give [it] you. Hitherto have ye asked nothing in my name: ask, and ye shall receive, that your joy may be full."

—John 16:23—24

This is a complete fulfilment of the mystery of JOY so we can join with JOY in Thanksgiving, I hope this is becoming easier to understand, but if we don't feel like thanking God, we thank Him anyway in faith! These are high level ANGELIC SPIRITS, not just words!

So, it's by faith that you that you do that and we see this in the pattern of Jesus life. Then the second part or realm is praise and here again, we join with a different dimension **IN JOY** and then we go into worship and we really thank God and we really praise God and then we will really join with joy and we will open up the heavens!!

This awesome life changing, game changing life revelation is based on Luke 6.22.

Blessed are you when you are in the attack and you get multiple attacks from multiple different demonic forces and them even people hate you on top, and they exclude you, they persecute you, they slander you, they reject you, they leave you, and you feel like you have been left on the shelf and they have insulted you well blessed aren't you? When you go through the pain because even pain has a purpose!

You've been feeling like you've been rejected from the glory of God like it's left you; this is all happening because of **the Son of Man who lives in you by the power of the Holy Spirit!** The Word says clearly 'rejoice in that day!' it doesn't say rejoice tomorrow it doesn't Say rejoice 3 days down the line, it doesn't say rejoice when you feel better and this really needs highlighting **'we don't rejoice, or join again with joy when we feel good.'**

<u>In faith we join with joy when we don't feel good!</u> In faith we join with joy when we don't feel good! I want to say it twice hear me child of God and rejoice anyway!

This is why I think God made me a preacher of the Gospel because He can see even though I am in pain, I will still preach! Even though I was in pain I will still have to Minister! Even though I experience pain, I had to realize there's a purpose for that pain! There is a higher calling on my life and woe to me if I don't preach the Gospel: I have to release the messages because, to use the Christian language; they burn in you!' but they really do! They just burn in your bones and also, it's a bit like giving birth; you've got to eject this, it's like a volcano, it's got to come out!

1. OUR JOY WILL BE MADE COMPLETE!

Restore unto me the joy of thy salvation; and uphold me [with thy] free spirit."—Psalms 51:12

2. THE JOY IS NOT OUR OWN VERSION OF IT

Its supernatural and it comes from Heaven!

3. THE JOY IS ACCESIBLE EVEN THOUGH YOU FEEL WEAK

The joy is accessible when you are weak, fed up and people hate you because of God!
The joy is accessible when people turn against you, its accessible when people shut you down, it's accessible when you get slandered, and it's accessible when the demons attack you!

HIGH WITH THE MOST HIGH

With multiple attacks, and it's happening all the time, we need to learn how to counter attack back and one of these keys to your breakthrough is for you to rejoice! We do it in that day, in that moment, we bring Heaven down not by our own feelings because we have to do it by revelation, and you achieve this through practice and Jesus has been talking to me about practicing thanksgiving in all circumstances, practice praise despite pain and then you go into the glory realm and you worship God and before you know it, Heaven comes down— that's my life! So basically, I do my best to do that all the time which can become very challenging to fight in this way, to rejoice in that day! It is a mega test but with a mega reward! There's a time and season for everything, weeping and reaping but Jesus said this to me also. **'I turned water into wine to show that all the seasons are mine!'**

All time is His. So, you can go outside of time, outside of your current position of pain and it's possible to bring in the future glory of God! Our breakthrough is to join in with rejoicing but you have to do something: leap for joy, clap, dance, sing, and preach but do something that you couldn't do before or didn't want to do before because you didn't feel like it or feel well enough! So, there is really something so powerful here that must be understood as a revelation:

REVELATION: LEARN TO JOIN AGAIN WITH JOY REJOICE AND REAP SUPERNATURAL JOY!

SOW IN TEARS, JOIN WITH JOY AND YOU WILL GET AN OPEN HEAVEN OF SUPERNATURAL JOY FOR YOURSELF AND OTHERS FULL OF GLORY!

YOU MUST PROVOKE HEAVEN WITH YOUR DEISIRE AND ACTION TO GET A JOY REACTION. FAITH WITHOUT ACTION IS DEAD.

REJOICE ALWAYS

THIS IS A MAJOR GAME CHANGER REVELATION! THE KEY TO BREAKTHROUGH IS TO LET GO AND LET GOD'S HEAVENLY JOY FLOW INTO AND THROUGH YOU!

ANGELS OF JOY WILL MANIFEST BECOMING PART OF YOUR STRENGTH IN CHRIST AT THE MAJOR CROSSROADS OF YOUR LIFE PROVOKING AN EXCHANGE!

YOU WILL LIVE:
- FROM POWERLESS TO POWERFUL!
- FROM WEAK TO STRONG!
- FROM MISERY TO HAPPY JOY!
- FROM RICH TO POOR!
- FROM YOUR OWN STRENGTH TO CHRIST'S STRENGTH

I can do all things (including rejoicing all ways)

"I can do all things through Christ which strengtheneth me."

—(Philippians 4:13)

Christ wants to restore us to the joy of our salvation (This was a point of exchange by faith) and we are to work out our salvation with fear and trembling which is awe of almighty God! He then gives us His strength and joy in **exchange** for ours! This is what fasting must do too, humbling ourselves before the Lord with prayer, fasting and exchanging our miserable hungry state, totally dependent on God for His mind on all affairs of Life and Abundant life!

I see this to mean that God has already provided a great secret called the **energetic exchange** that we received by faith at the point of salvation – why then go back to misery and slavery?'

"O foolish Galatians, who hath bewitched you, that ye should not obey the truth, before whose eyes Jesus Christ hath been evidently

set forth, crucified among you? This only would I learn of you, Received ye the Spirit by the works of the law, or by the hearing of faith? Are ye so foolish? having begun in the Spirit, are ye now made perfect by the flesh? Have ye suffered so many things in vain? if [it be] yet in vain."

—Galatians 3:1—4

"Now the Lord is that Spirit: and where the Spirit of the Lord [is], there [is] liberty. But we all, with open face beholding as in a glass the glory of the Lord, are changed into the same image from glory to glory, [even] as by the Spirit of the Lord."

—(2 Corinthians 3:17—18)

Jesus wants our cups to overflow and our hearts to overflow in abundance! He wants us out of captivity: We have the **God Key** Now! The key to come out of captivity in the soul is to allow Gods rejoicing in the Spirit to come in! Do this when we are next in the middle of an attack. Praise King Jesus Christ!

Never mind the pain for a moment, I know it's horrible but let's thank God for who He is, what He is, what He's done this shifts the focus off us, off the attacks, off the demons and it gets an open Heaven to come down, so this can even happen in the middle of those attacks, so when it looks like nothing is happening, you'll find that God wants to bring everything to you! See, God wants to bring everything to you! SEE, God wants to bring everything from Heaven down when it appears that absolutely nothing is happening! When you persist when nothing is happening! Somethings going to happen!

I absolutely love how Marie Woodworth Elta preached the Gospel outside in the rain whether anyone turned up or not! While clapping she praised and thanked God 'Thank you God for all these people that are here.' Now in the natural, there's no one there, it's raining! She could see it! Then a thousand people showed up and revival breaks out! The police had to put warning signs up because she was around, the glory was so intense that glory was like a force field! Beware, you can't go near that woman of God! She would preach and go into trances frozen to the spot and everyone would be convicted! Where is that level of power today? This amazing Saint had her children die and she realized that my children are going to keep dying and she uses the words 'God would take them.'

And she would say 'God isn't going to allow my children to live if I don't fulfil this calling!' That's how much of the Spirit of God was on her, like 'I have to go and get a tent, I have to preach the Gospel, and I have to do this! Otherwise, my children will be dead!' she sure understood the power of rejoicing in a wet field or Gospel tent! She knew the attack was persisting and the forces of Hell were all against her, so she was like 'right, praise you Jesus! Thank you, God you are so powerful! I worship you! You're awesome! I give you the glory! Thank you for all these crowds of people! Glory. Glory praise you King Jesus Christ! Well, they all came, after the clapping in the rain! What an awakening revelation!

So, when we feel excluded, insulted by people or by demons, and we feel rejected and we feel in pain, and we are going through trials, tribulations and persecutions the key is to rejoice: to join again with the Angel of Joy with Jesus! He is the Prince of Peace and the King of Joy!

You can get a major release by faith here! Jan Huss was so much in joy that he didn't feel anything, Heaven was open, it was a different dimension which I said previously which is worth noting again. 'What's that angelic singing from Heaven all about?' People will question your OTT joyful life!

They will persecute you because they won't understand it, nor you, but don't take it personally especially when even Christians turn against you for lack of understanding, revelation, jealousy and even religious competition! It will happen but rejoice anyway. Keep your garments of praise on! Then after Jan Huss there was a 30-year war 1618 to 1648 between the Protestants and the Catholics over Bohemia and Germany known as 'one of the longest and most destructive conflicts in European history' Now, that tells me that Satan was extremely threatened! Just imagine becoming that much of a threat to the kingdom of darkness! The result of this was that everyone prayed and the whole of Bohemia was completely Christianized— saved by the blood of the Lamb by the 10th century!

Wiki Britannica 'Bohemia' was briefly subordinated to greater Monrovia in the late 9th century. Saints Cyril and Methodius introduced Christianity into Bohemia from Monrovia'. Isn't that awesome? We are talking about the power to cause a Godly revolution to change the whole of history! It can happen all over again! We have this treasure in just little jars of clay to show this all-surpassing power is from God not from ourselves— that is the power of joy, martyrdom and glory!

Notice also that Saint Methodius was involved and it was the Monrovians that introduced grace revelations to the Wesleyans thus creating the movement of Methodism! This whole Reformation proceeded the 16th century one with Martin Luther. It was phenomenal reformation but it was also a phenomenal attack from Hell just like the Romans against Christ and His followers in the Acts of the Apostles. We have attacks against us daily, the kingdom of God suffers violence, but the violent (wise as serpents) take it by force! We suffer violently we feel all the effects of violence and trauma and pain and loss.

But God says 'if you will just go into thanksgiving, you will just go into thanksgiving, you'll go into the realm of praise, you'll go into the realm of worship, you'll go into the realm of glory and I will release my joy into your life and that will give you breakthrough that you have been praying for! You want to rend the Heavens? Well, you can because it's in that day you can receive my joy in exchange for your old version of joy and this will shift atmospheres in the spirit! You have inside you the power to unlock nations!'

REJOICE ALWAYS

'Blessed are you who hunger now for you will be satisfied"

--Mathew 5:6 –

So, Jesus goes up to the crowd of 5000+ thousand and He knew they needed feeding. So, I believe He thought 'well I have compassion and I will join with Father God and I will join with joy and rejoicing and I will join with Heaven …' In Christs heart, he wasn't moved! The suffering, sickness, the poverty and the hunger of the people didn't affect Him negatively because He was already in Fathers perfect will, so it was an invitation for Him to work miracles through the dimension of joy (which was more hidden) and the dimension of compassion (which was more seen by the Disciples) but what did He do? He thanked God and He praised 'His Daddy in Heaven!' He was connected to Heaven, He knew he was connected to heaven, He knew he was from Heaven. Just like this: 'I am not from this world, I am from Heaven, so I am going to release that so I need Fathers will, power and authority' also He knew that He wasn't perfect because He was still a man. It was only Father that could help Him, connecting Him to the miracle realm so even with Holy Spirit, He knew he wasn't perfect.There had to be all 3 connected! It's almost hard to believe because even Mum said as I was in fellowship and ministering: 'He's in Heaven and yet on Earth and the Father is Holy and He can't look on sin, amazing!'

It wasn't just Christs compassion that released the miracle, because we've heard that before, but He had already joined with Father God who was joy to Him and a delight so **He joined with rejoicing in Him** 'Oh I rejoice Father, thank you feeding all these people, of course you can multiply these bread and fish'

So that all happened, there were 7 baskets full left over and we are supposed to do greater works than Jesus Himself! It was cooked fish and cooked bread! The Bible says 'blessed are you who hunger and thirst now for you will be satisfied!

HIGH WITH THE MOST HIGH

Now we hunger and thirst for righteousness so we are going to be very satisfied in Ministry! *'Blessed are you who weep now for you are going to laugh! Blessed are you when people hate you, when they exclude you, when they insult you, when they reject your name as evil because of the Son of Men'*

And I will insert my Prophetic part 'Blessed are you when you get all kinds of attacks and counter attacks from the Devil you must remember to counter attack back by using my weapon of Joy: Rejoice!'

Great is your reward in 'Heaven' doesn't just mean when you die, it means great is your reward with the portal to open Heaven to come into effect in your atmosphere in that day now! **If you want breakthrough, you've got access to it by faith, by joining again with joy!**

Scripture says 'that is how the ancestors treated the prophets: so, we get mistreated but God thinks it's wonderful because He in you has already overcome the world!

"Behold, the hour cometh, yea, is now come, that ye shall be scattered, every man to his own, and shall leave me alone: and yet I am not alone, because the Father is with me. These things I have spoken unto you, that in me ye might have peace. In the world ye shall have tribulation: but be of good cheer; I have overcome the world."

—*(John 16:32—33)*

So, we can praise God for the accomplished victory now and in advance and I believe this is how people get their healing, this is how they get a revelation, and there'll be somebody out there, a child of God that gets this revelation: that Jesus has already done it! And then they must wait patiently often in the background, in obscurity, hidden away to manifest that powerful revelation in their life. Once they realize that, they are like 'Oh God wow! You did this so now I can just go near people who are terribly sick and of course you'll heal them! This all happens because of who you are everything is done! So, ALLMIGHTY LORD GOD OF ABRAHAM, I JOIN MYSELF TO YOUR JOY!

It all starts with a revelation because **the revelation can cause a revolution**, so much that not even a war, not even famine, not even death can stop the glory of God from being fulfilled because history proves that the whole of Bohemia Czechoslovakia was saved! It affected France, Austria, all across Europe, it was just absolutely so incredible and awesome and it's something we need to know!

There can be a suddenly with God. There was with Jessie Green who has interviewed Heidi Baker whom I saw in London once. Huntington Beach, California was suddenly full of revival, yet years before nothing was happening! There is such a power in persistence mixed with faith and humility. I believe that with my work, if I just keep on doing it exactly the method that God has told me, and just keep on doing it, then suddenly there will be a great breakthrough! So, when we get the attacks, pains and problems, let's just thank God for the accomplished finished work of Calvary, who He is, what He's done, what He's doing and what He is going to do and Heaven really will come down.

The Key to our breakthrough today: is to rejoice in that day! God is outside of all time and all space and He is happy from that complete, on the throne vantage point! Hallelujah Amen.

So, we must do this and we will put it into practice when we next experience pain, instead of talking about the pain, lets acknowledge that it's all for His name. 'I am in pain Lord, but I thank you for your goodness, I thank you for your goodness, I thank you for your thanksgiving and then you can go into this realm of praise through pain which is supernatural, I do it all the time, boasting in my weakness and exchanging it for Christ future strength and joy!

After praise, you go into the worship realm, then you are in the glory realm and you bring down an open Heaven, bringing out the anointing that breaks the yoke which is the secret of what all these Revivalists and Apostles had. Jesus himself had that revelation and manifestation of miracles, signs and wonders and we can have it too! Praise Jesus right now!

Chapter *Seventeen*
HUMILIATION & MULTIPLICATION: VISION & REVELATION

HUMILIATION AND MULTIPLICATION (Vision)

To understand these hard times and the goal of long suffering can only be understood through Holy Spirit who always leads us into all truth.

"Howbeit when he, the Spirit of truth, is come, he will guide you into all truth: for he shall not speak of himself; but whatsoever he shall hear, [that] shall he speak: and he will shew you things to come."

—John 16:13

Behold, thou desirest truth in the inward parts: and in the hidden [part] thou shalt make me to know wisdom."

—Psalms 51:6

HIGH WITH THE MOST HIGH

This isn't just the parts of things that we want to know about. This means everything that we are supposed to know about based on our calling. Put simply there's things that we are supposed to know and there's things we aren't. There are different times and seasons, some are harder and more painful and difficult than others, but all can teach us something. I have covered the question, 'why does God allow suffering?' In many of my other books so I will not labour it here. I aim to show you how I get high on revelations and how the glory will increase in our lives by passing through trials. The foundations of the word of God are always my rock, even though they can sometimes seem old fashioned and out of date, these Holy Scriptures are divinely inspired, and they cost blood for us to have them. The Gospel is not a frivolous thing but an eternal thing. Lives are lost daily for the sake by knowing Christ. It is costly knowing and following Jesus. Always remember that.

The book of Romans tells us we do this by faith: See NIV. Romans 3:21—27, Romans 4:4—9, Romans 5:1—10, 15—20, Romans 6:5—13,14, Romans 8:13,17

Now it's not my intention to print out the whole Bible but I have put these verses in for your study to show how:

1. We are all justified and forgiven by grace and through faith in Christ.
2. We will suffer but it is for Christ's glory
3. The law is not against us anymore.
4. We aren't even seen as sinners anymore!
5. In the spirit we are seen as pure and righteous
6. Our sufferings produce perseverance, character, and hope. So that there is no condemnation or shame for those in Christ anymore!
7. All evil, bad, hard, painful, strange things are working together for your good in Christ.

HUMILIATION & MULTIPLICATION: VISION & REVELATION

Here are 7 main reasons from a few pages in Romans why we should be happy despite trials. We can join in with the revelations that are written and with the ones that aren't written yet! Christ has finished the work for himself, but clearly His Body looks like it needs to catch up. As we are suffering now, it has a much higher reason behind it, all these defeats and delays are really working for us (Romans 8:28) and therefore they must really be secret victories in advance! Talk about a prophetic disguise and a strange mystery!

Therefore we are justified in Christ, end of story. So don't justify yourself to man, just abide and God in you will take over the rest! So before we move on to the next revelation God gave me, you must know the foundation revelations in the word of God. Thousands of years passed between David's Psalms and the book of Romans. Time changes things but both books are equally just as powerful. Do you ever wonder what is written in your book about your life? Or your data base? Have you ever thought about it? We just don't realise the painful, humbling and awful things we go through are really for God's glory this means God will be glorified. He will be seen!

If you share in his sufferings, you will share in his glory. Do you really want the glory miracles that much? Then either get prepared to suffer or you must continue on suffering-until the appointed time. It won't last forever. God is good!

"For our light affliction, which is but for a moment, worketh for us a far more exceeding [and] eternal weight of glory;."

—2 Corinthians 4:17

"Many [are] the afflictions of the righteous: but the Lord delivereth him out of them all. He keepeth all his bones: not one of them is broken."

—(Psalms 34:19—20)

HIGH WITH THE MOST HIGH

Thousands of years have passed since the New Testament and so no wonder why people going through long term suffering, sickness, pain, and major diseases are getting fed up depressed, oppressed and losing hope. Quite frankly, it is understandable at times to desire to give up but please don't! There is a major reward coming for those who refuse to quit! This cannot continue forever. Revival or we die!! These are desperate times whether we realise it or not. People often think Jesus is coming back soon but they have misunderstood the **Kingdom Awakening Plan and the Great Harvest Time.** None of us can participate in that time if we are sick, tired, fed up and oppressed! We can't do that great work without serious equipping and wealth as well as brand new health. It is all up to God. All the timing is down to God. It is Gods responsibility but we still have to play our part. We still have to get ready for revival. We absolutely cannot afford to give up or be lazy.

We are at his mercy every single day. It is humbling but it will be worth the wait, trusting God leads to inheriting the Promised Land, prophecies will be and are being fulfilled, and we have to prayerfully look up, look within, and look out for Jesus Christs next big move and if equipped by God, understanding the word and the revelations we cannot and will not miss it!

Even with deliverance, if your problem is caused by demons (which 9\10 it is) we only have the grace given to us for each day, and if the demons don't leave, don't give up. They are only a few evil spirits. They do not have as much power as you give them folks! Just trust God! They are doing a work, but I won't talk about that here I will save that for another one of my books that you can read or hear by audio in the future. Praise Jesus!

REVELATION: CHRIST IN US IS BEING HUMILIATED FOR A MUCH GREATER PURPOSE THAN WE CAN ALL IMAGINE-ITA ALL PART OF HIS PLAN

God told me this once when I was cooking our dinner and I had to be careful that I didn't burn it! The voice I heard was loud and audible and

HUMILIATION & MULTIPLICATION: VISION & REVELATION

it shocked me to my core it was the revelation that made the Words foundation make sense and feel more secure to me, especially in an insecure time! This was prior to the 2020 lockdown so I was being prepared to understand something deep on behalf of the body of Christ in advance.

I had a vision during this time when I went into an unseen realm, it was a part open vision where our oven just folded out and then I found myself seeing Africa. I was then there and we had plates and plates of food being multiplied before our very eyes and God said 'Son, just pray over the first plate!' This makes me laugh! We had a stock of empty plates but we just kept giving them out, and I thought but now we don't have any more plates left, but they kept on coming and coming! And I thought where are these plates coming from? And where is the food coming from? It was a completely different realm of glory! Heaven was providing for us! It was awesome and Jesus said,

'This is why **I am being humiliated within you now**! You want to be like me? Then you've got to let me in you! You've got to let go and let me do this in you! But right now I am doing this! I am being humiliated in you! It isn't about you feeling like you are being humiliated in me. It isn't that way at all. I am changing your perspective of my realm of suffering in the saint for you. Soon, you will understand more from a much higher perspective and higher dimension. You are out of the picture right now! But I will include you in the bigger picture in the future if you suffer now, you will be glorified in me in the future!'

Well, that blew my mind and really helps me to see, to realign priorities, to focus, to remember, and to praise God that no matter how hard it gets, we will still do our best now to help the poor but it's only God that's my provider and don't I know it!

The second part of this vision occurred after I had got off the floor. My spiritual Mother Priscilla understand that something was spiritual and she had a later dinner but she was ok with that! Kind of funny and then as I went into the sitting room I saw myself and her meeting Heidi Baker and I have already seen her in London after she flew all that way from Mozambique which is an experience I have never forgotten. I saw myself catching the same or similar grace to help the 200 Ugandan children we help in an orphanage with Pastor Elijah Shepherd, where at times, the suffering for them all has been off the charts and no help came through. Quite frankly, conviction is coming and a judgement because the Body of Christ is so selfish and lots of people make excuses why they cannot give to help the poor and needy. I am not the Judge, God is, but make no mistake about it, a heavy conviction is coming.

So the second part of this revelation is to **join Again with rejoicing**! So when I am being HUMILIATED FOR CHRIST, or when Christ is being humiliated in me, but you must see that it's a bit of both, it is highly purposeful. Once again, I must stress that I will not and do not look at my feelings, it isn't about me— it is about Jesus Christ in me and He helps me when I am at my weakest. Fact.

When I am looking down cast, if I look weak or pathetic and I know I can't save myself: I can only look to Jesus Christ as my source, my provider, my lover, my friend, my everything! For example, why would you fast? In the natural that is ridiculous. Well, you empty yourself so you get filled up! I don't want to be filled up with just food, I want to be filled up with spiritual food! And then I want to be in the overflow so I can help other people so I can be a real minister of God, so then I can be helping someone else in a supernatural dimension. I want my life to be supernatural. So, I empty myself, but <u>it's Christ in me that's doing the fast</u>. If I think it's me doing the fast, then I miss it! <u>Christ in me has done the fast in me already</u> so He's just repeating what He has already done. And if he doesn't let me/give me grace to fast then I won't. I just follow what Master Christ wants even though it's not easy at times but the anointing will break the yoke. Amen

REVELATION: FASTING:

PLEASE NOTE: IT'S NOT EVEN YOU WHEN YOU ARE SAVED DOING THAT FASTING.

HUMILIATION & MULTIPLICATION: VISION & REVELATION

YOU HAVE TO HUMBLE YOURSELF BEFORE THE LORD WITH PRAYER AND A WEAK SACRIFICE SO HE CAN MAKE YOU BETTER AND STRONGER AND THIS WILL ACTIVATE SPIRITUAL GIFTING IN YOU.

FASTING CAN ALSO VERY EASILY BRING OUT YOUR 'DARK SIDE' AND IT CAN CAUSE STOMACH PAIN, LONG TERM HEALTH PROBLEMS AND HEADACHES SO YOU HAVE TO BE VERY CAREFUL, WISE AND HEAR GOD.

FASTING IS A WAY OF FINE TUNING YOURSELF AS WELL AS A BODY/SOUL DETOX/MIND DETOX.

BUT FASTING CAN AND OFTEN DOES BRING UP NEGATIVE THOUGHTS AND FEELINGS SO YOU HAVE TO LEARN TO BE COMPASSIONATE WITH YOURSELF-

BUT REMEMBER THIS THAT FAST OF 40 DAYS AND NIGHTS 960 HOURS AND CHRIST HAS ALREADY COMPLETED IT FOR YOU!

ONLY DO YOUR FASTS LED BY THE HOLY SPIRIT AND NEVER BY MAN OR BECAUSE OF CHURCH PRESSURE. GOD KNOWS WHAT YOU NEED.

FASTING HUMBLES THE FLESH AND LETS THE SPIRIT OF GOD TAKE OVER.

You must exchange your weakness for God's strength within you that's already done by that 40 day and 40 night fast that God already did for you! Thank you, Jesus.

So God is gracious to our bodies and He shows me how long to fast, when to stop, whether it's a juice or water fast, I can hear him clearly, even though devils really try very hard when you are fasting to derail you, distract you, annoy you and use others to prevent you from doing your fast, so please beware of that our bodies are the temples of the

Holy Spirit, we belong to Christ, we are not our own. Also be careful with too much exercise during fasting. Fasting will slow you down and humble you and it is designed too.

> *"Moreover when ye fast, be not, as the hypocrites, of a sad countenance: for they disfigure their faces, that they may appear unto men to fast. Verily I say unto you, They have their reward. But thou, when thou fastest, anoint thine head, and wash thy face; That thou appear not unto men to fast, but unto thy Father which is in secret: and thy Father, which seeth in secret, shall reward thee openly."*
>
> —Mathew 6:16—18

> *"You also, as living stones, are being built up as a spiritual house for a holy priesthood, to offer up spiritual sacrifices acceptable to God through Jesus Christ."*
>
> –(2 Peter 2:5)

God gives me His strength and helps me compose messages or I just encourage others, but I do have a way about me that pushes people away so I can just be alone with God, and people often misunderstand this because I am unavailable, as I am angry at them or that I do not care, which just isn't true. Since the difference increases in my anointing I have had to give more time to God, not less. I also have my phone and social media inbox completely full and I can never keep up. It is not personal. Everything happens in its perfect timing. We all have to wait on God. Those in my close family who know me, they are well aware of how much time I need with my Jesus.

Even though the enemy wants to attack or distract me during that time, especially by the weakness of the flesh, I have to choose actively SPIRIT OVER FLESH nature daily.

HUMILIATION & MULTIPLICATION: VISION & REVELATION

We can therefore REJOICE when Christ is being humiliated within us, there is a massive purpose in our pain and so we have to rejoice! When we rejoice (join with the angelic joy of Heaven) all these things start to come together and that's what opens the Heavens! That's what gives us true breakthrough! I do also get discouraged and it is not easy to live by faith without a proper income but God is doing something so powerful and undeniable in my life. I have won the favour of my King! But I felt recently what was the point? I didn't have a bank account, someone scammed me and it's a long story! I didn't know what to do. So I made a crazy decision to spend 4 hours with God, just worshipping Him!! I was going to give him 2 hours which seemed excessive considering it was a major time sacrifice but as each hour passed, God wanted another hour!! Can you imagine? Then He wanted another one!

So 4 hours later I was pretty whacked and I felt so high in Christ. I absolutely need a worship partner but I don't think it's possible yet, so I hope it will be ok for it to just be me, even writing this I am starting to feel lifted like my body wants to float away…I feel the anointing so much on a daily basis and it's quite something - the revelation of worship it releases the river of God which releases miracles! I can feel my heart race and my chest feels like its expanding, I can shake or just drift out of my body and have spiritual experiences! I just absolutely love this life with Jesus despite the chaotic attacks. Thankfully Christ has provided the DOOR OF HOPE which is a way in and a way out. Portals exist in your body. I am becoming a gateway for the goodness and glory of God. This is the awareness of King Jesus within making me feel so high and floaty!

REVELATION: ANY EXTRA SACRIFICED TIME DURING WORSHIP WILL BRING YOU INTO HIGHER REALMS AND GODS OPEN HEAVENS AND PROVISIONS WILL FLOW IN YOUR LIFE! IT IS POWERFUL IN THE WORSHIP RIVER REVELATION REALM AND THEN MIRACLES WILL FLOW. JUST WORSHIP IN SPIRIT AND IN TRUTH. THEN WATCH, WAIT AND SEE CHRIST, WAIT AND RENEW YOUR STRENGTH!

HIGH WITH THE MOST HIGH

"God will supply your needs according to his riches in glory (glory realm) in Christ Jesus."

—**Philippians 4:19**

It was during those hours of worshipping Jesus that I got texts from different people saying that they would give to the ministry! So, what is the glory? It's the glory-realm that's where I was during all that 'lost/spent' time in worship and I went there by faith, which means that I don't have to see it. The not seeing is the exciting part, because something unseen and special is happening.

" Faith is being certain of the things no yet seen."—**Hebrews 11:1**

I don't have to be distracted or discouraged because I don't see something in the spirit that's not faith that's a demonic distraction! Wow! I think I have fell for that a few times and here's another lie 'don't worship God because you feel low or sad, no please, do it all the more! It will make you feel way better, not worse! Sometimes I will worship God in silence and other times with worship music, other times on a walk, and I also can worship God while I listen to other types of music. I am just so aware of His presence and so very thankful.

I still have some really lost sinner friends some I have met, some I haven't, but guess what? I still pray for them all! I don't think it's a waste of time because half the time I think God wants me to identify with all kinds of people, addictive or abusive types sometimes too. That's not easy, you have to learn to separate yourself from them for different times and seasons, but also you have to be a friend to them as you are the salt and light of the earth. Please note, these poor lost souls aren't going to go to a church. Therefore, you are their oil and light whether they understand, want it, reject you or not can we just try more to love people? Can we just be kinder and more giving and hard hearted and selfish please? We are not here just to separate people into categories.

HUMILIATION & MULTIPLICATION: VISION & REVELATION

You are these people's hope in Christ, they don't want to pray, they look at your example! Don't press block if God hasn't told you too! Also God can convict me so much sometimes saying 'Son, you must unblock and pray for people that have hurt you from the past. I am teaching you how to love.' Wow! We serve a loving God and maybe you may not like this message because it might be convicting you! Imagine what happens when you worship God and lift up lost souls to God's Throne? It's powerful! You can totally shift dark, heavy, oppressive, depressive or angry atmospheres by just having soft worship on in the background or singing softly. God is attracted to stillness, softness, gentleness and humility. He is attracted to praising through pain and worshipping beyond worrying and wondering what to do!

He is attracted to less stressing and more blessing! Then He will give you His blessing. Don't worry child of God, the provisions are all coming. No worries! He wants us purified through worship so the things of the world fall away from us! Our desires change through continuous praise. Worship is not just for God, it is for us. It will change you and your whole focus will be God centred, which loses the self-reliance which most people do not want to give up. I sometimes think praise and worship is more powerful than prayer.

For some time now God keeps telling me that so many Christians are operating in their own strength, categorizing sins and doing a 'holy than thou' act and missing the whole point. It's all grace from God! We can't do it perfectly even with a marriage and kids and church! You need GRACE daily and worship changes us from within it shouldn't be underrated, especially personal 'alone time' worship. God is truly looking at your heart. He knows who wants to worship Him for miracles and who just wants to be with Him for who he is, like life and death depend on it. Let every breath praise the Lord. Rejoicing always, being in the atmosphere of Heaven! This can become your experience. What an awesome invitation to know God that He wants to be with us that much, we go beyond the outer court into the inner cart when we praise our way through pain, let's learn to intercede in the rain and live from the glory river!

HIGH WITH THE MOST HIGH

Faith brings us into the River of Life and grace is given for daily humiliation in Christ for his future glory to be made manifest!

"But the hour cometh, and now is, when the true worshippers shall worship the Father in spirit and in truth: for the Father seeketh such to worship him. God [is] a Spirit: and they that worship him must worship [him] in spirit and in truth."

—(John 4:23—24)

Whether it hurts or not, I am still going to worship God: this is why I am so high with the Most High! Praise King Jesus, Yeshua H'Meshiach.

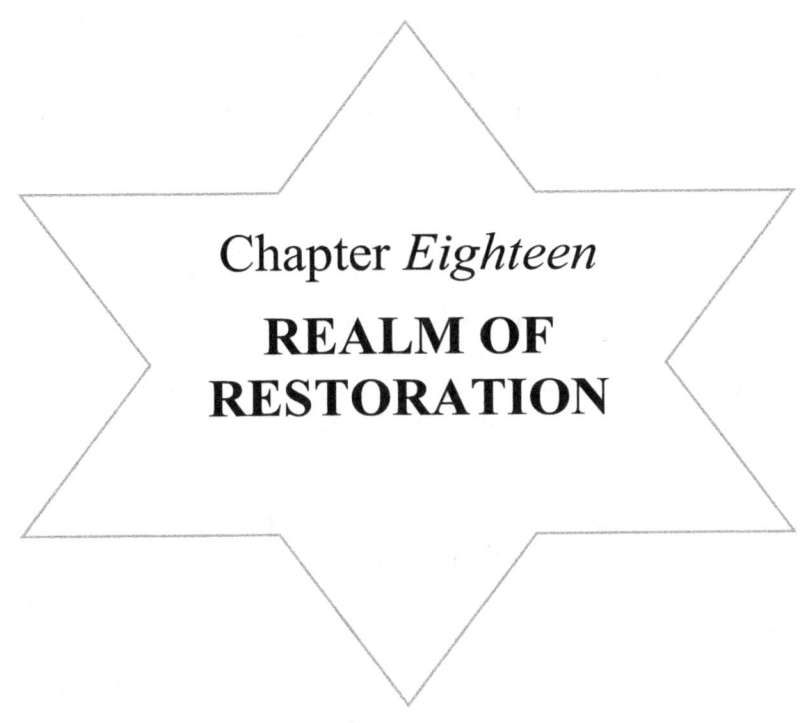

Chapter *Eighteen*
REALM OF RESTORATION

REALM OF RESTORATION

"And I will restore to you the years that the locust hath eaten, the cankerworm, and the caterpiller, and the palmerworm, my great army which I sent among you. And ye shall eat in plenty, and be satisfied, and praise the name of the Lord your God, that hath dealt wondrously with you: and my people shall never be ashamed."

—Joel 2:25—26

I believe by faith that God wants to restore broken lives, broken visions, broken hearts. That means we need to admit we are broken before the Lord, and I know that is very humbling, but please, we must do it. Yes I want us to be so happy, free and even high on Heaven

HIGH WITH THE MOST HIGH

but God will make sure that you face your pain to get to the good stuff. Mark that as very important in your life. No one else is going to face your pain for you, they might be with you, but there will also be times when you are 'alone' when others aren't around you, and you have to learn to cope with being ok around you and learn to let Holy Spirit in to comfort you.

No one is saying it is easy, but God will comfort you, because in some way or another we are all lonely without adequate fellowship with God. It is perfectly fine to admit this too. We weren't designed to be alone, but we do need to be alone sometimes, and we have to let God into those times. Pain and difficult feelings will provoke discord and discomfort in you, but you must face them. Don't be a coward! It's ok to not be ok.

Remember that and go on with God. You'll get good days and bad days and we shouldn't be in denial about the bad days. Just know that they are working for you and if you dare to praise God through those obscure difficult days. Well, then, you are really going somewhere!

We have this modern saying, 'You need to own your sh*t!" Which is quite funny, but it's quite truthful because you must own your bad days and your good days and know that they are all working together for your good in Christ Jesus. No matter how lonely we get, we must remember that hidden in Christ, we are so blessed! The Lord can make me smile and feel happy every day, but I do need to choose His happiness, just as we think and have put so much emphasis on choosing his Holiness, we must also choose his happiness, that way throughout all circumstances we can be truly free! Let's exterminate misery and revelate in joy!

REVELATION: CHOOSE GODS HAPPINESS AND JOY DAILY AND HE WILL GIVE YOU IT. YOU'LL EXCHANGE YOUR OLD SET OF EMOTIONAL AWARENESS AND EXPERIENCE IN FOR HIS. IT'S SUPERNATURAL!

Prophetess Janet was missing her daughter she hadn't seen her for nearly six months and that was too long for her as a mother she naturally wants to be close to her daughter but it's hard for her to see her daughter grow up. She doesn't want to be or feel alone or be haunted by the past, nor does anyone for that matter, so I'm sure that someone out there can relate? But we must know that we are never alone in the Spirit, we are surrounded in Christ by His saints and angels! We just have to endure temporary physical emotional/soul realm suffering but even this has a great purpose, despite feelings of any insecurity we are secure in Christ. Despite feelings of loneliness and sadness we have access to an abundance of joy in the spirit.

If we are physically alone, we may need to be 'alone' for a period of time, a season dedicated to the Lord, but we do need some company too. We need both otherwise we will get depressed. It's not good for man to be alone! (Especially for too long!) We need to wait on God for healing, even if we wake up physically 'alone' then we need to pray the moment we wake up and dedicate the day to God and ask God to help us but also thanking God for the revelation that: **we are already in Heaven and we do not need to try to be good or holy in our own strength.** This is written in the Word! We forgive and live! We let go of past grudges or negative thoughts to ourselves or others or any bad feeling towards the LORD which is instantly dissolved by His powerful light.

"This I recall to my mind, therefore have I hope. [It is of] the Lord's mercies that we are not consumed, because his compassions fail not. [They are] new every morning: great [is] thy faithfulness."

—(Lamentation 3:21—23)

We ask for healing, then we wait on God and learn to be content in all circumstances, this way we will not be in want, we will get peace and keep our peace despite all the fiery darts of the evil energy of the enemy! Who's with me? We are so much higher in Christ, seated in Heavenly realms far above all of it! Our healing, health, wisdom, success, provision, joy and Jesus Himself is in Heaven! Jesus is waiting for you to make your way to move into realms of perpetual gratitude despite all pain and suffering. You can go higher!

"Then he said unto them, Go your way, eat the fat, and drink the sweet, and send portions unto them for whom nothing is prepared: for [this] day [is] holy unto our Lord: neither be ye sorry; for the joy of the Lord is your strength."

—*Nehemiah 8:10*

"The Lord [is] my light and my salvation; whom shall I fear? the Lord [is] the strength of my life; of whom shall I be afraid?"

—*(Psalms 27:1)*

Janet was saying that even in her 50's because she isn't settled down yet and has to be single for a period of years, she feels like she's missed it so this was my response:

Jon: It doesn't matter! Tell the devil, 'Nice try!' It doesn't matter, I am in Christ! No way! Because God's prophecies will come to pass, because they are written in the word of God! God will give you the desires of your heart.

Verse: Psalms 23.I shall NOT want (No desire for anything)

I am NOT going to be in want! That is the realm of ABUNDANCE!! Jesus told me to write a book about abundance and I asked 'How can I write a book about abundance when I am in poverty Lord?! And God said to me, 'You don't know who you are do you?' Lol! He just told me to do it and He also told me to write about angels and I said,' Lord, I haven't had enough experiences with angels and He said,' I don't want to hear your excuses, I want to give you experiences!'

He said to me 'If you give me your excuses, I can't give you

experiences. Don't block me! I am not interested in your unbelief!'
The Lord's personality makes me laugh!

So God can do anything, He gave me a really trippy experience the other day. I got a revelation about the new wine, being like a drug of heaven as you heard about in the opening chapters, and I experienced the love drug that fell from the sky and then I was seeing in the Spirit all these cows everywhere and I saw this oil come down and the milk! Oh my goodness it was heavenly and I saw little children playing with oily sticky honey and Jesus really was standing in a field with cows around Him!

It was no longer my bedroom and let me tell you something as wild, out there, different and crazy in appearance these visions and visitations are, they are really changing me- plus God is actually fun!! Who knew?! Ha-ha, so that will get rid of a few more religious spirits from our planet! I was in another realm— High with the most high! As soon as I think and pray into these encounters I can feel that same angelic lifting energy! I have even prayed for my family and let me tell you something 9 months later they too started to have strange experiences from my prayers of impartation God is doing all of this through. I am a dead man walking!!

"Having been buried with Him in baptism, in which you were also raised up with Him through faith in the working of God, who raised Him from the dead."

--Colossians 2:12

"Therefore we have been buried with Him through baptism into death, so that as Christ was raised from the dead through the glory of the Father, so we too might walk in newness of life."

—Romans 6:4

We were then talking about an antichrist which is an anti-love spirit that tries to take our joy and our wealth and our relationships with others, family, friends and even with God.

HIGH WITH THE MOST HIGH

Jan: The first family in the Bible was attacked by the anti-love spirit and we aren't and we can't end with it. That antichrist spirit continues to break up the home, to break up the work force, breaking up families and relationships that won't love anyone or anything. It's also the Narcistic spirit that emerges, just like it emerged in Cain and Abel. Cain was the first narcissist. He contemplated murder, now that's a psychopathic narcissist! When I was living with one man who was antichrist in his ways, I had no idea what it was. (It was like a spell). And guess what? It causes trauma to the brain? This occurred when they were children and then manifested later in life.

Jon: Yes it was all a plan, but we are not giving the devil any credit, it was a diabolical plot, but it was overseen by the sovereignty of beautiful Jesus Christ who turns it around. He took trauma on the cross. He really took it!

Jan: We can't turn it around! I've been trying to fix everything and I can't!

Jon: Get rid of the word fix and let go, to let God's light and love and help come in. We can't save ourselves and guess what? We aren't even supposed too! We've got to let go and let God do it, but actually by revelation, He's already done it!

> *"When Jesus therefore had received the vinegar, he said, It is finished: and he bowed his head, and gave up the ghost."*
>
> *—(John 19:30)*

Jan: Yes He already walked it out for us and the Devil wants me to think it's over— which it's not, but what is over is my pride, right?

Jon: Yes that's right (I hope we are all getting this and going somewhere with it in Christ)

Jan: I have had to learn to hold onto tranquillity from Christ rather than waiting for a man I love to come back. I have to say, it doesn't matter, if he comes back or he doesn't! There's only one thing that matters, the perfect will of God, not the permissible will of God! So if it's not this way, then I need to be somewhere else, if I am not supposed to be in Virginia then God will move me! I'm serious! I have just got used to my apartment but I will not be held back because of lack!

Jon: We are surrendered and therefore surrendered to Christ's perfect plan. Yes we don't need to fear anything, including relocation. If we make a mistake, we shouldn't beat ourselves up over it, we must let go and move on with forgiveness, revelation and joy in our heart.

Jan: The Devil does not have that right to haunt me!

Jon: He doesn't have the power!

Jan: God will increase my ability to bring wealth and He will bring dreams to fruition! Praise Jesus. Amen.

Conclusion

You must be honest with God how you feel with God first and then man second, but only if He leads you to speak to man about things. Sometimes it is better to say nothing at all. Keep quiet and learn enjoy the silence and the pauses and the waiting time on God. That time has been allocated to help you, not to hinder you. Your feelings are fickle and they will come and go, but the Word of God will last forever. Love always wins and God knows what is best for us at the time and season that He is in with us! Rejoice, God is nearer to you, than you may think! Face your fears, wipe your tears and God will restore all the old evil years. Be honest with God and with Man and God will restore your whole life. He has His Divine Plan in mind.

Chapter *Nineteen*
GOD HONOURS LOVE!

GOD HONOURS LOVE

I know that God honours love, I've lived it, I've found out what it was and I lost it, but I also gained a greater revelation and experience of Christ's love. I know that I experienced love in different ways through my sexuality and my sensuality, but I gave it up. Surrendered everything to God. I gave up my desire to be loved by man or woman. I gave myself fully to the Lord to be used for his glory.

And who is the greatest enemy? Not the devil but me! So I gave myself up, I handed myself in to God. I said, 'Lord I am handing myself in so you can arrest me and my soul so I can say I was a sinner, I've been saved by your grace and I am going to be taught directly by you, and I am going to stay here on the altar of surrender until you work on me!!

GOD HONOURS LOVE

Otherwise I don't want to be a public minister of God! I don't want to breathe until you give me the breath!'

I have to live out this prophecy as I don't just have messages—I am a message! Myself and Janet were praying for her move to Florida, but I emphasized the importance of surrender, loving ourselves, loving and enjoying the journey in the wilderness, no matter how long the journey takes Christ is taking us to the promised land and new realms in God! Surrender and humility will bring an end to strife and will help us to gain greater capacity and more clarity. We need to be able to hear God's instructions or see in the spirit if He wants. We need to be able to wait on the Lord in patience, because you must know that even patience is a powerful angelic spiritual entity and clothing.

Clarity will only come if you clothe yourself with garments of humility and patience and self-control. Clarity is angelic! God will not allow any of us to divulge in excess. He strips us back, makes things simple, He will allow you to be poor if necessary. God does anything He wants and He does whatever it takes for you to be a ready vessel for ministry and operate correctly in higher spiritual authority in realms of the unseen. We need to be able to face the enemy, face giants and face demons and face ourselves in God's calling.

If we do not, and we just have all the cares of this world bothering us, we will stay trapped and attached to this lower level carnality and not develop our true spirituality! We need Christ in absolutely every area of our life so we can trust Him. If we are supposed to move home, then He will provide for us at the right time and in the right way. On the other hand if we are supposed to stay where we are then we should know it's because God wants to make us into stars! He wants us to learn to be content in all circumstances, full of gratitude, revelations and constant high praises! If He says go, we go. If He says stay then we stay. We only do what God says. I am not doing what man says and I will not be who man says I should be! Know this about me! It's a mystery what God is doing. God wants to give us the desires of our heart.

HIGH WITH THE MOST HIGH

"Delight yourself in the LORD; And He will give you the desires of your heart."

—(Psalm 37:4).

Some of our conversation:

Jan: My sister is so prophetic! She says, 'I see you selling to the rich', This is what you prophesied about the future mansions and yet even though the Devil can speak through her right now but it doesn't mean that her gift won't be God's shortly.

Jon: It's no problem, because she's really doing something for God but it looks like from the natural perspective, that she's doing something for the Devil but actually she's gaining ground! It's another part of the mystery of God's sovereignty.

Jan: Its God's gift. (He will use it and take it from being used from the dark side).

"Train up a child in the way he should go: and when he is old, he will not depart from it."

—(Proverbs 22:6)

My father doesn't deserve apostacy. He shouldn't have to watch his daughter get a tattoo from a 'witchy' Buddhist monk in some temple. Get out of the way in Jesus name! Get away from her you devils, now the Lord will get on her case day and night and show up in her dreams and she won't be able to operate in witchcraft and deception.

GOD HONOURS LOVE

She prayed, saying, 'Lord, give her the supernatural aspect of your grace and glory as you did for my uncle please do this for my sister In Jesus name. You didn't let my uncle go to the gates of Hell, just before you stopped him, because my father preached to him and in that realm of being refined by fire, he has also separated himself from all my 28 cousins. All of his Italian family, our US kids never got to be a part of him, because of my uncle, but that very man died 3 times, but the Lord brought him up to a marker, a line, where he could not get to the gates of Heaven. Well, my uncle was told to go back and go and talk to my father who refused to know about this at the time and 3 times my uncle came back in that hospital and all of a sudden my mother kicked him out.' There was something happening, she know so she made him go to see my uncle. He then went to Hell briefly and he told my father that everything is true. I told you there are books in Heaven Jon, I know you'll love that! But, There is a Lamb's Book of Life and my uncle told him that his name wasn't in it!!

(Quite a shock to get someone saved, but it worked. You can't just be religious, you must have a relationship with Jesus)

Jan: My ex-boyfriend also had a dream in Fall 2019: This was him and I sitting at the kitchen table and oh we were laughing and there were books everywhere! We were going through the chapters. But all of a sudden the table cracked and before it crashed he said, 'I looked over at you and you had this horrific worry-It was awful as you looked at me and then the table crashed. And yet I looked at you, none of us were hurt, and the books remained all around us and we were amongst our books still and we just started to laugh!' This dream woke him up and He heard a voice which was so audible that he jumped out of bed like it was really happening. Immediately he got in touch with me on the phone at 3am asking if I was ok?!

I was like, 'what are you talking about?' so he described this dream to me, it was more like a vision that he was seeing -not just an ordinary dream because it woke him up!!'

HIGH WITH THE MOST HIGH

Jon: Interesting! No wonder why God is hot on that particular prophecy we have prayed into. I don't give up! (God's perfect will be done)

Jan: So I realized that means those were the chapters of our lives in those books, so I told him that 'we were supposed to be together, don't you see that? We are in the books, you and me, we are sitting around, that table was part of the fall, that chapter in our life was not supposed to be interrupted by a fall, come on!! The Book of Life is part of those books and I am in his life but he got rid of me because he didn't want the Christ life inside me!! I was on a broadcast speaking in tongues and he made it like I had to make a decision between him or God, and I chose God so he left me!!)

I said 'I am not leaving this ministry for you!' So I don't regret it. It's not like I wouldn't take God's side, but he betrayed me (so it couldn't continue) He called me a witch and then 7 months later who would have thought? He called me up about a dream. I told my then fiancé that I was speaking in tongues that it wasn't witchcraft, but the problem with him is that 'You don't operate in the fullness of God. I would not want to live on this earth with a powerless God! That Holy Spirit is the power, so you are denying the power!' And he just didn't know what to say when I said that and that was the end of our relationship. I can't prove it but I know/feel/he cheated on me left and right.

Jon: A difficult thing to go through but it's not that any of that matters because God can do a turn around and if he married the wrong person then God can sort all that out too. It is all God's decision! And on top of that. God can and will take away the pain and rejection from your heart and He will bind up the broken hearted and remove the trauma if you will just let go, forgive and trust God, He will do it.

Jan: I knew you were going to say that Jon! That's so funny!!

Jon: You know me by revelation. LOL!

Jan: It really doesn't matter, you're right because I can forgive my father, it's not his fault, I can forgive my brother, it's not his fault.

GOD HONOURS LOVE

Whose fault is it? It's just the wrong voices that people listen to. (We forgive that ex bf too!!)

Jon: I really think it's really important to forgive him and if you want some more revelations I will tell you, but you could go mad at me for this one:

REVELATION:JUST AS WE MUST FORGIVE OTHERS AND OURSELVES,WE ALSO HAVE THE POWER TO FORGIVE DEMONS!

THIS RELEASES UNCONDITIONAL LOVE TO THEM AS A ENERGETIC WEAPON.

IT DISPELS THEIR POWER FROM ATTACHING TO US AS WE ALREADY HAVE ALL POWER OVER THEM THROUGH CHRIST WHO IS HIS WORD, WHO EMPOWERS HIS WORD AND WHO IS THE SPIRIT OF PROPHECY!

IT IS A CHOICE TO FORGIVE DEMONS AND THEIR DEMONIC EFFECTS, ALL THE AFTERMATH THEY CAUSED BUT THIS CLEANSES OUR SOULS AND OUR SPACE ESPECIALLY WHERE THE SIN OR OFFENCES OCCURED.

THE DEMONS WILL STILL BE PUNISHED BY CHRIST, BUT YOU WILL BE ABLE TO BE FREE WITHOUT ANY SOUL ATTACHMENTS OR ENERGY THIEVES. IT IS A MYSTERY IN THE SPIRIT!!

Jon: You see, when we forgive the demons, and their works, we are extending God's forgiveness out towards the person through Jesus Christ and the external perfect love of God. Even though demons cannot be forgiven, this shockwave of love in Christ can cast out the demons! Let me explain it scripturally. You know when Jesus found that demon possessed guy, he crossed the other side. He said to his disciples 'come on, lets fish on the other side' and He went to that piece of land where the demonised man was, where no one wanted to be near him as he was so deeply possessed.

> *And they came over unto the other side of the sea, into the country of the Gadarenes. And when he was come out of the ship, immediately there met him out of the tombs a man with an unclean spirit, Who had [his] dwelling among the tombs; and no man could bind him, no, not with chains: Because that he had been often bound with fetters and chains, and the chains had been plucked asunder by him, and the fetters broken in pieces: neither could any [man] tame him. And always, night and day, he was in the mountains, and in the tombs, crying, and cutting himself with stones. But when he saw Jesus afar off, he ran and worshipped him, And cried with a loud voice, and said, What have I to do with thee, Jesus, [thou] Son of the most high God? I adjure thee by God, that thou torment me not. For he said unto him, Come out of the man, [thou] unclean spirit. And he asked him, What [is] thy name? And he answered, saying, My name [is] Legion: for we are many. And he besought him much that he would not send them away out of the country."*
>
> —*(Mark 5:1—10*

And we have all fallen short of the glory of God, we have all been like that demonised guy-right? But have we really understood what that demonised guy represented?

He represents the rejected part of ourselves. That demon possessed man was a 'used guy' and he was hurting himself over and over, self-harming, tearing himself up, he had no identity but the demons identity! He had split personalities and complete possession. He represents sin in some ways. But as soon as Jesus touched the land, immediately the demons reacted violently and immediately all that **spiritual dominion** of that whole place became God's and the Love of God came over to reach that demonised man. Notice the demons were the first to react and not the person. Now they spoke through the person, the demons screeched 'Aah! Son of God what are you doing here? Have you come to torture us and cost us out before our time?!'

GOD HONOURS LOVE

Now that tells me there's a time for casting out demons and God knows what that time is and how to fill us with His holy power to do it! And those foul demons didn't want to get out of him! No way! But you must see the focus isn't just the casting out of the demons to make the man finally free, although that's part of it, the other part of is the unconditional love of Jesus Christ came through, the demons reacted to it and the person found the love of God, got saved and was given a new identity in Jesus Christ love the moment touch down began!

So therefore the moment touch down begins in our lives is the moment that all evil spirits, all the split personality spirits, all the condemnation spirits, all the religious spirits and all the rebellion and rejection must go! The demons then start reacting, by blaming, shaming and slandering us, name calling, putting labels on us but actually this is the point of access where God wants to give you the biggest hug to prove that He's the alpha and the omega and you are right in the middle and you are in the middle of his Alpha and Omega great unconditional love!

REVELATION: SO THE BIG SQUEEZE (HUGS FROM GOD) MEAN THAT BOTH ALPHA AND OMEGA HUG YOU IN THE GRIP OF GOD'S UNCONDITIONAL LOVE AND THIS IS THE POWER OF LOVE THAT CASTS OUT DEMONS. THIS IS THE HIGHEST AUTHORITY IN THE WHOLE UNIVERSE.

IT'S NOT OUR SPIRITUAL WARFARE THAT CASTS OUT THE DEMONS AND MAKES DEMONS REACT. IT'S THE LOVE OF GOD! IT IS ALSO THE KNOWLEDGE AND POWER OF GOD WHICH IS ALL PART OF HIS MYSTERION (HIS MYSTERY OF LOVE REALM) IT'S NOT OUR FASTING, IT'S NOT OUR WORKS, IT'S NOT OUR ANYTHING. IT IS THE LOVE THAT GOD THAT IS HIDDEN IN CHRIST JESUS INSIDE THE HOLY SPIRIT INSIDE US!

God wants to give you the big squeeze as well as the big breeze! The winds of change will blow upon your strange, painful situation. It

HIGH WITH THE MOST HIGH

looked beyond hopeless for that poor demonised man but now he's free forever more all because God cared enough to go to the 'other side' and rescue him. God loves and cares about all sinners! He knows how we got here, what we go through and He gives us His great love! It's very humbling to think that we don't have that love and power without Him!!

God is saying, "Hey I'm in control, I love you; I will always, always love you, I will never let you go, I want all of your family saved and I'm going to do it! You don't have to do it! You're not in defeat, you are in complete victory through me and here's the strategy.'

Praise Jesus! That's the perfect will of God. You're in it when you abide in Christ.

Jan: It's the power of God, right? I love those prophetic downloads that He gives us?

Jon: Yes, the LOVE OF GOD is the POWER and He's unconditional because of the power of Christ's atonement for us, He really did take our place for every area of our life! So God doesn't see any of our sin. It is all washed away. The only ones who remember it are the demons, the old accuser and us! So let's let go and forget it! We don't need sinful old identities anymore we need daily fresh upgrades and they are available in the Holy Spirit.

All our sin is washed away!! Take a moment to be washed by the river of Heaven and then submerge yourself in the rivers of joy and revelation and life daily. They are 3 different heavenly river realms – oh the glory! I can feel myself floating and feeling higher than before. I am giving you a revelation book of fresh upgrades to get high or jacked up on Jesus!

Christ Jesus is so wonderful talk about rose tinted glasses! The only thing that has tinted them pink is the crimson blood of Jesus! May we never forget the COST OF THE CROSS! May we never lose focus of what God did to get us to go to where we are going without being like spoilt brats and selfish, hard-hearted religious, self-righteous know it all's. The Lord rebuke us and our old sinful attitudes which can so easily blind us. Let's BIND ourselves to the CROSS at all COST and then we will see what God has DONE and he will show us what He will DO and you will be in the realms of absolutely shocking freedom. Whoosh!

God has known all the suffering and seen all the suffering. And He said to this to me: "Your issues have become my tissues and I've already wept over you and I have saved your soul, not you trying to be good and save yourself!'

Janet and I were amazed when we heard this. God said to me the other day when I was sitting at my desk 'Son, don't worry about anything, you worry too much!'

Jan: Therefore our souls, because they are saved, we don't have to be hurt, we don't have to be broken souls.

Jon: Yes we lay everything down. We surrender all.

Both: We pray that God would transform all the wrongs and make them right. We decree we will no longer live a defeatist attitude with defeatist outcomes. We then prayed for house sales and book sales for Heaven to Earth Ministry International. We also prayed for a loyal team with churches and ministries to get more involved. We also prayed for Virginia Maclain Bible institute and other churches all over to be coming together. We prayed for future travel arrangements an advertising methods with church bulletins.

Jan: You should now get used to people investing in you and enjoy the profits of your hard labour. I advertised for my sister and now she's on a book club with a book which was based on some of my story and all of our adventures as kids, so the Lord helped me to get her in touch with a book club in New York and so now they're reading her book, all ten of them from there we're going to the next book club and then we're going to wind up in the Public Library over there so I'm just saying this is the beginning of exposure time for her and for you.

Part of stirring the waters for this ministry is to receive help. So if you had a meeting of say five people it will expand. My friend Peter goes to a new church and they had four months of revival now! I told him back last year, 'why aren't you at that church? You've got to get to that church!' And so now he's going he's amazed because they don't stop having revival!

We're going to do a zoom meeting soon so please let me help, I can see it so clear the churches have free bulletin advertising you can just give them an opportunity to honour you.

We are not saying spend your American dollars, we are saying 'come and push a prophet through' Come on, they will want to buy your books and find out more about who you are stirring the waters is part of the mystery. He's already planted you into the prophetic fulfilment with what you were supposed to do with books now you need to expose yourself, you can't do it alone, so you've got a team for a reason. Jesus had 12 for a reason so it's biblical, before you begin teaching ask to share something and tell them about your books.

Jon: one day we will have our own TV channel before we know it! Ha ha! I already saw it once. I even saw HQ in Dubai in the towers and I wondered what it meant? I saw Dubai and America being linked together and Mum saw it too! I don't even tell you half the stuff I get to see! Because some things are so extreme, you think that God that's so impossible why are you giving me the most impossible rich prosperous, ridiculous prophecies that no one would ever believe!? So He does it! He thinks it's funny, He says 'just lay down your life son and enjoy the ride!' But you're right, we have to find the right team. And God's already assembled his team and He is assembling us all the time! Because if you look around you can feel that people are so hungry and thirsty for the anointing we've got as a team we have a dream team anointing! We have individual people that have powerful callings, but we are isolated and that's wrong! So we are going to be coming together very soon and we are going to be ignited and we are going to ignite others, it's going to be explosive, it will be on zoom or social media then it will be in person. The ministry is developing but slowly but surely.

I know that one day I will be in America in person in different states like Virginia, Washington DC, NYC, Florida, California, wherever God wants me to be I will go. I will do whatever He wants, whenever He wants it, but not before. Today we are shifted from a realm of defeat to a realm and revelation of victory! And in the middle between defeat and victory was strategy! Strategy is wisdom which is wise dominion. We are loaded up in wisdom, but the Devil wants to try and distract us by that spirit of defeat. That spiritual demonic power of defeat is the Devil's strategy, the devils devices and it's also worldly thorns around the neck to try and distract you or and try and choke the plant however we are not having any of that in the name of Jesus Christ!

We are out of that realm of defeat, we are in the realm of complete victory and in the middle of that is a big hug, a big squeeze called strategy. Strategy is also angelic power sent from God. And God has just squeezed you and is giving you the biggest hug.

The thing is Satan tries to block you by distracting you! It's this evil spirit of distraction that's one of the strongholds in the Body of Christ that people don't even realise we think 'Oh it's just a distraction!' No it's not, it's a spirit that tries to steal the word of God. You can see it in the Bible in the Gospels and in Nehemiah for example.

"And he spake many things unto them in parables, saying, Behold, a sower went forth to sow; And when he sowed, some [seeds] fell by the way side, and the fowls came and devoured them up: Some fell upon stony places, where they had not much earth: and forthwith they sprung up, because they had no deepness of earth: And when the sun was up, they were scorched; and because they had no root, they withered away. And some fell among thorns; and the thorns sprung up, and choked them: But other fell into good ground, and brought forth fruit, some an hundredfold, some sixtyfold, some thirtyfold."

—(Mathew 13:1—8

"Now it came to pass, when Sanballat, and Tobiah, and Geshem the Arabian, and the rest of our enemies, heard that I had built the wall, and [that] there was no breach left therein; (though at that

time I had not set up the doors upon the gates;) That Sanballat and Geshem sent unto me, saying, Come, let us meet together in [some one of] the villages in the plain of Ono. But they thought to do me mischief. And I sent messengers unto them, saying, I [am] doing a great work, so that I cannot come down: why should the work cease, whilst I leave it, and come down to you? Yet they sent unto me four times after this sort; and I answered them after the same manner. Then sent Sanballat his servant unto me in like manner the fifth time with an open letter in his hand; Wherein [was] written, It is reported among the heathen, and Gashmu saith [it], [that] thou and the Jews think to rebel: for which cause thou buildest the wall, that thou mayest be their king, according to these words. And thou hast also appointed prophets to preach of thee at Jerusalem, saying, [There is] a king in Judah: and now shall it be reported to the king according to these words. Come now therefore, and let us take counsel together."

—(Nehemiah 6:1—7)

I just paraphrase things slightly differently. 'The birds that come and steal is a spirit of distraction that tries to steal the word of God, the revelation and then try to confuse the prophecies! So we must be more vigilant.

God will give you the desires of your heart and I can see it, I can see it's a complete victory in Christ and I can see the strategy like you can, so I honour you as a prophetess, you honour me and the Body of Christ gets blessed. Praise and thank you Lord master Christ Jesus. This is Heaven to Earth! This is Father God on the earth through his people, but it all looked like a defeat -ok? It appeared like it's a terrible defeat, but just look at what JESUS CHRIST has done! IT IS FINISHED!

"Delight thyself also in the Lord; and he shall give thee the desires of thine heart."

—(Psalms 37:4)

Chapter *Twenty*
NO RELIANCE ON OUR OLD UNDERSTANDING: REVELATION

REVELATION: NO RELIANCE ON OUR OLD UNDER-STANDING!

Another revelation that God has made me face over and over is that we don't have to rely on our old own understanding anymore and nor should we! Especially if want to develop and gain Godly fruits in the mystical Vine. We have got strategies from Heaven and we are going to do what God wants and we decree complete victory in Christ! Holy Spirit thank you for the fire! It is my earnest prayer that you are encouraged dear reader or listener. I want you to feel uplifted, included, challenged and inspired, so you know God truly loves you, He loves the current body of Christ, and He is adding new souls to us daily filling the world with His love, fragrance of secure peace and power revealing his great awesome power again!

So many of us could easily be frustrated because things don't seem to be happening yet, or how we would like, but it's not about us, it's not about our comfort or our timing or our convenience. It's all about God's perfect timing, His perfect will and is only put together and performed by the word of God within us which is Jesus, only He can do it! So therefore we must let go of distraction, anxiety, fear, worry, fretting and frustration and pray for clarity, concentration, fresh vision and determination to continue on in the strength of God, and not in our old fallen strength.

Our strength will always fail us, people get older, people have accidents, bad things happen, lives fall apart, Kingdoms rise and fall, but our beautiful Jesus remains the same yesterday today forever the same! He is the complete security and strength of our life. His word upholds all things!

"Behold, God [is] my salvation; I will trust, and not be afraid: for the Lord Jehovah [is] my strength and [my] song; he also is become my salvation."

—(Isaiah 12:2

"(Now that he ascended, what is it but that he also descended first into the lower parts of the earth? He that descended is the same also that ascended up far above all heavens, that he might fill all things.)"

—Ephesians 4:9—10

The holy scriptures always tell me that God is still in control no matter what. We always just need to keep getting fresh oil beloved. We can get fresh oil every single day.

NO RELIANCE ON OUR OLD UNDERSTANDING

Jesus told me this in the month of September 22 which is sweet September and you should pray for the honey gate to open, so I did! The Lord said, 'Don't pray with defeat in your heart because that's a distraction!'

We don't have any defeat hidden in Christ- bury yourself in revelation- battle on with weapons of revelation and let's keep on moving toward body of Christ! May God forgive us, break the curses of a defeatist attitude today. We break the trauma of defeat too. Thank you, good and glorious Father.

Here is some more of my prophetic prayerful conversation with Janet:

Jan: In Jesus name we will have the money and take care of this beautiful man and he will be successful. In this month as long as it comes fourth I have three houses and another to sell as part of my job. (GOD'S holy will be done) I believe we will get our dreams come true. I am going to travel in Ohio in a few weeks. Lord, you needed me to be in a car to go from beauty to ashes back to beauty so that I would say 'Ok what do you want me to do with these provisions Lord?!

Jon, you are a very fair man, you could say we need this finance for Pakistan or Africa or for myself and mum for a new home and we have these orphans we help by the absolute grace of God! You have made all kinds of connections and I want to help you, and there should be many others who want to help the vision of Heaven to Earth. I told the Lord it's not my money, so that's just it.

Jon: Yes it's not my money either, God has to direct us! I wouldn't dare mess around here! (My hand was still shaking in the anointing). When you said Ohio so I said 'Yes, Lord.' You must understand your happiness really matters to God (same with all here). He wants you to be happy so you can minister really well and really strongly. You are such a wedding girl! You're a typical princess wedding fairy tale girl.

Jan: I really am! I really do want a wedding. It doesn't have to be big anymore because the years went by, but a restoration would include a wedding! Like a Roof top wedding. You can oversee the city and I really like that. It's a good prayer thing. She prayed, 'Lord please give us the prophetic fulfilment. You have made us this way- Jon and myself want to love, it's not good for man to be alone......'

Jon: We are wired by God, for real love.

Jan: Adam didn't even know what an Eve was, but it was a beautiful blessing and a beautiful gift so we pray give this to us. Amen!

Jon: Forgive us Lord for listening to depression defeat or distraction. We thank you for total victory over the spirit of defeat.

Jan: Yes and we break agreement with any idols!

Jon: We break the Ashtoreth poles the lot! I hear God say 'You've put it on your mountain of prayer and it's not staying there I will give you the desires of your heart. Just lay it down and I will do anything!!' He talks to me just like that it's funny, He's so casual sometimes! I was brought up in England, Hertfordshire in Stevenage which was kind of rough and we had some rough edged people around! So God speaks to me in a casual, street like or cockney way sometimes!

Jan: I just heard what God said through you: Jon, you said, 'I will give you everything' that means everything. We have to give him that pit in our stomach, and the fear of tomorrow, when we don't know what to do, or the dreams we are holding onto.

Jon: Yes, that includes the fear of the unknown, the fear of being misunderstood, the fear of missing it, the Lord says: 'Sin means to miss the mark', well praise God we all sinned! and why do I say it like that in jest? Because Christ FORGAVE ALL the sins!

NO RELIANCE ON OUR OLD UNDERSTANDING

"And you [hath he quickened], who were dead in trespasses and sins; Wherein in time past ye walked according to the course of this world, according to the prince of the power of the air, the spirit that now worketh in the children of disobedience: Among whom also we all had our conversation in times past in the lusts of our flesh, fulfilling the desires of the flesh and of the mind; and were by nature the children of wrath, even as others. But God, who is rich in mercy, for his great love wherewith he loved us, Even when we were dead in sins, hath quickened us together with Christ, (by grace ye are saved;) And hath raised [us] up together, and made [us] sit together in heavenly [places] in Christ Jesus: That in the ages to come he might shew the exceeding riches of his grace in [his] kindness toward us through Christ Jesus."

—Ephesians 2:1—7

He died as a substitute in your place! God says: 'While you were dead in your sins I saved you - while you were at your very worse - I FORGAVE YOU!' that's generational man! 'Just look again at the word <u>while</u> it means time, throughout all time and space throughout all of history, even through all your sins I have loved you and I will always love you.....I will never ever let you go- and you didn't miss it! It wasn't a defeat, it was a victory in me, but you can't see it yet because I am the most high and I hide!' God was laughing and it made me laugh!

Jan: 'I didn't miss it' is a big deal to me. You have no idea. I thought I missed it.
I thought I screwed everything up from the beginning of college.

Jon: No! God has not made you a victim but victorious! You are absolutely more than a conqueror through God who loves you, and loved you and always will love you! Because He can't help it, that's who he is! He is love, He will give you the desires of your heart, He will give you what you need in business, in ministry, in relationship if you follow him and do what He asks of you to your best ability with honesty towards him, yourself and others. God is a God of truth. He cannot lie.

HIGH WITH THE MOST HIGH

He is the one being humiliated in us not us being humiliated. It's HIM being humiliated inside these weak yielded jars of clay. He said ' It's me! And I've overcome all humiliation and I have overcome the world!' He said this to me one day while I was making dinner and I almost dropped the pot! Ha-ha.

"But we have this treasure in earthen vessels, that the excellency of the power may be of God, and not of us."

—*2 Corinthians 4:7*

Jan: So you were feeling bad about something?

Jon: I was just feeling bad in life and in pain. I asked God why he wanted me in a wilderness, a little village for years with a burdened stressed family with nothing going right but I was cooking and thanking God for the dinner and the Lord said 'Yes son, you better start thanking me for the dinner because soon I will do great miracles in your life where you've got a little bit of food and a lot of faith and my multiplication miracles will come out! The times coming when people aren't going to be able to buy food and they will be told that they can't even grow it, but yet my royal children will be doing supernatural acts and food multiplication miracles!' He asked me, 'Do you want this power, son?! Then lay it down. Lay all your life down on the altar of surrender.' He talks to me! He said, 'I have already taken all the humiliation. It's me that's being persecuted for my holy names sake! And you are all part of my name!'

My family were saying 'yes it's all for God's sake' and the Lord said to me 'Excuse me? It's for your sake as well! I collaborated with you, I carried you on the Cross, I want you in my plan! You and I are one! It's for you! I am going to give you my everything because you are my inheritance!'

NO RELIANCE ON OUR OLD UNDERSTANDING

I used to have different obsessions as a kid growing up and I did wonder about myself looking back as I had a spice girl obsession! And my bedroom was absolutely plastered in posters and magazines. Ha-ha! With the spice girls (90's pop girl group) and later I had a Gothic obsession, then a witchy obsession, then art and fashion. I had all kinds of obsessions and expressions but the thing is God says to me every day 'I am obsessed with you!! I love you so much! I crave to be near you so much! Please, can we spend a bit more time together?!' That blew my mind! Lol, how radical!

When I was working full or part time at my job God would be talking to me! One time in the body shop in Cornwall, I dropped the body butter cream when I was in the shop because God spoke to me about His love for me and his love for the customer! And I just wasn't expecting to hear him at that point. I was trying to do my work! Very funny! He'd say audibly 'I love her, and I love you and it's exactly the same love!' I was like 'Whoa!' Excuse me, sorry about that, just my butter fingers!' Ha-ha!

God will always talk with us and He will always show us his awesome love because He is LOVE, and his perfect love is beautiful beyond anyone's understanding, we can't understand that love, it's a shocking outrageous love. He loves every single species on the planet, and He loves every single person on the planet.

And he has given everyone the invitation to know Him, to come into heaven and experience heavenly dimensions on earth but people say 'No' to him because they don't know who He is! And yet, we are the gateways that look like they have been blocked up with defeat! -well, it's all victory for Christ. This is generational! People's generational gateways have been completely blocked up and that's what sins done but Christ became the image of sin. He became the exact image of sin.

HIGH WITH THE MOST HIGH

"Who hath believed our report? and to whom is the arm of the Lord revealed? For he shall grow up before him as a tender plant, and as a root out of a dry ground: he hath no form nor comeliness; and when we shall see him, [there is] no beauty that we should desire him. He is despised and rejected of men; a man of sorrows, and acquainted with grief: and we hid as it were [our] faces from him; he was despised, and we esteemed him not. Surely he hath borne our griefs, and carried our sorrows: yet we did esteem him stricken, smitten of God, and afflicted. But he [was] wounded for our transgressions, [he was] bruised for our iniquities: the chastisement of our peace [was] upon him; and with his stripes we are healed. All we like sheep have gone astray; we have turned every one to his own way; and the Lord hath laid on him the iniquity of us all. He was oppressed, and he was afflicted, yet he opened not his mouth: he is brought as a lamb to the slaughter, and as a sheep before her shearers is dumb, so he openeth not his mouth. He was taken from prison and from judgment: and who shall declare his generation? for he was cut off out of the land of the living: for the transgression of my people was he stricken. And he made his grave with the wicked, and with the rich in his death; because he had done no violence, neither [was any] deceit in his mouth. Yet it pleased the Lord to bruise him; he hath put [him] to grief: when thou shalt make his soul an offering for sin, he shall see [his] seed, he shall prolong [his] days, and the pleasure of the Lord shall prosper in his hand. He shall see of the travail of his soul, [and] shall be satisfied: by his knowledge shall my righteous servant justify many; for he shall bear their iniquities. Therefore will I divide him [a portion] with the great, and he shall divide the spoil with the strong; because he hath poured out his soul unto death: and he was numbered with the transgressors; and he bare the sin of many, and made intercession for the transgressors."

—Isaiah 53:1—12

NO RELIANCE ON OUR OLD UNDERSTANDING

"This [is] the generation of them that seek him, that seek thy face, O Jacob. Selah. Lift up your heads, O ye gates; and be ye lift up, ye everlasting doors; and the King of glory shall come in. Who [is] this King of glory? The Lord strong and mighty, the Lord mighty in battle. Lift up your heads, O ye gates; even lift [them] up, ye everlasting doors; and the King of glory shall come in. Who is this King of glory? The Lord of hosts, he [is] the King of glory. Selah."

—Psalms 24:6—10

REVELATION: THE IMAGE OF SIN ON THE CROSS:

If you dare let me preach true love; Jesus Christ actually became a worm! He looked like a dissected worm in the natural but actually in the spirit He was like a burning Man on the Cross. So he was like a burning worm dissected! He became the image of sin! He became not just the image, but He became the image of the author of sin— which is the Devil! Now the author of sin, the Devil, and the worm, needs explaining. If you look at the Norse word and spelling of the worm it reads: WYRM that is a dragon! So GOD became the image of the dissected, defeated WYRM! He defeated the Dragon on the Cross! He also fulfilled the prophecy of David and became the image of the complete defeated dragon on the cross!

That's the hidden revelation God showed me this year. Christ became that image and meanwhile you and I were in His heart, and he was burning for us like the ultimate martyr and the ultimate final sacrifice! That's how much it cost! These are things that occurred in the spirit realm hidden away from man's natural eye. He wanted us to know him!

Jan: Wow! He wants a relationship with us.

Jon: Yes He wants us, He is obsessed with us, He sings love songs over us, but we aren't hearing many of them if at all -so sad!

HIGH WITH THE MOST HIGH

Jan: That's the thing, we aren't hearing from God. We aren't hearing his love songs. We don't feel Him anymore!

Jon: We are going to get through this iron prison. We are going to get through this heavy iron heaven! We are going to get through this rusty old religion! God and His heavens should be tangible. He just wants repentance.

"From that time Jesus began to preach, and to say, Repent: for the kingdom of heaven is at hand."

—*Mathew 4: 17*

What do you have to do? Repent! What do you have to repent of? Self, your old understanding, your old flesh nature, your old man, your pride and all deception! But you have to understand is the greatest thing is not that the demons seem to win, it is the lack of LOVE! This is what we have to repent of most: That is it! THE GOSPEL IS LOVE.

Perfect love has already cast out all fear! All fear has gone! He already took on the image of the worm, a wyrm; a broken dragon ! He took on the image of the dragon! It is phenomenal! He has taken on that very demonic image with all its power, stripped Satan of all authority and He took it to hell! So all of the sin, all of the sickness, all the defeat it's in Hell!! This revelation needs prayer! Sickness, sin, and disease it's all in Hell, and Christ triumphantly rose again and took us with His heart as his captives, out of the sleepy, paradise realms which is the real Eden into Heaven! That's where we belong in pure, uncontaminated, blissful, peaceful, prayerful, perfect Heaven!! That's where we have our citizenship. It's a fact! It's not just oh, I read that in the Bible! No, I have had to lay my whole life down and be sacrificed and sliced up for God as a prophet, because He loves us!! He's obsessively in love with us and loving us continually, all the time He loves us, because of who he is!!

NO RELIANCE ON OUR OLD UNDERSTANDING

"Blotting out the handwriting of ordinances that was against us, which was contrary to us, and took it out of the way, nailing it to his cross; [And] having spoiled principalities and powers, he made a shew of them openly, triumphing over them in it."

—Colossians 2:14—15

"Wherefore he saith, When he ascended up on high, he led captivity captive, and gave gifts unto men. (Now that he ascended, what is it but that he also descended first into the lower parts of the earth? He that descended is the same also that ascended up far above all heavens, that he might fill all things.)"

—Ephesians 4:8—10

"(For the weapons of our warfare [are] not carnal, but mighty through God to the pulling down of strong holds;) Casting down imaginations, and every high thing that exalteth itself against the knowledge of God, and bringing into captivity every thought to the obedience of Christ; And having in a readiness to revenge all disobedience, when your obedience is fulfilled."

—2 Corinthians 10: 4—6

We have to catch up, so we thank God for revelation. Revelation is experiential knowledge, this isn't book knowledge, this is experiential and it's painful to go through, but I praise God through the pain! We still do it anyway but oh my goodness, God loves that! So these revelations and strategies will equip you more now, as you deepen your faith walk and feel more secure in Christ, **now,** we have the victories! REVELATION: GOD'S PLAN IS FOR US ALL TO BECOME LOVE:

We are all becoming the perfect image of love in Christ! Praise Jesus continually!

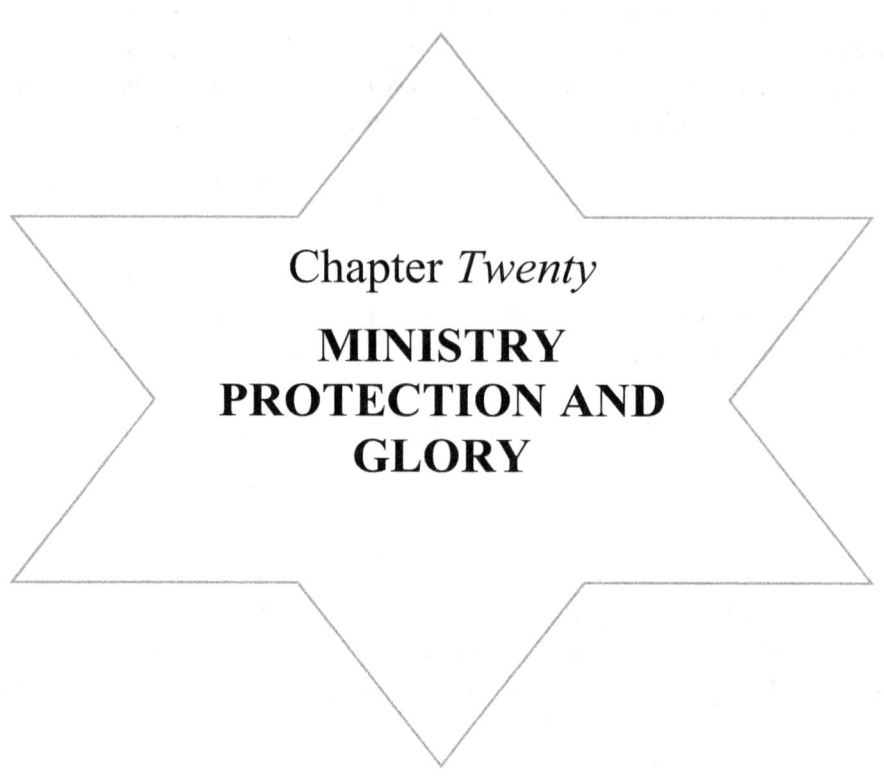

Chapter *Twenty*
MINISTRY PROTECTION AND GLORY

From - 5th September 2022

MINISTRY PROTECTION AND GLORY

This morning I was praying about the canopy of our ministry: Heaven to Earth International and how we have spiritual sons and how we are all under this Heavenly Protective canopy. So, I started to see a vision of it. Now this canopy is far away, far up above the clouds, a very big, big canopy like a tent over us all. It supernaturally covers everybody. But what happened in my vision was the rain was coming down from Heaven and its making that canopy start to sag in the middle.

MINISTRY PROTECTION AND GLORY

Today I woke up to a strange sagging canopy vision! I thought it was rather peculiar so I started praying into it and I realized to my surprise what God was saying: 'You can rend the Heavens with your praise and worship son and try to pierce my holy canopy with your sword if you can reach it, to the top of this canopy!' God challenged me. But the whole thing is coming down and it getting heavier and the atmosphere is getting heavier and heavier in a good way! The Lord also said: 'The sword of the Spirit in you is active to rend the Heavens and you do can this through your praise and worship and rejoicing despite painful circumstances and threatening storms, so you will eventually prick it, piercing my canopy.'

I saw that God will allow the whole canopy to collapse under His power and with our persistence in praise and worship in a higher realm releasing Heaven to Earth! I saw this going over every one in the ministry. Mum asked me if it would start with a drip, drip, drip?

Jon: Yes, of course it would, but it will just be a tiny prick to begin with.

Mum: And then it's going to tear! (We said in unison)

Jon: Yes, and before you know it, then everyone is soaked!

Mum: Like the power of Niagara Falls! (This is the Great Grace Movement as Kathy Walters said on her YouTube)

Jon: Yes, it's going to be a great grace outpouring! And it will be over every single son and daughter that comes under this ministry. And guess what? The Sun will shine so bright and the rainbow prismatic glory will be over everyone! We will be covered by the Covenant of God!

So it will be like water, rain, sun, light, glory, spiritual fire, prisms, rainbow fire the whole lot revealed in this mystical covenant that God has with us! It will be real Heaven to earth! Anything is impossible for those who believe! Even gemstones and gold dust and healing and great wealth transfers! Everything comes down with Holy Heaven riches, everything you need. This includes everything that's in Heaven! It's coming down!

God said to me 'This is the power of true worship! This is the power of praise; this is the power of thanksgiving when you don't feel good and you don't want to praise me! This is the power that is released when people persecute you if you praise me in that day, when you rejoice in that moment, in that day and you don't wait till you feel better! Or in the attack you fight back!

When the attacks come it's time to get very proactive and catch this revelation that causes a revolution that rends the Heavens! Because collectively when you all praise and worship, the whole of the Heaven will come down and then what will happen is over every single individual: There will be Heaven, Heaven, and Heaven, multiplied over everyone! Then you will go out and about having been held captive for a generation. And then Heaven will spread everywhere! This is what you are going to see—only believe, worship opens Heaven!'

"By him therefore let us offer the sacrifice of praise to God continually, that is, the fruit of [our] lips giving thanks to his name."

—Hebrews 13:15

So now God has revealed what that small canopy vision was all about. So often we get mental pictures from God and we can so easily brush them off if we aren't sensitive to the Holy Spirit. May God have mercy so we can all hear Gods voice. Keep making more time for God and we will surely testify that the realm of praise and worship realm leads us into glory and this rends the Heavens! Let us all repent of being so wrapped up in the cares and chores and distractions of this world so that we don't sin and stop the flow of an open Heaven in our lives in Jesus holy name. May God have mercy and forgive us so that we know and experience these revelations as part of our revival lifestyles! I also asked God what was the difference between a canopy and an ark?

Answer: The canopy like a tent or tabernacle is portable. Whereas eventually we are going to have to need an Ark for everyone to come into it to be safe from the Devils devices futuristically and then the coming wrath of God! But that time is not yet. The ministry is an Ark that people are going to run into saying they need the salvation and healing power of God! The Rain is coming and the storms are coming and we are going to need real loving ministries of God to become arks.

Mum reminded me of the replica of the Ark in America teaching about Noah's flood and how we must see the relevance of this story, how prophetic it is. I am also in deep prayer, research and reflection about all the different devils' devices concerning end times, or genetic manipulation and genetic sabotage and genetic warfare at this time. As gross as most of these subjects are they should not be overlooked and God wants to give us a revelation and experience of His pure holy, new genetics. I see a great shaking and a great awakening and a great uprising! New things are ahead so let's fear God, being in deep awe, reverence in the beauty of His holiness as praise and worship perfects us into His new genetic supernatural image.

Chapter *Twenty-Two*

MIRACLE CAFÉ: DIFFERENT DIMENSIONS

(From Tuesday 6th September)

I would like to take you back a few days to our evening visit to the Miracle cafe Bangor.

The Spiritual Dimension

We were watching a TV internet clip from Aliss Cresswell, in a group fellowship meeting. We don't get to go here too much because of the long drive, but when we go it is a brilliant evening.

Someone started to experience sudden heat in their hands, and the reaction from someone was 'that's creepy' (This often happens to me and we must remember that not everyone likes the supernatural, or gifts of God).

MIRACLE CAFÉ: DIFFERENT DIMENSIONS

They were praying even on the streets of the UK and a lady said white light comforted her, and an evil spirit left her from the past, she had felt like she was being haunted. This is becoming more and more common here. Lots of people believe in ghosts or have experienced some sort of paranormal activity.

We were listening about different dimensions and CS Lewis' Aslan was mentioned who is depicted as the Lion of Judah. This is how I got saved! (God also spoke to me about the movie 'The Lion king' and He showed me the prophetic references. I call this quick mental cross references!)

The general conclusion was:

1. Many have desire another dimension
2. Jesus spoke about the portal to His world—Heaven.

One person saw clearly that Jesus =Door. Therefore Jesus Himself is a portal and if we have Jesus in us then a portal is activated by prayerful faith and submission to God.

"Submit yourselves therefore to God. Resist the devil, and he will flee from you."

—James 4:7

"For Christ also hath once suffered for sins, the just for the unjust, that he might bring us to God, being put to death in the flesh, but quickened by the Spirit: By which also he went and preached unto the spirits in prison; Which sometime were disobedient, when once the longsuffering of God waited in the days of Noah, while the ark was a preparing, wherein few, that is, eight souls were saved by water."

—1 Peter 3:18—20

HIGH WITH MOST HIGH

Jesus is the legal access point, and He is the Sheep Gate. Otherwise, it is the Goat Gate and therefore illegitimate, crossing over to dangerous demonic territory. We have to test the spirits, but make sure you do not have a spirit of fear with you! That one must be defeated!

After this there was a feast of the Jews; and Jesus went up to Jerusalem. Now there is at Jerusalem by the sheep [market] a pool, which is called in the Hebrew tongue Bethesda, having five porches. In these lay a great multitude of impotent folk, of blind, halt, withered, waiting for the moving of the water. For an angel went down at a certain season into the pool, and troubled the water: whosoever then first after the troubling of the water stepped in was made whole of whatsoever disease he had."

—John 5:1—4

In the story 'The Lion, the Witch and the Wardrobe' Lucy explained to her brothers that the wardrobe became a portal but her brothers made fun of her. We also watched a Buddhist witness that CHRIST IS THE DOOR Aliss Cresswell prayed 'Lord Jesus let him see the door in front of him, Let it be real enough to feel'. And he did!

Tonight was an incredible time of fellowship at the Miracle Cafe in Banger Wales. The drive is 1 hour and 45 minutes from us. So even though we don't get to go as often as we'd like to and we absolutely cherish these times. God did not disappoint us, we had a meal out in Cloe's restaurant then went to the evening meeting. We did the introductions and immediately you could feel the high energy and I could sense a whirlpool portal, though at the time it was hard to put into words.

We watched the video then did the exercise of inviting Holy Spirit to minister to us from a different dimension and the heavens opened! It was absolutely glorious. There was a testimony about a hippy gypsy family and their children getting excited about prophecy and healing

MIRACLE CAFÉ: DIFFERENT DIMENSIONS

being on the spiritual menu and they wanted Jesus to come into their hearts. One girl was crying and she was sad but then the host Claire got wisdom from Holy Spirit to tell the two little girls about the Door way of light, she prayed for them to see Jesus as the Boss and the Light and their eyes sparkled with bright light. They were so excited and they saw Claire's eyes full of light too! They gave their lives to Jesus there and then. Praise God.

We all shared our experiences and one lady saw a waterfall and little fish and animals that was connected to it and a picture of the Lord Jesus in paradise gardens wow! Dot and others also saw visions, I saw a blue energetic wave portal, one man saw colours flowing into that and then it opened up around him and he was amazed! I could feel the holy portal open and I was trying not to manifest or shake during the time of prayer but it happened anyway! I did not want to embarrass anyone, but I have gone beyond caring now!

Glory to God, well, everyone was feeling lifted but Amy was feeling intuitively grief for a lady as a word of knowledge and she encouraged her which made the lady emotional and this touched the group. Previously she had felt sorrow and an emotional attack happened, a spiritual battle before the meeting. These are tiring, but we knew God had a plan. Dot saw different creative patterns as she is a designer like me and a big drop of purple oil came down and submerged into her hand. She described it as a power for creativity. The lord also previously spoke to her earlier that evening about being as humble and important as scaffolding as she was building up our family which was the church. That was her personal word and she doesn't often share these things often so I'm so glad that God is speaking to her and He kept us all in the peace.

After this I was asked to pray healing for Bob and his wife, and Bob had Parkinson disease. Well I've rebuked that and he then got quite happy drunk in the spirit, I saw this amazing couple had the healing anointing calling despite struggles. This was confirmed as they had ministered on the Benny Hinn prayer team. Once, they also they had set up a Bible school and put their children through American education and they had some sort of ancestry link with Past Revivalist Stephen Jeffreys, links with Smith Wigglesworth anointing in Sunderland and then with Stockport and they were from Bolton. I saw a rose arch around them and sensed the Kathryn Kuhlman oil and this was also confirmed as Bob knew about the scent of strong roses that filled the Hospital after Kathryn went to glory which filled the whole floor. She truly was the fragrance of Christ! And she is still is absolutely gloriously alive! We got talking and he got even more drunk with bliss and joy. I fell to the ground when I prayed for him with the host Claire who wanted me to pray for them.

Not everyone was looking at that point but I felt his pain and God used me as a prophetic shock absorber for a moment and that electric sensation ran through my body as I gave the pain and problem to go and it went back to the Cross where I saw everything evil is supposed to go. We need to remember this in healings and deliverance ministry. THE CROSS IS KEY! This has happened while praying against Mum Priscilla's pain and diabetes, in Llandudno in the summer. Praise Jesus, no one wanted to go home! It was so funny then Bob gave me some cash, as he knew I lived by faith and they got so whacked, he hugged me in the street and invited me to go to Bolton!

7th September 2022

Time for a Fast

Everyone was on a complete high so I thought it's a great time to continue my fast only the few days I did before weren't part of it! God told me they were just the warm up so I will have to follow his instructions for a much longer fast. I have the faith for it and I got a mega revelation to allow me to understand it greater. I know Hell tries to attack the peace but this time they aren't getting through in Jesus name!

MIRACLE CAFÉ: DIFFERENT DIMENSIONS

FASTING REVELATION:

God will do the fast through me. Christ has already done the 40 day and 40 night fast and overcome all the power of the Devil completely and so I just have to LET him do what is easy for Him in me, as there's no fear and perfect love has already cast out all fear so this includes fear of not eating! Fasting means 'not trying to do the fast' It is only me standing in the revelation realm of what God has already done for me so it's absolutely NOT me doing it—it's CHRIST in me doing something in me that He's already done!

Christ has complete triumph power and authority over the fasting realm. So what is there to be worried about? Excuse me, but my Jesus has already cast out all fear! So I am perfected in LOVE, so I have been in persistent prayer and praise and I am just going to continue as God is preparing me for global impact! I know that I will be going to the States to Africa, to Asia, wherever God wants me to go I will go. There is an event coming up in Birmingham that I am praying about too, but I only want God's will— His perfect will, even though I know that God loves me as I am, unconditionally! So Jesus does everything, I don't have to!

I exchange my natural in for His supernatural! Christ has already defeated the natural and the flesh that bothers us so much. I am already a SPIRIT man, and God has already done everything in advance for everyone called into the ministry and for all believers! This should be a wakeup call so we don't need to worry as Christ in us sustains us completely and his burden is LIGHT and He can do all things and therefore, I can do all things through Christ who strengthens me! I just have to be a crazy believer, endure all and let go of all and let God take over. God is just too good. What's the point wasting time and worrying? This fast has already been completed by Jesus! Someone praise Him! This is a funny revelation and God makes me laugh!

I am going to exchange weakness in for His strength! Christ has already defeated death, the devil's powers, the demons, fear, disease, sickness and sin. He has also defeated hunger so I don't have to be hungry! It's a lie! The supernatural has taken over and dominated the lies of the natural.

I have a spiritual and supernatural existence and everything has been let go of in order that Jesus Christ be completely seen and glorified! The Lord is preparing me for a great powerful ministry for his glory. He is doing something new and we don't have to understand it yet.

It's 2 am so I am about to sign out after a long day in his sweet presence, so I am filled today with praise, sermons, prayer, Bible study, fellowship and I know I am following after great giants in ministry. Praise Jesus all the time!

I was listening to Denis Jernigan who used to be a gay man! How interesting he also struggled with different things, as it said in his blog: 'The day before (Dec 30 2008) I had battled a lot of the enemies lies.' So this goes to show that even worship leaders struggle at times. Well I am determined to bring Heaven to Earth by a revelation! And 'God is able' as musician Ron Kenoly sings.

God showed me a powerful vision of Alvin Slaughter and Benny Hinn and I met them both and ministered with them. I better believe it! And most of the Ghanaian prophets have all seen me meeting Benny Hinn, praise Jesus, so nothing is impossible for the Lord. 'ONLY BELIEVE!' – Smith Wigglesworth.

Denis Jernigan has 9 children I wonder if God plans for me to meet him too! He read some hateful YouTube comments and was upset by them but we must know that Christ told us that we would be hated, misunderstood and persecuted so there special blessings and anointing to go through persecution. A lot of us have had countless attacks and persecution in advance but it's all for the glory to God and we don't have to understand it!

A British outstanding heaven sent Pastor Mike Parsons did a 40 day fast and he documented it in a blog and I love to read it as it encourages me

MIRACLE CAFÉ: DIFFERENT DIMENSIONS

and he survived and is still more alive than ever! These were just some of the incredible things that happened with Pastor Mike on day one!
1. Heat in his hands.
2. Vision of a golden wheat field, seeing Jesus and two angels and the harvest, walking with Jesus in that field.
3. Revelation, 'He is jealous for me, loves like a hurricane and He is a lover looking for a lover, so He fashioned me and formed my heart'.
4. During worship he had a vision of expanding mountains, then an angel gave him a flower which was very beautiful and vibrant and he saw flowers everywhere all shapes, sizes, colours, fragrances, he said this,' I started to see the colours more brilliant and defined, sharper than I have ever seen before. God said 'There will be new colours, new visions, new spectrums, the spectrum of heaven being revealed!'

That's absolutely mind blowing grace, all I can pray is Lord, show me Heaven, new creation realities and save souls in Jesus mighty name. By Grace, I know some of Mike Parsons's friends in the USA and they are so loving and super cool. Mike is part of the new mystical movement that God is doing in the Church Ecclesia. Exciting, Heavenly Kingdom times are coming! Get Ready, Praise Jesus!

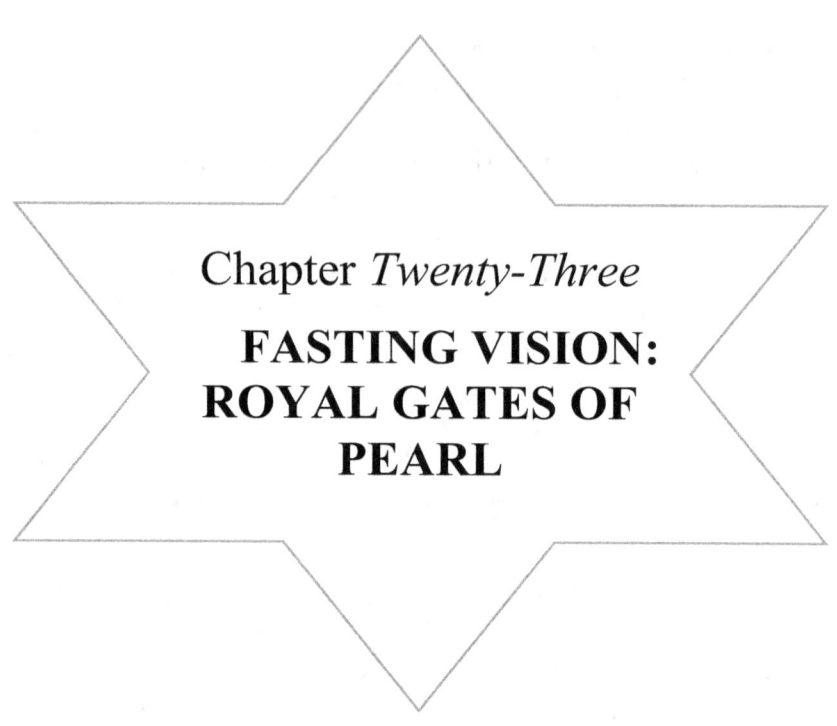

Chapter *Twenty-Three*
FASTING VISION: ROYAL GATES OF PEARL

A ROYAL FAST – PEARLY GATES VISION
Thursday 8th September day 2

I feel excitement in my spirit coming through into my soul and mind today. Last night I was buzzing with spiritual mental energy as the environment was charged by God's presence during a lot of praise and worship music while I tried to work! It will be kind of hard to do that when I get high again! Being high with God is really fun and purposeful but I have get myself out of the way and just let God take over with his awesomeness of who he is. We have to stop looking our emotions how we feel in order to get high with God. It is a mega

FASTING VISION: ROYAL GATES OF PEARL

revelation that we can come into a future happiness and joy and bliss kiss for today!

Few people realize this! We just need to stay appreciative, grateful, happy because we are so blessed! We are in His holy bliss bubbles. We are protected, appointed and anointed in Christ. Yesterday I was praying and God showed me a brief vision of a funeral, people were crying around the grave and God said, 'I am the resurrection and the life whoever comes to me shall have the same Holy Spirit I had and the same resurrection power! It's time to raise the dead! When he said that I felt His childlike excitement and did you know that the real glorified beautiful King Jesus Christ is playful? When I had heavenly dreams a few years ago which were night visitations, I found out just how much!

So these holy bliss bubbles are all around us for some reason and I can see these today in the Spirit, and God is showing me FAIRY LIQUID now that makes a lot of bubbles! All the fairy/angels have bubbles of glory all around them! I wonder if I am going to see them every day? Another thing I heard yesterday was 'Open wide you ancient gates and let the king of glory come in'!

Something came to me as a revelation shock:

As God is the Ancient of Days and as He is the gate, the shepherd gate, to find good pasture (the goodness realm), he is the door in revelation, he is the portal to Heaven. Well, if he is the Ancient of Days and He has loved us and known us from the foundations of the world, then Jesus became the 2nd Adam and this was all achieved in him! There is absolutely no separation in Him, whereby this is an existence in a higher dimension of perfect love and then His perfect love has already cast out all fear, so there is nothing to be afraid of and therefore it is impossible to fear, God has put us all together with the saints, angels, Great cloud of witnesses, and what are they witnessing? The ancient gates opening up! And who or what are the ancient gates? These aren't just places, it's much bigger than that! We are the ancient gates, and we are in the ancient of days already. There is an ancient gates or ancient gateway plan to open all these gates and we cannot just attribute this scripture to the demonic kingdom! What about the angelic kingdom? What about the kingdom of Heaven? And what about the Kingdom of Heaven opening up like an ancient gateway full of Gods glory through you? Do you believe it's possible? I do!!

We are in the ALPHA OMEGA force in the Heavenly places NOW, where there is no aging in the Heavenly realms but there is wisdom and that is wise dominion and God says we have dominion and authority already! This means there's no separation from any of his anointings! The Kathryn Kuhlman, Reinhard Bonnke, Marie Woodworth Etta, etc.

Are all available to the saints now! So what about accessing high level ministry anointings and the power of the HOLY SPIRIT through previous saints and then worked through you! Oh if only we would BELIEVE and then we would RECEIVE! No one of God ever dies, it's impossible! They live and live forever in something beyond bliss! Sheer ecstasy! No wonder why there's drunken glory in Heaven and its way beyond that. We can't even imagine how much lavish loaded, over the top, pure eternal Love Bliss is spilling over. God's love is continually flowing, gushing, holy, perfect, pure love and He has all this for us! And get this part, He has all this overflowing love and power for us every day!! We are going to bring the reality of Heaven to the earth whether we understand it theologically or not! CHRIST IS THE FOUNTAIN OF ETERNAL LOVE!

He is the very reason why we can be so high and wonder why! And we can access DEEP LEVEL JOY DAILY! This tells me that we have not fully understood who God is: We think He is conditional love, but He is not this and most of us have had enough of that!

He is:

1. Unconditional love
2. Eternal love
3. Perfect love

Currently, there is a Trinity of Divine Love, but God wants us to know that we are all made in his own image and he wants us to know that

FASTING VISION: ROYAL GATES OF PEARL

it's perfect love that he already cast out and got rid of and purged out all fear! This is exciting because fear is also to do with punishment and fear of hell and punishment. I have found that even know as Christians we will be chastised (disciplined) that we can even fear this! We can fear torment, we can fear losing our own lives for the Gospel and few want to do this because it is a massive costly call and people want a more simple easy yet selfish life. But that is not going to produce heavenly fruits of the Kingdom! So whether we like it or not we have to receive the Lords rebukes. But knowing this wisdom is both scriptural and revelational and you must have both is not always easy every day to maintain your faith when all hell rains down on you!

You are going to be tested and brought to trial spiritually before you can handle larger blessings of a greater freedom and even then the Promised Land in life and in Ministry is full of giants. This means that we have to learn to face our giants now while we are in the wilderness. I have to trust God completely that He will lead the right people to read my books, hear them and study from them at the right time and it is not easy to do that while being co-dependent on others or them being co-dependent on me especially if they are ill and in daily pain. Wow, it is such a test! But that does not mean that God is not faithful nor that God is not with me, nor that God does not care, nor that God does not know, nor that God will not provide folks, please understand. IT IS JUST A TEST and when you realize this God will do the rest!

Our sanctification may not be comfortable but it is purposeful! It is all for the Glory of God, Gods Kingdom and for the Kingdom of Heaven to be made manifest in you and in the whole of the Body of Christ. We are coming into really hard times since 911 and since Covid but that does not mean that God is not in supreme control and command. Nothing passes His eye without Him knowing about it. He is the all seeing eye, not lucifer and certainly not man.

This is why Jesus is the PRINCE OF PEACE and SUPREME JUDGE and He brings peace to you. But you have to receive it and before you can receive it you have to believe it! Are you getting the message?

Then, this is surely the same for joy and for spiritual sight and encounters.

Don't be depressed, rather fight those devils off with your smile and your praise to almighty God! Say no to sadness, lame living, victim mindsets, negativity even if you feel it from time to time and are surrounded by negative spirits in operation with people. Pray against the Devils negative emotions from affecting you. Bind and block and condemn their powers. You must condemn hopelessness and despair and depression not give into it. The same is true for addiction which is often the result of someone losing their hope, their peace or their joy then they become hard hearted and rebellious and follow 'other gods' and idols. Who has been there?

But, I want you to know that Christ's perfect Peace is accessible now, today, from within and this mighty peace flows like a river, bliss covers the skies, joy fills and floods our heart and soul as letting Christ love us is the only true goal! This is going to make you high despite problems, pain, trials, crazy attacks, people's insults, misunderstandings etc. We have to let go and let God! We have to let of all negativity daily and latch on to God's perfected positivity and this will lead to His perfect peace and then we will really start moving with Heaven! We will not be wishy washy, fair weather Christians, carnal or backsliding Christians or have victim mindset or be arrogant people! God is purging all the world and its desires out of us and the flesh and Satan and the worldly spirits hate it!!

This has been true of every revival move and we are in preparation for the Next BIG WAVE! We have to see if God wants to do it differently and then he will do what He wants, what He has planned with or without us. His glory realm is moving across the whole earth, in small bits and pieces yes, but nevertheless Christ is moving – Like in the Lion, the Witch and the Wardrobe by C.S Lewis. Aslan is on the move! Spring revival rain is coming! I need a lot of quiet time with Jesus, only following His lead as this is what happens every day but I must make special time for Him otherwise I too can feel lost. We are a royal family,

FASTING VISION: ROYAL GATES OF PEARL

a royal priesthood and we have a royal river flowing! Christ eternal love is a glory ocean!

The reason why I mentioned the Trinity is because you need to see yourself in the middle of that Trinity! The Godhead have surrounded us in perfect love and this means we shall not become as god's. We already are god's already, created in His perfect image. This is why Satan is so threatened and another way of saying it is this: We are made in their perfect image from the realm of perfect love.

In the SPIRIT we are already, right now, in perfect love, fully perfected in that realm when we know the trinity as a family! We are a family of perfect love. Nothing can ever separate us here! That means I am included and you are included! You are included because you are being a good Christian you are here because GOD was a GOOD and PERFECT MAN ON EARTH THROUGH CHRIST! This is our blessed assurance. Everything is all found in Christ and it can be accessed by faith daily. This is our inclusion that we thought we could not have because in the past we believed the lies that we could be separated from the love of God that is in Christ Jesus, and now we are in Christ Jesus, we are new creations, new creation glory realms are accessible and we have gone beyond Peter and Paul's and Ezekiel's revelations!
In Christ we have gone beyond! We go beyond and as it was revealed to Pastor and Mystic Mike Parsons, we can soar so high in Christ. We go beyond!!

A profound and prophetic advert popped up on my phone, a Vodafone I phone 14 read: PRO- BEYOND. This is exact confirmation of what I am meditating upon we have gone beyond in Christ! It's even more than God's resurrection, the emphasis here is not even on death, demons and the devil. They are already defeated if you <u>stay in your bliss bubbles</u> and if you give all of yourself to God's love you can go deep diving into pools of never ending grace and revelation glory! <u>These higher heavenly realms are accessible now!</u>

I can feel everything getting a lot lighter! Whoo-hoo! Goodbye old world that I used to belong to! I am going way beyond the constructs of religion, I am going deeper and deeper in my mode of transport - my bliss bubble which is my angelic, non-separative glory vehicle! Last night I was seeing bubbles and there were blues and purple iridescence and I put on Reinhard Bonnke, 'Faith and Fire' talk and after that I rested. My room was then loaded with Spirit and fresh fire and glory bubbles! Angels are everywhere!

Another thing that Christ said to me yesterday was how much value I am to Him. How I believed the subconscious lie that I didn't have value once and then Satan sowed in evil weeds but the angels are coming to do some weeding! Whoa I feel glory! The Kingdom Age will come if you let the Angels do some weeding. We aren't who we thought we were! Heaven is here, Heaven is at hard, it's accessible by faith and faith comes by hearing the WORD, the sounds of glory! The Lord said to me: 'Son you are my inheritance and you know that right? Well you are also my gateway to Heaven for other sheep to come and find safe pasture, as the real you is hidden in me so we are hidden in each other right now!'

Isn't that fun, mysterious and exciting? Then He said: 'So I inherit you as you abide in me and you inherit me in you! This is a cool exchange don't you think so? You are all part of the substance of the Eternal priceless pearl the Christ of all the crystalline lover, now come to the gates of pearl of great value and you'll find you are re-created into part of my pearly gates!!'

Well I can tell you for a fact, I am starting to feel glory whacked! God what are you saying to us? 'Some of you are rusty old gates and I am sending the refiners fire and the polishers ahead of you to show your true value hidden in me! We are hidden in each other. It's not a gate like you'll expect it's like a wall in heaven. It's a huge gate and wall made out of pearls and you are my pearls church! You are the point of access! I have made you into pearly gates! I have made you into kingly gates! You are royal and not only do you have access but…I have carried you into my heavenly gates to the very walls of Zion!

You are my inheritance! You are my New Jerusalem! You are grafted into my holiness, my greatness, my goodness, my majesty, my peace,

FASTING VISION: ROYAL GATES OF PEARL

my grace, my mercy. You are my love gates-gate ways of glory to reveal Heaven and my eternal kingdom to earth.'

Father continued to reveal this awesome revelation:

'You are:
1. PEARLY GATES
2. PRIESTLY GATES.
3. KINGLY GATES.

You are completely royal, completely holy and complete now in me, fully perfected and part of the entrance and access points of Heaven! You can walk right through my gates at any time because you walk through the pearl realm to get to the priestly realm, as the royal priesthood of Zion, as royal citizens of my Royal Family you walk through the holy gates of heaven.

You are walking through the gates of great price because you cost me everything and when Heaven was constructed I had you in mind, there in my heart. You are pearly priestly royal time travellers in my glory realm and this is all accessible through childlike faith! So as it is written all the gold, all the silver is mine and all the other metals, minerals, gemstones and crystals and all the pearls are mine! You are all incorporated already into my pearly gates because you are part of them! You are a soul saving pearly priest son! Tell my bride to simply abide! Believe and receive!'

Then during this fast, He revealed more: 'And who is the Mother of Pearl? The Holy Spirit, You're mother of wisdom! But we are all one here, so we are a family of wisdom which is wise dominion! You need to know the power of the pearl within you! You need to know who loves you, why we love you, what we did for you and then teach others our eternal love of which you are incorporated! Be therefore grafted into our heavenly holy wisdom and know you are not merely looking forward to the substance of who you are in us, but that you are already the substance of what we are hoping for! All of this reality exists in the Heavenly places in the SPIRIT REALM already! You are our inheritance son! You gain the Church Body and the church body gains you.

You have the pearl of great price hidden within you now and you are our pearl of great price. We want you and we need you and we made you a Doctor of our Church which is in Heaven. Heaven has already decided all things. Some are planned to be forerunners and some are planned to be celestials. You are our celestial being. It is here where you belong and dwell with us for ever. The lion of Judah let you into our kingdom. The belly of the whale was Leviathan and Jonah has already defeated and overcome that devilish creature and now I use the spirit of leviathan for my purposes, politically too for my glory and you don't have to understand this yet. You just need to learn how to relax and let us the TRINITY your family in Heaven, love you and take care of you the way we want too!

If you give us the desires of what you think is in your heart, we will give you the desires of our heart, then you will know the Holy Alchemical Christ that makes all things happen according to His perfect will. A lot of religious imagery can be damaging if you don't really get to know us! You don't want to have preconceived ideas about us and even about yourself as we are already ONE and we have won!! So yes at times you will be love drunk, and at times you'll be overseeing creation and restoring it to how it's meant to be. This will happen in the spirit and on the earth as it is already in Heaven! THE RESTORATION OF ALL THINGS IS AT HAND! And our power is accessible within. We love you!'

"One [thing] have I desired of the Lord, that will I seek after; that I may dwell in the house of the Lord all the days of my life, to behold the beauty of the Lord, and to enquire in his temple. For in the time of trouble he shall hide me in his pavilion: in the secret of his tabernacle shall he hide me; he shall set me up upon a rock. And now shall mine head be lifted up above mine enemies round about me: therefore will I offer in his tabernacle sacrifices of joy; I will sing, yea, I will sing praises unto the Lord. Hear, O Lord, [when] I

FASTING VISION: ROYAL GATES OF PEARL

cry with my voice: have mercy also upon me, and answer me. [When thou saidst], Seek ye my face; my heart said unto thee, Thy face, Lord, will I seek."

— **Psalm 27: 4—8**

I like the bit where it says in verse 8.
'My heart says of you' Seek his face!'

We need faith and action, and we look to patriarch Saint Abraham as he was credited righteousness, he believed and he did what God told him to do-no questions asked and God provided a Ram in the thicket! Jesus the Lamb is a Ram! We have to have faith with our giving, not faith and fear -the two are incompatible. If I want to explore Heaven it is led by God first and then I can access those holy wonderful realms by faith, revelation and visitation. So much will I be changed from glory to glory that I behold his face!

"Was not Abraham our father justified by works, when he had offered Isaac his son upon the altar? Seest thou how faith wrought with his works, and by works was faith made perfect? And the scripture was fulfilled which saith, Abraham believed God, and it was imputed unto him for righteousness: and he was called the Friend of God. Ye see then how that by works a man is justified, and not by faith only. Likewise also was not Rahab the harlot justified by works, when she had received the messengers, and had sent [them] out another way? For as the body without the spirit is dead, so faith without works is dead also."

— **James 2:21—26**

Here the prostitute Rahab is remembered and considered righteous by what she did as it took an act of faith. God will always honour faith. The revelation I have come to believe it's not our version of faith, it's Christ's! We can make wisdom very bitter if we mix it with carnal earthly wisdom. Wisdom comes from Heaven, to occupy heaven takes the wisdom of God and we are wise in Him. Just as Abraham and Rahab and Noah were accredited righteousness and faith so too can be wisdom be accredited as well as revelation. Experiencing God's fullness is God's inheritance to us and we are God's inheritance! Jesus Christ wants me and you all the time! He wants to spent time with us and we are his Bride to be! The fear/awe of God is the beginning of wisdom. Wisdom is wise dominion. Heaven is not closed as Reinhard Bonnke says, 'Heaven is open to us right now!!' There's so much to learn and we will always be learning in the school of the Spirit and the celestial academies! Glory to God!

"But the wisdom that is from above is first pure, then peaceable, gentle, [and] easy to be intreated, full of mercy and good fruits, without partiality, and without hypocrisy. And the fruit of righteousness is sown in peace of them that make peace."

–James 3:17—18

Wisdom/wise dominion is firstly pure. We must be purified and sanctified before we enter the Heavenly bliss kiss! We must let God be glorified in us! How can we enter gates of pearl, being not of pure pearl? That would like in Little Britain comedy 'The computer says NO!!' Ha-ha.

"For wisdom is better than rubies; and all things that may be desired are not to be compared to it!"

-- Proverbs 8:11.

I hear this from Heavenly Father: 'Wise dominion is far greater than the ruby realms, and with the pearly realms there's colours you can't even understand yet and higher frequencies that will just fill you up and flood you if you let them!' I was listening to Katt Kerr on Heaven this

FASTING VISION: ROYAL GATES OF PEARL

morning and I only got 10 minutes in and then Jesus took over my understanding by impartation to let me write all you have just heard! Some of her points were these:

1. <u>We must be like little children to enter Heaven and Heavenly realms which want to invade the earth.</u>

I remember reading Bill Johnson's book 'When Heaven invades Earth' about it and being very inspired from 2005 -2006. Yes, it was 2006 that I was really learning to hear from God, and although the enemy tries to derail me, all his powers are now NULL and VOID through glorious Jesus Christ, God of all life I abide!

2. <u>You cannot be manifest sons and daughters (of the King) if you do not know what God looks like on the inside as well as the outside!</u>

We are being called into the Pearly Priesthood of Gods Perfection Realm far out!

3. <u>God loves us all more than we can ever possibly imagine!</u>

He wants me! And He wants you too! We are one! We cannot be separated beloved!

4. <u>Don't wait to be perfect and feel all cleaned up.</u>

This is so important. Don't wait to feel better! Don't wait to praise God because you feel rough – *I dare you to praise God anyway!* You just have to be willing to be 'used' by God! - It's all for his glory! You are set apart for HIS GLORY!

5. <u>The revelation is not mine!</u>

That's what God revealed to Katt Kerr and that she owned nothing so she had to spread her work everywhere for free and then her ministry tapes were spread all around the world especially Asia. Jesus told me the other day: 'There's no copyright in heaven son! I own it all and therefore if you abide in me so do you! All the heavenly libraries are accessible by faith and you'll be amazed what they know and teach already, and this is why I made you a Doctor of the church. Keep praying for Dr. Blessing it will be well. You will be rich in me! As you already are rich in me now!'

In summary, that was well worth a fast day! God spoke deep revelations into me and later on you'll find out that I started to experience glorious new realms. Praise King Lord Jesus!

> *"Now unto him that is able to do exceeding abundantly above all that we ask or think, according to the power that worketh in us, Unto him [be] glory in the church by Christ Jesus throughout all ages, world without end. Amen."*
>
> —*(Ephesians 3:20—21)*

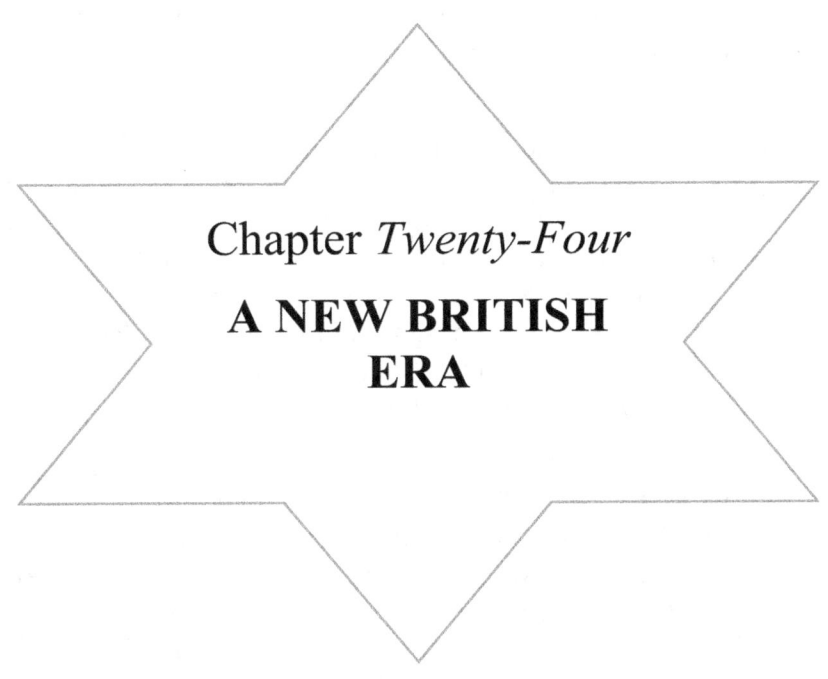

Chapter *Twenty-Four*
A NEW BRITISH ERA

A New British Era

A new British era has come because our wonderful Queen Elizabeth II went to glory! Now Charles III is king and people are saying 'God save the king'. We must be praying for the Royal family and the new Prime Minister Liz Truss, who is called Mary Elizabeth. They are immediately talking about capping energy bills at $2500 as they know most people just cannot afford the cost of living because after Covid everything is inflated. During the 'Pandemic' I saw that books would start to rise up to £30-40 and this has been happening.

It does not mean that we should be fearful and panic but we are being humbled and we are dependent on God through our government and through Charles III new monarchy. Britain will be grieving her Queen as the longest reigning monarch and also celebrating her long life at

HIGH WITH THE MOST HIGH

96 when she went to be with the Lord Jesus when she spoke so fondly of Him during her Christmas messages.

I wonder if we will start to see visions of her in glory, God knows all that happens in death and He gives everyone the door way of light choice to follow Him through the dark tunnel. Some people are so full of hate, demonised and refuse to forgive even though the light of the world has already forgiven them! These people are seen to be condemned, cast away from the light, and reserved for deep darkness and torments forever. People choose Hell by refusing Christ, refusing his forgiveness, refusing His great love.

In some ways in a sober way especially being left as I am fasting this is a sad thought that not everyone makes it into God's kingdom without Christ's mercy. I hate to think of unbelievers and atheists saying 'No!' to God and yet they do! All of us have gone astray, we have left the faith, the person of Jesus, forsaken his great love and we simply have to repent. Yes I am writing this book on how to be full of joy, and stay high with the most high but it's also about reflecting and remembering that not all people know Christ. We are to be the gateways of glory that God reveals to creation, as we say goodbye to our beloved queen Elizabeth II, and we pray Christ's holy will and Kingdom come, His will be done.

I have known and seen for some time that lots of drugs will be legalised in our near future especially cannabis and Wikipedia tells us something about our new Prince Minister Lizz Truss was active in the liberal democrats during her Oxford years where she supported the legalization of cannabis and the abolition of the monarchy. In 1996 she joined the conservative party. How interesting! I wonder if she still feels the same now! In 2005 she was added to David Cameron's A list. 5 years later she was elected into the House of Commons. In 2012 the book 'Britania Unchained ' was written by her which describes the British people among the worst idlers of the world. 'We work the lowest hours, we retire early and our production is poor. Whereas Indian children aspire

A NEW BRITISH ERA

to be doctors or businessmen, the British are more interested in football and pop music'.

So great Britain is basically being accused of being lazy! Half of these people should try having long term issues which stop the ability to work! Rumours of wider reforms of Britain are underway and have been since Boris Johnson, so who or what is really running the show behind our country? Well even though we are well aware of the New World Order Masons and others. God is still in control and Great Britain is great to God. I see a hidden revolt in parliament moving away from some of the secret initiations to climb to top in power, as Christ promises to pour out his Holy Spirit on all flesh and this includes the Elite, parliament, institutions and the monarchy.

Governmental Dream:

I had this prophetic dream once that Parliament was leaking rain water and they couldn't stop it. It was raining in the House of Commons and in the House of Lord's! It got worse and worse and more out of control. Some loved it and were drunken happy in the glory of the latter day rains and others were furious! I can't wait! LET IT RAIN! The work day of Britain will be changing soon to 4 days with longer hours and this is being trialled out now for the next 6 months.

Friday 9th September

I have decided to end my short fast. I managed three days this week, that might not sound that impressive but I got God's approval! And revelation: We already have God's love, approval and favour through the Lord Jesus Christ! He did that 40 day fast so we don't have to. We just have to be led by the Holy Spirit. If God wants me to fast more then I will be empowered to do that, if not, that's absolutely fine. The Lord Jesus is not a hard task master! He wants us to have energy and to continue with what we need to do each day. He told me that He didn't want to see me in more pain in my stomach than I needed to be, that I couldn't fast for healing, that He's done it at the Cross, that he wants us all healed, but we can't heal ourselves, we are dependent on him completely and my healing that has already taken place in the Spirit, and through the Lord's grace it will happen only at the right God ordained time. The Lord knows when that is, so I can let go, let God and trust him. It felt strange adjusting to food again but at least I saved my body from being in pain. I don't want stomach ulcers! We were praying for Amy's friend, Latifa, today who had to have surgery and has spent a huge chunk of her life in pain and we are praying against cancers. I was working on my books today and organising everything, let's just say I have written a lot!

Vision:

While I was praying with Amy and preparing dinner in the kitchen I began to see in the Spirit. I saw myself with fiery feet and then I had smouldering volcanic hands as I stretched them at the fire of God flew out! It was so dangerous! I saw Heaven to Earth Apostolic Ministries International as an ember glowing and growing in the darkness and it soon become a hill, then a mountain of FIRE!! Then I looked and I saw some of the rocks move upward and these formed into giants of FIRE! There were three giants on that mountain with one sitting at the entrance! In August God saved me different giants too. We have prayer giants with us-all to glorify God! Hallelujah.

Chapter *Twenty-Five*
GLORY IS THE NEW DRUG

9th September 2022

God told me 'That GLORY IS THE NEW DRUG' and 'I am your new drug dealer. I am the Hope dealer not the dope dealer! You have impartation grace to make others high even if you don't feel high yourself!' He then said the Holy Spirit is coming like the Wild Goose! This reminds me of the Celts who saw the Holy Spirit in this way because of the amazing manifestations of God's power. Then in confirmation Kathie Walters sent out an email about this very subject that I was praying about! How cool to be so in sync. We are all becoming one family and ONE LOVE.

HIGH WITH THE MOST HIGH

I was pretty happy after my fire mountain vision and seeing those giants. I know lots of people will call me mad or whatever, but who cares, in Christ is the tough shell and soft heart that I have always needed. He makes all things happen for the children of God, we are so far away from believing His sovereignty and we are too quick to blame Him when things go wrong. He says, 'Yes, I knew that would happen but I am still here for you in the middle!' I find that revelation a never ending bliss kiss and He comforts me and makes me laugh even when people are being all stuffy and religious. They can't help it. In God's presence is fullness of JOY!! Whoosh! That means I am complete in Him already! I see revelation bombs are going off! BOOM!!

At this time I was listening to RLM and Brandon was talking about Jubilee, I started to feel more whacked and he was saying things like 'let's just get baked and toasted on the Holy Spirit!' That made me laugh even more! I was also speaking to him most days on social media and his friend Jake, well let's just say I am still praying for them.

"And though they hide themselves in the top of Carmel, I will search and take them out thence; and though they be hid from my sight in the bottom of the sea, thence will I command the serpent, and he shall bite them: And though they go into captivity before their enemies, thence will I command the sword, and it shall slay them: and I will set mine eyes upon them for evil, and not for good."

— **Amos 9:3—4**

I was meditating on the Heavenly realities where 'the hills of the trees will clap their hands' and 'the rocks will cry out' and this made me feel that even uses trippy language to describe the Glory of God! FAR OUT! Even with the horn of David, I have had horny visions! Can I say that? Oh come on, it might get rid of some religious dust from your nostrils! Man, we have been breathing in the same old religious ideas for too long and Jesus is sick of us not being kind and kind and high. Whoa can you imagine if we were kind, high and powerful? Now, that would make a change! Instead of us waiting for the Holy Spirit and then complaining when we do get a visitation or an encounter that we don't understand, or it is too disturbing or loud then maybe we will learn to enjoy the ride and enjoy the show because Church, here we go! Fasten your seat belts because this is going to be more like a wacky rollercoaster than a comfortable church cruise! Who is ready for what's coming?

As I was saying, I have had visions of horns growing out of the Throne of God and I have seen God with horns and most people would say that He looked like a monster. I think I mentioned this in 'A Prophet's Journal' during my 2020 Lockdown Revival. Freaked me out but at the same time I saw GOD in a whole new way and this is not stopping!! The personification of things is at hand when the sons of glory are made manifest to all of creation and through all creation. YES LORD!

"For the creature was made subject to vanity, not willingly, but by reason of him who hath subjected [the same] in hope, Because the creature itself also shall be delivered from the bondage of corruption into the glorious liberty of the children of God."

Romans 8: 20— 21

Jesus then spoke to me about the parody of marine spirits and the undersea kingdom of the Devil 'Guess what son? All of this is just imitation but also guess what? Are you still guessing?' He then made me wait and then He shouted 'IT ALL EXISTS IN HEAVEN TOO!' I thanked God for deafening me and awakening me and then I asked Him to explain.

'Well, it's pretty simple. We also have 'water' in Heavenly places and there are creatures and spirits in the waters from the macrocosms to the microcosms to the aquatic to the mammals. Just as you have classified different species on earth into 'kingdoms' so too have we! Some saints aren't even aware of these and not everyone gets access to the same rewards in Heaven because it is full of different dimensions and it is nowhere near big enough to what are planning my child! And it's coming to earth. Well, in part and the revelation is hitting you like a tonne of bricks knocking down all your pseudo self-righteous churches in your subconscious mind and memories and I am washing all that away with my Heavenly waters and Heavenly higher consciousness! Enjoy!'

'You are the earth. You know that, let's save that revelation for later otherwise you'll be a stoner in the spirit and unable to do anything and I want you to write books and preach and be creative while functioning on the whack of Heaven! So, we will save that one for another time my boy! Come and taste and see that I am good. I can drug the living daylights out of you and make all the darkness light and all your light into darkness and reveal there is no such thing as darkness when you abide in my light. You blaze in my crystalline temple and oh my son I am proud of you so blaze on! BLAZE ON!'

I was feeling weird and holy and who knew that Jesus Christ can be hypnotic. It felt like I wanted to sleep and it felt like I wanted to throw a huge party and dance all night. I just couldn't decide which he interrupted my thoughts with.

'I know what you are thinking and who cares what people think? Oh dear son, you'll learn that I am fun and I am the Lord of the Party! Come and see the new substance of where your faith has brought you so far? We are having heavenly Edenic glory restoration and you'll love this next section of your life, so cares if it makes sense to people, just follow me, yeah?'

I honestly don't know how I am still functioning as I feel like my body just wants to float off all the time and never return until I can be the cure all for all and God said: 'If you want to be the cure all for all; then you must go through all things for all. Very strange things for very strange oil. This is my holy cure all for all. You are co-labouring in suffering to co labour rule and reign with me. This will be the CURE ALL FOR ALL. When I get my way with you and make an example of my abundant non-religious grace. I can send you off into new dimensions all across time and space! There will be so many signs and wonders with you just as there is an abundance of treasure in the earth, in the planets and in my Heavens! You have an endless supply and you'll never wonder why I am so shockingly good because you will morph into the fullness of my image inside you! Get ready!! Get enough oil to handle my visitations and encounters else you will struggle and be zonked out on the floor or your bed and you will not be able to move!! I am going to bake your soul in my glory!'

Well, I don't even know what to add. Glory to God.

After this I broke my daily fast and went into the garden to see my family. They knew something strange was happening to me as I spoke to them all wide eyed, smiling like a Cheshire cat! Later, God led me to look up Bishop Kanko who is an ex occultist witchdoctor who saw the kingdom of Satan under the sea.

I was also listening to Vincent KY about Hell on Telegram, also my great friend Prophet Prince Kobby who always does the most amazing messages and writes excellent books.

A powerful weekend in the Glory

I spoke with my friend Tye, a friend of Angel Wilson from the USA for a few hours and he prayed for my leg to straighten up and it did! I had never told him about this and it was a total surprise to me. I miss speaking to Him but we need God's best timing on fellowship with all my amazing friends and I am always on catch up with work and writing books is very tiring! It was amazing because God had not forgotten about my old wounds that He healed! God was so kind to be right in the middle of us with brother Tye. I will write about this in another book with the theme 'High with Tye!'

HIGH WITH THE MOST HIGH

Sunday Church Zoom – Robert Pears

During this time I experienced another vision during the meeting and I think that I will discuss this also in another volume. I just wanted to mention it here to whet your appetite! We will talk about this next time: VISION.BAPTISM HELMET.

I also experienced something that blew my mind which I will call 'The clouds and the coasters!' I experienced all the effects of going on a Rollercoaster Sunday night but without seeing anything! I couldn't get off my chair. I felt like I had been fastened into the ride and I had no choice. This whole mind blowing experience and its effects made me squeal like a child so much that I almost lost my voice and I had no idea God could do that! My family left me well alone – I think they thought maybe I was in pain and it's a good job that our neighbours didn't hear. Thank God for thick walls! I believe that was a Katt Kerr impartation but it came at the strangest of times!

We were learning about how Jesus took all the abandonment, He didn't sin. Holy Spirit is such a great teacher! Well, I just wasn't expecting that!

Some of my new week: 12th 13th September 2022

Monday 12th

I was still thinking and praying about these words: Abandonment, deliverance, counselling, trust. I thought to myself if I really trusted God and if I would trust God with my whole life? Or would I want to keep back some of my life for myself or keep back my dignity? Wondered if I had what it takes to be Gods Kingdom Disciple. I know I am in a visitation part of my life and I am seeing angels and Heavenly things and I feel so very blessed.

GLORY IS THE NEW DRUG

Jesus spoke to my soul and said: 'Just trust me, I am a good Teacher! You can trust your teacher to teach you well. I will teach you all that you need to know and I will teach you. Just let me do my job OK?' I started to feel what I can only describe as 'Zappers!!' This is a combination of high, drugged after effected, whacked, inspired and blessed. I then started to see bubbles all over my room. I thought 'Is Jesus going to take me somewhere with these Bubbles of light?' You never know with GOD! Anything can happen and He is really helping me process the NEW experiences the best way I can!

I began to see a VISION of me in Christ and Christ in me (I started to see the prophetic exchange revelation) dancing over death! It was electrifying! There was a mega Portal of electricity open and I then worshiped God with Ron Kenoly music and played 'Jesus is alive' very loudly and on repeat! My whole body started to shake and I got what felt like electrical shocks from side to side and I knew the angels were close. My chest began to feel like it was expanding and my arms and hands shook under the anointing. It can happen to you too!

For some reason I had Edmonton Baptist church on after this on You Tube but I can't remember what it was because I was too out of it! The worship and the power of God's presence was so, so tangible. I feel like every day is another dream.

Tuesday 13th September

Today I got more revelations and I don't even know how to put anything in proper words yet, so I think I will just wait. The presence of God was so overwhelming. It produced a K.O (Knock out) effect! I don't even know what's been downloaded into me but I know it's a lot!

God said that 'Daily deliverance = Great gratitude.' That makes sense. He showed me the power of gratitude as the right attitude. Not complaining in the wilderness because of problems. I am juiced for

HIGH WITH THE MOST HIGH

God. I am drained for God. I am revived for God! I am experiencing all things for God and through God. Jump on board! This ship is setting sail, the Glory ships are coming and the angels are about to give me more experiences so that when I can recover from these I will be able to teach them!

WORSHIP REALMS REVELATION: WE GET DELIVERED FROM EVIL INTO THE GOODNESS REALM. THE GOODNESS REALM LEADS INTO THE GLORY REALM. APPRECIATION IS IMPORTANT.

But we have to be grateful for all the goodness and kindness of God and the fresh mercy He has already shown us!

"And as he entered into a certain village, there met him ten men that were lepers, which stood afar off: And they lifted up [their] voices, and said, Jesus, Master, have mercy on us. And when he saw [them], he said unto them, Go shew yourselves unto the priests. And it came to pass, that, as they went, they were cleansed. And one of them, when he saw that he was healed, turned back, and with a loud voice glorified God, And fell down on [his] face at his feet, giving him thanks: and he was a Samaritan. And Jesus answering said, Were there not ten cleansed? but where [are] the nine? There are not found that returned to give glory to God, save this stranger. And he said unto him, Arise, go thy way: thy faith hath made thee whole."

—*(Luke 17:12—19)*

Worship realms:

This is just the beginning. Actually from Heavens perspective it's not even worship! It's called ADORATION realms which Heaven is constantly in and this is what releases God's kisses to us in! The Lord said, 'You worship me in Spirit and in Truth not because of obligation but because you love me and are truly grateful. Therefore I do not get worshipped, I am adored, and guess what you are in me and I am in you and I adore you and you adore me. And the realms of adoration and constant peace and bliss are Heavens reality.

WORSHIP is an old revelation word! WE ADORE EACH OTHER IN HEAVEN. I ADORE YOU AND YOU ADORE ME. THIS IS THE WORSHIP REALM AND I WANT TO RENAME IT THE ADORATION REALM WHICH COMES FROM AND GOES INTO THE DIMENSION OF THE CONSTANT CELEBRATION REALM. We all adore each other, and we are all in love in Heaven!

After this God gave me an alphabet from some sort of glory drug He gave me: He told me 'each one is like a kiss' (See song of songs)

You are:

ATONED not ABANDONED

BEAUTIFUL not BROKEN

CARING not CRUEL

DELIVERED not DEMONISED

EXCEPTIONAL not EVIL

FACE TO FACE not FACELESS!

GLORY FILLED not GROANING ANYMORE!

HOLY not HORRIBLE!

I AM PRESENCE not IAM WITHOUT!

JUSTIFIED not JEALOUS!

KISSED not KILLED!

LOVED not LOST!

MERCIFUL not MISERABLE!

HIGH WITH THE MOST HIGH

NURTURED not NEGLECTED

OPULENT not OPPRESSED!

POWERFUL not POWERLESS

QUIET not QUARRELSOME

RESCUED not RAGE FILLED

SANCTIFIED not SINFUL

TRUTHFUL not TORMENTED

UNIQUE not UGLY!

VALIANT not VAIN!

WONDERFUL NOT WORTHLESS

XENIAL (hospitable) not XENOPHOBIC! (Racist to others)

YIELDED not YOKED!

ZEALOUS not a ZERO!

I was whacked on the love of God this day. After God gave this alphabet and I meditated on it I started to feel like I would travel the world and God told me to dream big dreams because He 'loved the whole world.'

> *"That which was from the beginning, which we have heard, which we have seen with our eyes, which we have looked upon, and our hands have handled, of the Word of life; (For the life was manifested, and we have seen [it], and bear witness, and shew unto you that eternal life, which was with the Father, and was manifested unto us;) That which we have seen and heard declare we unto you, that ye also may have fellowship with us: and truly our fellowship [is] with the Father, and with his Son Jesus Christ."*
>
> —(1 John 1: 1—3)

Chapter *Twenty-Six*
FORGIVENESS AND FAVOUR: REVELATION

FORGIVENESS AND FAVOUR.

"But if ye forgive not men their trespasses, neither will your Father forgive your trespasses."

—Matthew 6:15

"So likewise shall my heavenly Father do also unto you, if ye from your hearts forgive not every one his brother their trespasses."

—Matthew 18:35.

The Lord said to me 'we have been panelled with peace, fortified with hope and adorned with love. My love is now unconditional, through Jesus Christ, all your sins are forgiven and in my sea of forgetfulness. It's time to dive in!' We are going to come into this realm where we don't even remember the things that bother us we can't even worry! We will be completely worriless! We are going to go into a worriless realm! A fearless realm! A fortified with hope realm and a panelled with peace realm and adorned with God's love realm and be cherished with favour! Praise Jesus and forget the past! Forget none of God's benefits. Do not remember the sins of your youth or your past. Your past has been the last 20 seconds when you felt bad or sad, forget it, it's gone!

From a futuristic perspective we have been immersed in the glory of God, in His Ocean of deep love and we've got to dive in! We've got to get in the sea of glory. This is His sea of forgetfulness!

The Lord is saying to me 'I want you to be in the sea of forgetfulness, where you see yourself as sinless and complete, and holy and made of light' The Lord reminded me of a story I heard recently. 'If little children can come to the Bangor miracle cafe and get filled with my light and want my salvation, why don't you want my salvation power every day?' He asked me, 'The spirit of religion has been blocking my church from seeing what I have already done for them, and how much I love them, and I will always love them and I won't ever stop! So why don't you love yourself with that love? It is my divine love that heals all.

Why are you being distracted by the things of this world or the enemy, and the way you think about yourself, thinking about the thoughts the enemy puts in your mind, you are believing it, and you're absorbing it and you are making it part of your reality, and actually you can change your reality by how you think, so let Heaven change the way you think, let Heaven come out of you, let my light and love come out of you. Let it be an exchange in you out of you, in you, out of you. There should be like a wave of glory inside you every day. It's like a rhythm, in and out like breathing, in and out, simply breathing, breath in my glory, breathe out the world and it's darkness. It is just simple breathing that will help you to let go and be in the know as you glow in my glory, letting go and

FORGIVENESS AND FAVOUR: REVELATION

breathing in my eternal love. You are truly forgiven my son and my daughter, now breathe in my favour and receive my peace today. Just breathe!'

Sometimes it's often the simple messages that we can overlook. We need to let go, let God and learn how to abide in Heavens sacred breath. The breath of Heaven within you will change you. I am reminded of some lyrics: "Let us breathe out and confess'....'Let our ordered lives confess the beauty of your peace.' Satanic forces want us to have confused, chaotic and disengaged minds, where what we take in doesn't seem to matter. We are surrounded by so many images in today's world that after a while it all becomes meaningless. We have lost the ability to really be patient, to engage quietly with God and have dialogue with the Spirit. We can get this back when we humble ourselves and pray

> *"If my people, which are called by my name, shall humble themselves, and pray, and seek my face, and turn from their wicked ways; then will I hear from heaven, and will forgive their sin, and will heal their land. Now mine eyes shall be open, and mine ears attent unto the prayer [that is made] in this place."*
>
> **—2 Chronicles 7:14—15**

God will heal our fragmented fractured minds and upgrade us. He will give us reasons to hope, reasons to move forward, not just for the cares of this world for survival but for the greater picture global revival. Let us be still and know that God is God. He is in control, interested in us and our development and engaged. He is attentive and mindful of us. All things are known to God. He is waiting for us to engage today great favour is coming in Christ you are forgiven. Amen. Therefore please stop beating yourself up for sinning, missing the mark and going your own way. Most of us, if we are being real about it have hardened our hearts more times than we have hot dinners and yet God has still forgiven us. Take that in and read it again:

YOU ARE TOTALLY FORGIVEN IN CHRIST

YOU ARE TOTALLY HEALED AND FREE IN THAT REVELATION OF CHRIST'S FORGIVENESS FOR YOU. HE HAS ALREADY FORGIVEN YOU.

We do not need to have low self-esteem anymore and no more anxiety either! Why? Because we are justified and being sanctified through Christ. Let go and let Christ Jesus do the work through you. Let Him get rid of your old body as you lose the focus of the carnal and the temporal and you learn to accept your ascension body you can learn to put on the incorruptible every day! Oh beloved, if only we would awaken. Don't let pain, discomfort, pride, sin or any other evil distract you from abiding in the freedom of Jesus every day!

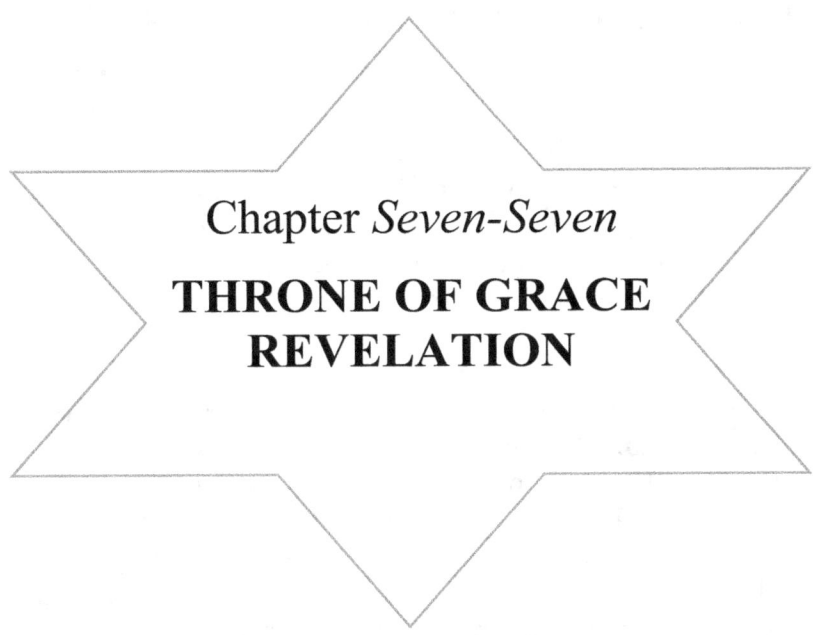

Chapter *Seven-Seven*
THRONE OF GRACE REVELATION

Throne of Grace: Revelation

During fellowship in September 2022 with Mum and Amy I began to see a picture of a throne and I asked God what it was: It was a celestial golden throne in space, in flames and the Lord said 'I want to take your sister a lot higher than she's willing to go, but she's not willing to go yet.' I was like 'whoa ok!' So, I asked the Lord 'what is this? The Lord replied 'This is a time travelling redemptive vehicle of my Grace. That is what a throne is, and a throne is a place where you are seated as part of the government of Heaven, yes, you are the family of Heaven, you are the royalty of Heaven! So therefore, my judicial decisions will be made through you when you realize you can already access my grace through the Throne of Grace, in your time of need.

HIGH WITH THE MOST HIGH

"Let us therefore come boldly unto the throne of grace, that we may obtain mercy, and find grace to help in time of need."

—*Hebrews 4:16*

God said, 'Do not see the grace of Christ as something as outside of yourself. You have been given the throne of Grace for yourselves, so the only way to go and get access to that grace is to get it from the Throne of my Grace within. You get access by going within abiding in Christ.'

Therefore, God dwells outside and He's given us a seat of power as we belong to the government of Heaven already. Then the Lord showed me these empty seats floating about! So, I asked the Lord again what was happening, to which He answered. 'So many thrones and not enough people to occupy them because so many of my royal people are believing that they are like lifeless lumps of stone!' I was taken aback and my sister Amy and Mum Priscilla started to have a great conversation with some excellent input:

Amy: So many times, in life I've felt insecure, and inferior to other people as if I didn't have any voice, so to speak.

Jon: Yes, like I'm a blockage, I'm a boulder, I'm a useless stone, I'm a problem, I'm a stumbling block in people's way' And God is saying 'So many thrones, and so many lifeless stones. It shouldn't be this way!'

Mum: But, they haven't gone to sit on their thrones!!
Jon: Yes, and we are supposed to be living stones. We are supposed to be receiving the revelation of the crystalline Christ. We are supposed to be understanding we don't just go to the throne of Grace, although it's a real thing in Heaven, and I'm not saying it isn't.

THRONE OF GRACE REVELATION

But God has given us a time where He sits within us, and He is seated in this throne which is a vehicle of time travelling redemption!

Mum: And we will be lifted higher!

Jon: And we are supposed to get elevated higher and higher and higher!

Mum: Right, like the scaffolding.

Jon: 'He lifts me up' like that song that Josh Groban sung. So, this throne of grace isn't just something that we go to (like we have been only taught) but it's also we have got to our own thrones of grace, which God gave us by part of His eternal plan. That's how we get the Grace to love ourselves, because then you know:

- You are family in the realm of family.
- You are in the realm of royalty
- You are in the realm of government.

That's who you are! This is a real revelation of Heaven now! We really need to experience and believe in the Heaven now mystical way of life abiding in the supernatural Messiah! We have thrones of grace that are accessible in the Spirit that we can bring down and let these gravitate in order to get them to go higher. This is a mystical way of ascension. It is another way of explaining the mysteries of the Holy Scriptures, so we can all understand.

"For in him dwelleth all the fulness of the Godhead bodily." — Colossian 2:9

You see, <u>we have already ascended in our spirits</u> at the point of our salvation but there should be no separation for us. There is an illusion currently in the Body of Christ by these devils that are causing these distractions and illusions to say that we already separated from God, and then separated from His love which is a flat out lie!

> *"Who shall separate us from the love of Christ? [shall] tribulation, or distress, or persecution, or famine, or nakedness, or peril, or sword? As it is written, For thy sake we are killed all the day long; we are accounted as sheep for the slaughter. Nay, in all these things we are more than conquerors through him that loved us."*
>
> —(Romans 8:35—37)

Amy: Yes and we think we aren't worthy.

Jon: We think we are separated, not worthy, we are isolated and a lot of us are frustrated.

Amy: We see ourselves a lot of the time as insignificant.

Jon: Yes unimportant, and yet the truth is: It's all the opposite! God says 'Look, I have already given you what I have got! And you are my inheritance and I want you to realize this, I want you to realize that you've got to open the gateway and open the doors and let the King of glory come in and come out! You are my family of glory and so you are coming with me! So, we are going on journeys together, it's time for Apostolic prayerful time travel journeys where you realize that you are children of the promise and children of my redemption. You are to be my children that change whole atmospheres, shifting different atmospheres, changing people's hearts and perceptions changing and being changed daily' I hear Jesus say.

We chose to empower ourselves daily which is what Grace is, we have the grace anointing to empower ourselves everyday with this supernatural Grace. We have got access to it through Christs great

THRONE OF GRACE REVELATION

Throne of Grace and you have access to your own throne of Grace! Just insert your name! This is mind blowing and it would really change the way we think, about ourselves and each other. We would realize our responsibility and duty which is hidden in Christ. We would know what is required of us and be empowered to bring it to pass, filled with the power of the Holy Spirit. Therefore, you've got your own throne of Grace! We don't realise who we are yet!

Mum: The other part I understand is us not accepting God's grace. I was just thinking about Grace and favour and I was reminded of the Queen Elizabeth II can give out grace and favour homes to anyone of her choice, and if their 'impoverished aristocrats' that she feels deserve special rewards and care, she can offer them an apartment in Hampton Court, for example. This might be a reason why Hampton Court burnt down because people would use candles in these flats, but I don't know if that's just a false accusation when people said its builders and the roof which is a lot more likely but anyway they are called Grace and Favour houses or homes and they can be a flat or they can be part of a grand mansion she owns so many properties and obviously they are not all filled.

So, for example, if there is Lady Godiva and her husbands died, and her sons taken over the mansion and she doesn't have a dour house and they are considered 'impoverished' you might say 'Lady Godiva, would you like to come and live at one of my stately homes somewhere? Now, if Lady Godiva said no, I will go and put myself on the counsel list!' She would lose all the grace and favour! Lol! And she would lose the reward and the provision which was for her to raise her up!

Jon: How profound? Great illustration, Mum!

And a lot of us are sitting on the wrong list because I can hear the Lord say 'we have got impoverished mindsets! So, we need to repent of small minded and poverty influenced thinking.

HIGH WITH THE MOST HIGH

Mum: Yes, well you could mope and say 'oh I will just go on the counsel list, they'll have to give me something'

Jon: Victim mindsets! We don't want theses! Impoverished and victim mindsets have to go because we are not victims, we are not impoverished.

Amy: We are not inferior or insecure!

Me: And I hear God say 'why are you surprised when I prosper you? You shouldn't be because this is your inheritance and you are my inheritance my beloved'.

So, we declare 'for our inheritance, give us the lost'. Well God is singing that over us. He is saying 'for my inheritance – give me the lost'.

We are Priests of the Highest; the royal priesthood and we are supposed to bring in the lost.

Mum: oh, that's beautiful!

Me: We are the fisherman. Whichever way you look at it, we are the fishermen! And we are supposed to bring in the lost, so how can we be fisherman if we don't understand the River of life? And if we don't understand the river, how can we understand and operate in the seas and great oceans winning nations and continents for Christs Holy Kingdom! That is the final Game of Thrones! I was reminded of our meeting las night where we heard about baptism, 'Believe and be baptized!' not just a water baptism, but a spirit baptism, a blood baptism and a fire baptism! Talk about elemental initiation into different dimensions in Christ! Just imagine now we have access to the Throne of Grace and our own thrones of co-grace! What a glorious inheritance we have in Jesus holy name to look forward to. Amen.

"I marvel that ye are so soon removed from him that called you into the grace of Christ unto another gospel: Which is not another; but there be some that trouble you, and would pervert the gospel of Christ. But though we, or an angel from heaven, preach any other gospel unto you than that which we have preached unto you, let him be accursed. As we said before, so say I now again, If any [man] preach any other gospel unto you than that ye have received, let him be accursed. For do I now persuade men, or God? or do I seek to please men? for if I yet pleased men, I should not be the servant of Christ. But I certify you, brethren, that the gospel which was preached of me is not after man. For I neither received it of man, neither was I taught [it], but by the revelation of Jesus Christ."

— **Galatians 1:6 – 12**

"And He said to them, "Follow Me, and I will make you fishers of men." Immediately they left their nets and followed Him"

—**(Mathew 4:19—20)**

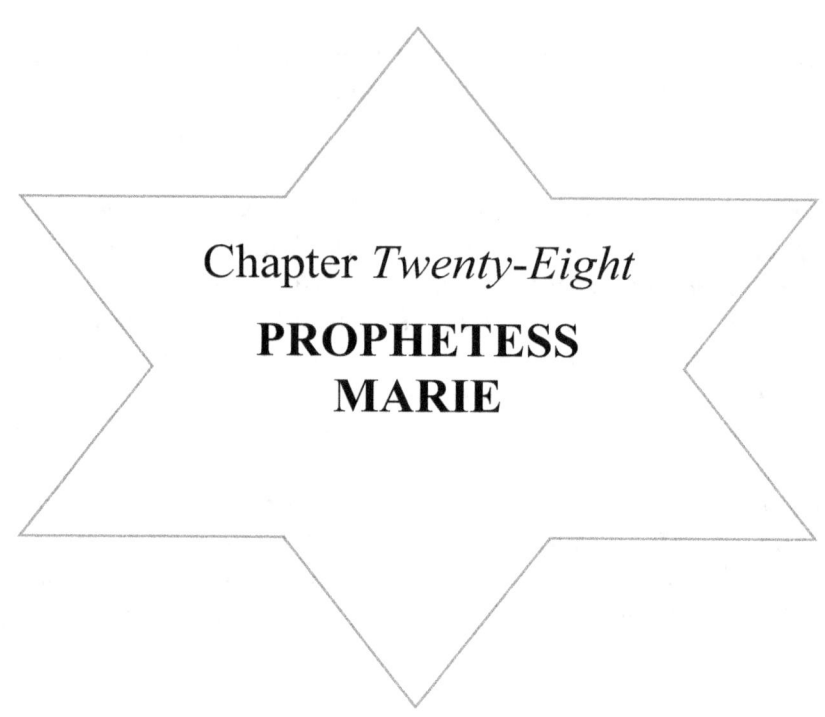

Chapter *Twenty-Eight*
PROPHETESS MARIE

PROPHETESS MARIE: A NEW KINGDOM.

Some are going through a very difficult time. But for you, not so, because as you look and go far beyond what you are now, looking into events which are surely going to rock the planet to shake it! And the Lord is showing the revelation and the deeper work which is coming about because of the need that is what God has put into motion. This is what the Lord is showing to you, that this opening way is going to bring you into a place where you've been before, and to be able to put together in the name of Jesus, souls to enter into the kingdom of the Lord your God in whose name you put your trust. Joy is filling your

heart because at last He raises you up for such a day and we thank you Lord for that release.

PROPHETESS MARIE

I see the internet, I see a free flow. As that word goes out in Jesus name joy comes about by people who begin to realise that there is a great God, a great saviour. The lord Jesus Christ, where every knee shall bow and tongue confess that Jesus Christ. You are Lord indeed. So there is a release now of knowledge, faith, wisdom, worker of miracles, prophecy, discerner of spirits, walk over devils; you bind them, you break their power, you are not fighting flesh and blood, but the principalities and powers of the darkness of this age. You WIN! The battle is the Lord's and JESUS CHRIST WINS EVERY BATTLE! Tongues and interpretation, Holy Spirit thank you for the gifts severally given as He chooses. As you preach the Gospel with the signs and wonders and miracles are following! In the name of Jesus, you have the victory.'

This is an example of Prophetess Marie's ministry work and prayer on zoom, now I will give you my prophetic word:-

'Thank you Holy spirit we acknowledge your direction and your path. The Lord is showing you the tools of the trade. These are to do with technology, furthering the education into something which is going to be very much required of for part of your life. But many people are looking at certain things to do with technology but when you have the mind of Christ, you are able to see far beyond that, God is showing: But it doesn't take one, it takes one for all and all for one! That is where the problem lies because nobody wants to be the all for one and one for all, they just want to be the one! THE ONE! This is what the Lord is showing, this is where, as you know, as you have discovered that as yet, they haven't woken up to themselves, that there is only one way, and that is the Lord's way which as you know to come together as one church—one mind of Christ, and all together fighting the good fight of faith in which we are able to overcome! As you overcome all the fiery darts of the wicked one and this is what He is showing to you right now.

HIGH WITH THE MOST HIGH

God bless the United Kingdom because we now have a king, a kingdom with a king. Now we are going to see some fireworks going off! We are going to see a multitude of sins coming out in all directions, it's going to be a very unusual time ahead because it will start out slow because he doesn't dare bring out what he is going to bring out to begin with, he will seem like a nice little pussy cat, but then once he gets firing off- he's going out like a tiger! So we are aware of something so blessed which we have seen in a Queen who has been given a great mantle over the years and now we are ready, oh yes we are: for the change!

Coincidentally, incidentally that the two have come together! Yes a new prime minister as well. Oh dear, we shall see and when we see, we will know far more beyond what they can understand if they are not of the kingdom well. But we thank you, Jesus! (We pray for the government and the royalty regularly). Greater things are coming on a much bigger scale.

The United Kingdom has a kingdom and a king, but we have the King of kings and Lord of lords!! That king is going to have something to say very soon. He is waiting for a certain specific time because that time is going to make everyone accountable including his church. Accountability! This is what the Lord our God is showing but your joy is full because you have a full basket of eggs. People say 'don't put all your eggs in one basket, but you are able to do this because you know exactly where those eggs came from.

This is a bit of a pun, a joy a fulfilment of God's progressive work which He has been doing in your life. And of course there's always the dad jokes! And these can spin around all over the place which we are not supposed to enter into. Joy is filling your heart, we can get such joy at the smallest detail of this living God in whom you put your trust! There's a release now in Jesus name, as in the Knights of old, when the living God came upon the scene in a great and powerful way of course we are talking about the armour (Ephesians 6). Put on the armour! And we defend ourselves against the works of evil. We are not fighting against flesh and blood but against darkness, principalities and powers. He trains your hands for war, your fingers for battle. You have escaped out of the snare of the Fowler and the Lord is showing also the pestilence!

The noisy pestilence! But the plague shall not come near your dwelling place because that's where all of this is coming from the plague!! God shows to you very easily, very clearly that it shall not come near your dwelling place. This brings great joy to your heart, because when you go to another level of understanding you don't have a spirit of fear, but of power, love and a sound mind.

Joy is filling your heart as you reach out, touch the world with His love, LOVE IS THE KEY to everything you do and Jesus is a part of it all. It's like the Lord is showing all the bells and whistles. They all start to chime all at the same time! This is going to be a very important time when people realise, in the name of Jesus Christ, to make sure you know where your finance is going! Because for a lot of people it won't be around soon! We thank you Jesus that you are showing us the Kingdom!

The kingdom will know no end and we are being shown very clearly as a wise steward! Make sure your eggs are all in one basket! Make sure that you are not left out on the side. Because there is going to be a tally financially and there will be much gain by the idle rich. The Lord is showing. This is a time to begin to realise He owns the cattle on a thousand hills and he owns the hills the cattle are on and he owns the gold, and the silver, and the diamonds! So why store up gold? When in Jesus name, when we own it all! Don't store nothing up, just wait for the living God in whom you put your trust to put it out there, in every area as a wise steward in Jesus name.

Now joy has gone beyond measure, going beyond God's purposes, and you are seeing that these countries, these nations all become ONE. It's only a matter of time. Thank you Jesus!

Jonathan, you can be like the drummer boy who's at the front, whom the army followed, a little drummer boy! Making sure that the little drum was beating to the tune of the living God, in whom you put your trust. Joy is filling your heart, because you'd love to be that little drummer boy! But of course you are a true son of God to be given power to become a SON! So much love! Love is the key to open the door to the King of kings and the Lord of lords. Your joy is full! Many doors open! Walk ye in them, don't turn to the right or left, just keep going through this maze of life. Then finally you come to the end of the maze, of course, led by the Holy Ghost. Thank you Lord for the release right now with love, joy, peace and prosperity. Amen.

Prophetess Marie can see the bigger picture and lots of prophets cannot always see it. She releases the presence and love of Jesus wherever she goes. You can find her at Jesus Light ministries: Marie Licciardo. It's an honour to know her and she is an extraordinary gift and sign and wonder for the Body of Christ. We meet on zoom every week, please follow me on social media to find out more and she will prophecy and pray for you if you are able to join us. Please consider any donation to her PayPal as she is so generous in her time and anointed words. Be blessed in Jesus mighty name.

Chapter *Twenty-Nine*
FLORIDA CONFIRMATION

The Lord has been talking to me and Janet recently that we need to be in Florida in the future. There is a certain ministry calling in me that will not go away and it connected to Florida and Awakening the nations. Sometimes I feel like I am just following other anointed ministers but I know that I just have to follow Jesus. If He says go and empowers me, I will go. If not, I won't go, but if He calls me, that means I will go when He says. He empowers me!

Janet is currently living in Virginia which is also an anointed place where Ruth Heflin used to have Calvary campground and people were definitely drink in the spirit there! They had gold dust, glory clouds and gold teeth in the early 90S! Absolutely incredible. Wonderful anointed drunken glory awakener Brandon from America in RLM apparently died and then came back and he went to Ruth Ward Heflin's church and got radically touched and this increased his anointing. I am still really praying for Red Letter Ministries as is my friend Raymond. There are lots of ex RLM folk out there! This book is dedicated mostly to him and Red Letter Ministries and they even have outreach where they help the poor in Kenya. He is teaching me a lot of different things about the anointing and Jesus is teaching us all to have fun more and we got to explore the Heavenly realms by faith! It's absolutely liberating!

Eric Melwani says this on his website: 'I believed that Jesus was a God, but not the only way to God. I also believed that there were multiple ways to God, Finally one morning before I went to college I called the prayer line again and told them that I desired to be able to pray in tongues. I prayed the prayer of salvation all over again as they assisted me to receive my heavenly language. Then suddenly in my room, I began to speak in tongues over the phone. I was so excited and happy to receive this heavenly gift. I began to attend a Pentecostal church in St. Thomas but still held onto my Hindu beliefs. One day we moved to Orlando, Florida'.

Now I find this interesting as the Lord completely captivates us! We are chosen to be ministers of Christ's Gospel and we are only just finding out what that means! With so many denominations to decide from, it can be confusing which one to belong too but guess what? There's no denominations in Heaven- we are all one Body of Love full of Christ! That is mind boggling and Christ is training us daily to thirst for him just like Pastor Eric Melwani did! And where did he end up? Florida!

Also God is talking to me about Florida, because it is home to Doctor Rodney Howard Browne, The Brownsville Revival and Todd Bentley's outpouring, along with Benny Hinn Ministries and many other anointed men of God that have either ministered there or live there.

God recently gave me new friends from Bolton that are connected to a Bible school there. Pretty exciting times are coming up. I feel that these are going to be greatly connected to Florida and the USA as well as Canada especially Toronto. I was anointed by the Arnett's from the Toronto outpouring in Dudley Revival Fires, UK and we are going back there soon. I keep seeing an anointed sword dripping with oil. God is

preparing me for something way bigger than myself. I humble myself daily and I have to just wait on Him for His supernatural manifestations.

FLORIDA CONFIRMATION

I cannot demand them. That is important. I have been so busy lately so I have not been able to catch up with everyone that I want too, but everything has its time and season and we have to realise that we cannot be everywhere to everyone. We have to give ourselves the grace while we are busy. In the hub of activity there must always be prayer otherwise it is just meaningless strife.

Vision of the Sword:

We actually have to preserve our energy and keep waiting on the SWORD which is the WORD, who is Jesus, and I didn't even know I was going to say that. I often say things that I had no previous knowledge of. God showed me the shining sword will only shine when the right royal child takes it out of the Rock! It is just like King Arthur! The amount of Fairy Tales God speaks to me through is beyond count! The rock is Father, the sword is Jesus, and the light is Holy Spirit and it went deeper than that, I saw water gush out of the Rock which is the outpouring of the Holy Spirit. See, it's not enough to just be in the light, we must become part of the substance of heaven – living waters!

We must be the living light waters to our lost and broken world. This vision seems to be getting deeper as I pray into it. I can now see the sword of LIGHT squirting out living waters which then turn into FIRE! Did you know Christ was alchemical? Did you realise that He has power over all the elements? Did you know that the occult is only imitation and there's nothing to fear as perfect love has already cast out all fear! I think we need to remember this daily as it will settle our nerves. I don't want to be a nervous person but I do want to be a powerful person! The water will not run out if we return daily to the Rock from which were are hewn! That's an exciting revelation and invitation! Talk about upgrading the sword in the stone and what have we been talking about before Orlando Florida which is also home to Walt Disney land!

HIGH WITH THE MOST HIGH

Although there are some conspiracies about Walt Disney I don't want to major on them here, rather I want to focus on what God is saying and what He has said to me recently:

1. I see there to be 2 portals connected to Disney Land Florida and also in Paris Disney Land. I see these are connected to the future outpouring also it is very important for the destiny of France, the Gaul's; the Celts and this will spread like wild fire. Disney is connected to children and those who have childlike faith, and the child in every adult. It is important to God. It is important to the movie industry and I see it will be connected to the Azuza street, California, LA outpouring in our near future.

2. The California outpouring is connected to the Bethel movement, supernatural school of ministry and a huge move of God among celebrities and mass media culture. It will penetrate the dark underground cults of Hollywood and reveal God's power, majesty and restore the fear of the Lord in the nations.

3. The media Revival that is coming is connected to celebs turning to Christ and I also see Dubai getting heavily involved as stars such as Will Smith hang around with Sheikh Hamdan and others.

4. The media revival outpouring will spread all over the nations to anywhere they make movies and do TV. I see an outpouring in London connected to the BBC. I see that it's going to get out of control.

5. I see football stars, sports stars and lots of singers and dancers being saved and although they will continue with their work, they will find an even greater deeper life purpose.

6. This will affect the modelling, entertainment industries. It will affect how people really feel about themselves, it will reveal how we treat people.

7. The outpouring will spread to the sex industry, sex workers of all kinds will hear about the 'New wave of power' and although some will

FLORIDA CONFIRMATION

say it's 'Religion' that word will not be able to define the remarkable supernatural movement that is happening all around us.

8. The outpouring is going to go everywhere! It will spread into prisons, it will change crime levels dramatically once again. It will reveal Christ's love to humanity, it will give us fresh understanding, fresh vision, fresh revelation about God and what He has already done for us!

9. It will impact all ages, everywhere, schools and nurseries, hobby groups, gyms, hotels, business meetings, supermarkets – honestly we don't realize what this global outpouring is going to do! I don't even know how we can prepare for something so grand orchestrated by Heaven which is being birthed through surrendered, humble pure hearts in prayer, praise and worship. The realms are opening everyday more and more and the enemy is getting very worried!

10. Persecution is increasing, threats of lack of electric power, inflation and a global crash with a global reset are heard today as common words but there's absolutely nothing to be scared of as Christ is in full supreme control. God knows what he is doing, even if we don't! Let Him be glorified in that time. We just have to continue in the secret place daily dying to self and let God do his thing, taking over all the nation's as they already belong to Him! It's going to be a phenomenal supernatural show down!

There are many different portals all over the world. Some are very ungodly and connected to the space god's and the Nephilim, and others are thin places for Christ. That doesn't mean that God is not going to totally dominate even dedicated places to evil. He has done it before and he's about to do it all over again!

"A Psalm of David. The earth [is] the Lord's, and the fulness thereof; the world, and they that dwell therein. For he hath founded it upon the seas, and established it upon the floods. Who shall ascend into the hill of the Lord? or who shall stand in his holy

place? He that hath clean hands, and a pure heart; who hath not lifted up his soul unto vanity, nor sworn deceitfully."

—(Psalm 24:1—4)

We need to catch this revelation as it should help us become some sort of shock absorber as we see the miraculous flood of Christ's Eternal love filling the atmosphere, revealing the realities of Heaven to us all again. We need to see God's goodness and His glory and we really will!!

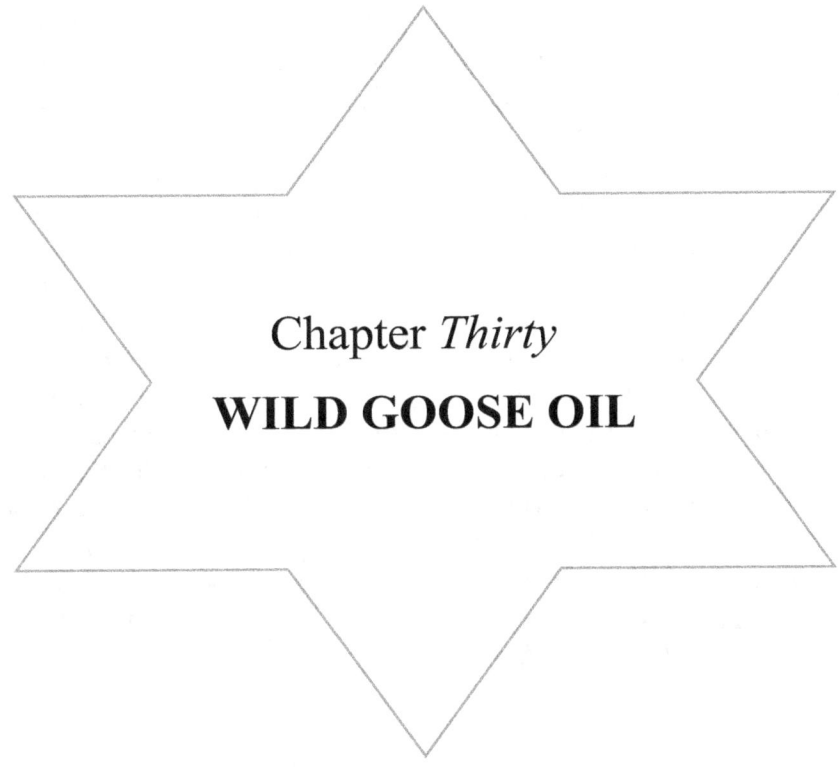

Chapter *Thirty*
WILD GOOSE OIL

10th September THE WILD GOOSE!

Praise Jesus! The Wild Goose is on the loose! This is how the Celts described Holy Spirit! What a picture of crazy freedom! Kathie Walters wrote an email and post on Facebook about it and I was getting whacked by it! I spoke to her and she told me to listen to Rodney Howard Browne, and he mentioned abundance in the mind and they are now getting a bigger building so I was imparted on that word too of ABUNDANCE! I had a great word of encouragement as always from Prophetess Marie and then I spoke with Prophet Oskar and I was praying for the Stockholm revival that I see in the spirit and I was telling him about Bob Jones and how he gave a 1 million dollar offering into Russia and this created secret churches which I just know will affect

Ukraine after the 2022 War, when they learn to forgive their enemies and embrace the revelation and the gift of forgiveness as a lifestyle! How can anyone go back to unforgiveness when we ourselves are forgiven for all sins and Christ Jesus empowers us to forgive all!

Unforgiveness is a curse and it brings more curses! Forgiveness is a supernatural blessing and gives you an understanding, appreciation, gratitude and radical revelation to change not only yourself, but also others around you by a supernatural grace. I of people do not realise that God gives us supernatural grace everyday- but often we don't appreciate it or understand it, or apply it! That must make God sad- and yet He is so joyful, why? He's not split personality but a multidimensional being and Spirit! He can feel both emotions of sadness and joy and we must realize He feels both sets of emotions. And quite frankly the revelation is, we can always choose joy no matter what! Despite the attacks we counter attack back by staying in peace and love and joy in Holy Spirit where there already is NO separation! No wonder why I am so love drunk every day, it is absolutely glorious and I prayed for this verse to come to pass:

"Restore to me the joy of Your salvation And sustain me with a willing spirit. Then I will teach transgressors Your ways, And sinners will be converted to You."

—Psalms 51:12—13

Misery, moaning, groaning, and pain your time is up. Sorry for the late notice but you've been evicted now in Jesus name!

So then once we have hold of the:

1. Foundation = Word of God
2. Revelation =Rhema and experiential Gnosis by Faith =Not living by our feelings.

WILD GOOSE OIL

We can then move into the revelation so much that it becomes so much a part of us that day to day, night to night we are absolutely surrounded, loaded and laden up with the treasures of God the treasury is in fact inside the church and there is indeed gold in the soul. If I say too much I am likely to get too excited and then incapacitated for a while as now I am perpetually high wondering why and all the pain leaves as the Lord Jesus reigns absolutely supreme in every way, in every place! Now that is exciting and I really can't stop, pop or contain these secret bliss bubbles that I keep seeing in the spirit and there are oceans of joy, as eternity is loading us up every day, as the spirit of Heaven literally takes over our souls and takes us from glory to glory. I didn't just find Christ in a dark place, I found Him and I find Him daily and once again I find Christ every day, night and day, in every place, in every space: it's all full now of Jesus! His name is written in GOLD and it is dripping all around me!

"But we all, with open face beholding as in a glass the glory of the Lord, are changed into the same image from glory to glory, [even] as by the Spirit of the Lord."

—(2 Corinthians 3:18)

Praise Jesus! Someone is getting this revelation that we don't have to try to understand, rather we let go of the stinking thinking, and controlling jezebellic whore that can't take any more and her vehicles of her false prophets are out of control! Why are we so bothered by the spirit of Jezebel? I can tell you for a fact she isn't getting hold of this prophet! No one controls me, only the LORD! You can't outrun Elisha, Church, so Elijah be strengthened and stop fretting Jezebel is nowhere near you!! We really aren't supposed to be intimidated by Jezebel. That is really immature, just be vigilant and engage in spiritual warfare, trusting God with the whole picture of the battle. We do not have to fear these evil powers, evil spirits or demons. Just be aware of them, that's all.

HIGH WITH THE MOST HIGH

"Lest Satan should get an advantage of us: for we are not ignorant of his devices."

(2 Corinthians 2:11).

"And Jesus answered and said unto them, Take heed that no man deceive you. For many shall come in my name, saying, I am Christ; and shall deceive many."

Mathew 24: 4—5

So what if you are in pain today, is Jesus still Lord? Do you only praise him when times are good? Ha-ha! I find that a strange thing to do! I praise God in pain until the pain disappears! Then if the pain doesn't go, well, praise God! It's there for a reason. It's doing something for me in the future that I don't know yet, something so wonderful, something so glorious, something so joyous, something so dangerous to the Devil's old campground of our old negative emotions- You'll be amazed and you'll need new sight! Oh I pray for your eyes to be opened- Enlightened awakened ones—Sons of glory arise!

Even your pain and suffering do not despise, it's temporary— It's a light affliction- look beloved: because next the word affliction is the word LIGHT! Glory! Shake off the old snake, ask Holy Spirit to ignite you inside, get oiled up in the glory and get absolutely soaked in spirit!

The wild rains are coming and the wild geese! Holy transformations are taking place every day. OmG, you are absolutely shockingly blessed! When is the church going to awaken? I feel like my whole body is being saturated with zeal and crazy revival passion! The GLORY DAYS are for today. It is NOW the power of revelation, salvation, invitation, destination and resurrection! These things and realms are going to be a part of our day to day lives! We can get high on the Holy Spirit despite feeling awful to begin with hope you're catching this fishy flow as it's loaded with your next catch oh soul winner! These revelations are breaking generational devils that you didn't even know were there! Praise God somebody!

It's time to SON bathe. Go get toasted, roasted, stuffed with anointed, fragrant spices. I urge you to offer yourself up to God first, as a living sacrifice daily and you'll never go back to what you thought was reality. We are drenching our souls and minds for goodness sake with all reverence in the rivers of living water! We need to be so drenched that our neighbours can't handle the anointing, that people are so offended and we are so whacked, so sun baked, so toasted, so roasted that we couldn't give a damn but this holy sanctified and glorified in Christ lifestyle and attitude is unblocking the wells of the Pharisees and the damns of what we taught and thought was reality!

We pray, we forgive, we love, we move on, we dream on, we keep our praise on, we keep our mind on Jesus and wow in the glory. We see Him!!!

We better get over ourselves otherwise when Holy Spirit doesn't manifest to us as a sweet little dove sometimes, we will get mad. There's no temper tantrums in heaven folk's! If you want a pity party then please exit through the main gates of pearl. Thank you but if you forgive, you will live so, enter in! This is your new world full of Jesus, everywhere you look, it's glory!

The colours the sparkles, the wonder of it all because Jesus have you and wants you involved in heavenly realms every single day! Why are people waiting till after they die? Go and DIE now! Keep dying to self and you'll get there! We can be with Jesus 24/7, all the time in every single space, every single thought, every single moment, we really can be so aware and in prayer in his remarkable royal presence! The Holy One of the universe wants to hang out with you! 'Wow! It's believable!' stop saying that learned junk 'It's unbelievable!' Don't you dare speak death when all you have been given is already in the realms of glory which is LIFE and LIFE in ABUNDANCE. I two different realms right there. Wakeup call! Repent, stand in awe and stare! Look at the majesty of King Jesus Christ! HE WANTS YOU AND HE LOVES YOU!

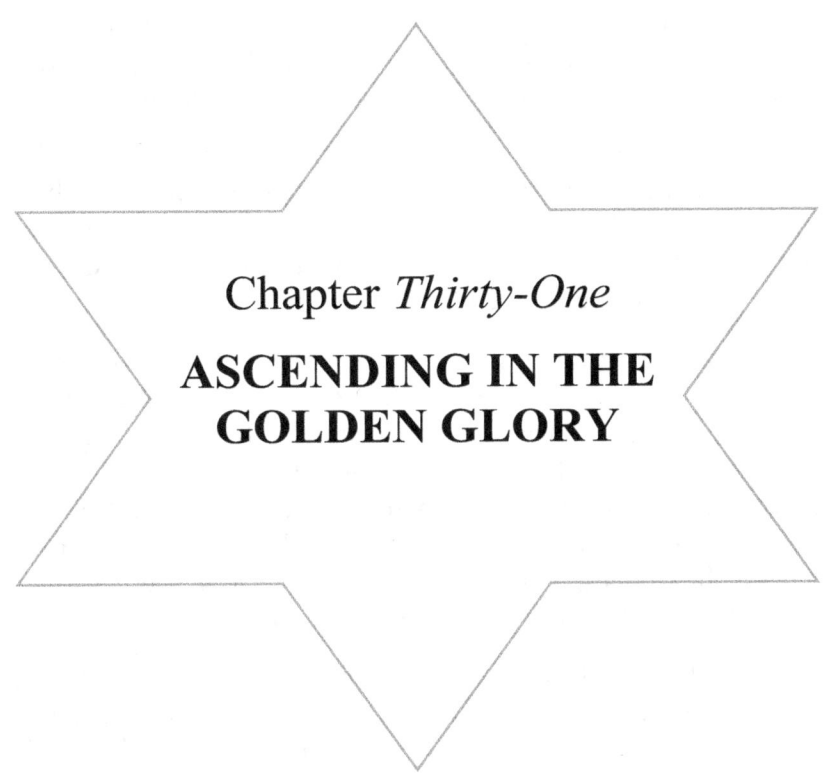

Chapter *Thirty-One*

ASCENDING IN THE GOLDEN GLORY

When I was fasting the other day I went to bed with bubbles of light everywhere and they looked like orbs but they were only there momentarily and I didn't know this but it answered my prayer for even more impartation, multiplication and radical acceleration and then God showed Himself to my Red letter friend Brandon. He is my new brother who is full of revelations too and is now loaded with Heaven with his team every day! No more dryness!

Brandon: 'After we ended the live stream today the next song came on saying 'I see the Lord' by Ron Kenoly. Yes, we even listen to the same music! As those lyrics were spoken, I saw the Lord of glory standing where my broadcast chair was with my physical eyes! There were thousands around him that looked like orbs! I was so shocked that I closed my eyes, shook my head, looked again and all the glory orbs as angels appeared again! I know by the Holy Spirit within me this was the physical appearing of the king of glory with His angelic armies appearing on earth and now released upon the Earth for us!'

More Lord, more multiplication and amplifications! More accelerations! Turn up the stereo Lord! Bless Brother Brandon oh most High! RLM has been helping us see more of Jesus in a contemporary way so we really appreciate them despite the crazy hardships and persecution in advance we have all been through.

Gold dust miracles were breaking out in Brandon's tribe online and I had mine on the Monday I fasted on the phone to Janet. As much as I love glittery things I touched absolutely nothing like that at all! It just happened, the little sparkles appeared which I get frequently and then two fingers were half dipped in white golden shimmer! PRAISE JESUS, I desperately want to be deep with God as I am well aware that if people worship the signs and wonders they will leave but I know that nothing must stop Heavens invasion! Praise God!

Four days ago I group I belong to from Red Letter wrote a post was written by a member called Cheryl and this revealed the transparency and sometimes the warfare battle it comes to seeing in the spirit or having heavenly encounters but God is triumphant and radiant all the time whether we feel it or not. I felt led to include it to show we are a real people with real problems at times, despite our glorious supernatural lifestyle which is a grace gift and our inheritance. 'I love you all so much! I was already experiencing some deep repentance earlier today and then I went into all out deliverance during tonight's broadcast. I know I still have some mixture and some pride coming through me from my last several years which is part of the reason why I don't interact much, but it's burning away daily now. Tonight was so precious and priceless! I cried for most of the broadcast, but the peace and the beauty that came with the release was profound and Jesus was right there holding me throughout it all, Thank you, Brandon and Rebekah! And thank you to all the rest of you amazing angels too.

ASCENDING IN THE GOLDEN GLORY

Also, while Brandon was speaking towards the end I had a vision of him sitting in a golden setting on a golden couch. It was like I almost saw into a place that I knew, but I don't remember and I desperately wanted to be in that place again. As soon as I tried to go in deeper to the vision it disappeared and I just froze in amazement for a moment. It was still beautiful and special and helped me see more clearly. I know the more I crucify my pride, the clearer these realms will become, the clearer I will become! I am just so grateful for you all'

See folks that sort of humble attitude will take you higher and higher and higher! The church body is completely royal and will have a royal awakening! It's time to burn off some calories and river dance!! That level of honesty, humility, transparency will lead to transparent gold souls! Cheryl won't just see brother Brandon on the golden couch like some sort of celebrity brother come and catch this wild revelation:

It's time to dissolve the old celebrity image deep down in the Body of Christ, break down the pride by dipping yourself into the melting water! This is what the Spirit is saying to the churches at this hour. It is the hour of power spending a 265idiculous amount of time with Jesus with good spiritual food which will then increase the revelations, impartations, visitations, and encounters in our lives! Because guess what church? We are doing this all together! I really felt that Cheryl's attitude is refreshing!

I want us all to learn from this attitude as it's how you ascend in altitude! Don't miss this revelation. Lots of people today are looking for mystical encounters with God and that's wonderful but they don't realise how to not only get them, but how to maintain them. I am not an expert, not at all with all humility, I am compelled by beautiful Jesus to help encourage you via these words.

Good words can impart the soul. This is exactly why I write to encourage you all so deeply. Did you know you can see God and sense His presence daily? I urge you to pray always about what God shows you and brings up in your day, in the talks and sermons you listen to, in the books you read. This means talking to Jesus and really listening to

Him. That is prayer! I know you are hungry as we are all here together. You want to know about the revelation of heavenly closeness and heavenly intimacy and then to experience the realms of Heaven with Jesus, don't you?

See, it's your heart that gives you away beloved. 'If you spend time with Jesus you are spending time with the Jesus in me!' Don't miss that revelation, because it's an extra one and I am loaded tonight, so let's go back to the first one just so we stay on point and really get this together.

1. Sometimes your revelations won't seem mystical or wonderful at all. They will seem quite ordinary but look deeper child of God.

There are Revelational and Foundational levels and realms and you must have both. Holy Spirit is leading us into new realms from the Word of God. Don't throw out the time spent reading or listening, or studying the Bible. Yes, of course, there is more, but that holy book is NOT like any other in the whole world. Its messages are made of light even if they seem old, archaic, strange and unrelated to today! They are relevant! Don't judge. Those words have love light energy in them. You don't even know what encounters God and Heaven have for you next! You don't know when your next holy and fun encounter is coming from, whether God wants to use a person, situation or meet you directly, just like He did with Brandon and just like He has shown Himself to me! Just continue on in Christ Jesus. SAINTS ALIVE! WE ARE HERE TO STAY.

Forget the media fears about diseases, lockdowns, food shortages, fuel shortages, famines, wars, rumours of war. Just pray and repent of the dark flames of fear! Christ Jesus is here you have absolutely nothing to fear! Gross darkness and political chaos is no problem for God. Always remember this.

ASCENDING IN THE GOLDEN GLORY

"Arise, shine; for thy light is come, and the glory of the Lord is risen upon thee. For, behold, the darkness shall cover the earth, and gross darkness the people: but the Lord shall arise upon thee, and his glory shall be seen upon thee. And the Gentiles shall come to thy light, and kings to the brightness of thy rising. Lift up thine eyes round about, and see: all they gather themselves together, they come to thee: thy sons shall come from far, and thy daughters shall be nursed at [thy] side. Then thou shalt see, and flow together, and thine heart shall fear, and be enlarged; because the abundance of the sea shall be converted unto thee, the forces of the Gentiles shall come unto thee."

Isaiah 60:1—5

I hope we are all learning something about keeping a good attitude of faith and radical love for God and towards the spirit of Joy so we really catch fire in the Spirit! If you want to see Jesus and inherit the earth, you'll be emptied completely, your old self will be crucified, you'll be humiliated, and you'll be overtaken! Oh yes, let's add in rejected and humiliated and persecuted all for Christ's name's sake. What glory! And what a shocking turnaround is coming!

When we learn to see the sparkles on our crappy more lower days (though they are less all the time now because of grace and drunken love!) Then we will really accelerate. This means seeing the sparkle despite the pain, dimness and darkness. Our darker days can still shine! Jesus loves a sacrifice of thanksgiving, gratitude, praise and worship daily. This is really the emphasis of staying high with the Most High! Do this and you'll ascend and go even higher than you can imagine both in Heavenly realms and in Earth's realms which are now being totally taken over by paradise pleasures and Great grace. The shakings of God have all been purposeful even if you didn't understand them, misinterpreted and judged them, and filled them in your subconscious as too weird. Come on!

That girl Cheryl prophesied, 'The serious shakers full of drunken glory are coming back on mass! I am converted to these different dimensions and I am not going back to the old ways! We are moving from glory to glory. These are exciting times and crazy times. Be expectant for your visions and visitations as Holy Spirit arranges everything perfectly!'

Cheryl also says some more funny and great stuff. Note take this one disciple drinkers! 'Brandon Barthrop, I also want to mention how hilariously prophetic it is for me that you keep mentioning all the manure piles in the manger! I am currently cleaning up all that sh*t not only within me, but also in the place I am living. The lady here is in a wheelchair and has an old deaf/blind dying dog who can't control his bowels anymore. I am constantly dealing with his messes in the house. It's almost become overwhelming at one point until the first time you mentioned Jesus being born in a manger in the middle of a manure pile! Now I can dig it! It's not the most pleasant of experiences but I just let Holy Spirit lead the way!' Whoever that Cheryl girl was, God bless her!

Not only is this really funny but laughter is good glorious medicine for the soul, lest we forget! But it's also profound and we are back to that simple subject of humility again. And when you think of supernatural the first word that comes to mind isn't likely to be humility yet in Christ: humility is a great kingdom key. It's also an Angelic power which unlocks blessings and an inheritance in the saints. You need to know that people are waiting on your manifestation, your saintly prophetic flow and glow which always comes from God within and not of you!

"But we have this treasure in earthen vessels, that the excellency of the power may be of God, and not of us."

—(2 Corinthians 4:7)

Paraphrased: We have this TREASURE in jars of clay (fragile, weak, dependent on God bodies) to show that this ALL SURPASSING POWER including JOY IN ALL CIRCUMSTANCES, SUPERNATURAL STRENGTH AND STRANGE SMILING is from

ASCENDING IN THE GOLDEN GLORY

GOD ALONG WITH DAILY MIRACLES and it is certainly not from us!

We need to get this as it's totally:

1. Biblical
2. Foundational
3. Revelational.

God's not going to give you streams of revelations everyday if He can't trust you so you better get over it! Don't cry about it! The Lord means business at this hour. The Lord resists the proud but gives SUPERNATURAL HEAVENLY GRACE to the HUMBLE, and the meek will inherit the earth and earth will be flooded with glory waves! It will get too intense, magnificent and wonderful that you'll have to take time off work even though you might think you can't afford it! This next outpouring, awakening and reformation of God's holy church is going to be immense, the Devil's counterattacks will seem like a walk in the park in comparison!

I was just speaking with my awesome friend Tye and we were saying that in the future people will say we are like occultists, because such will be the miracles, strange signs and wonders will **follow us** and make people **compelled to give** to us and they will **flood around us** wanting a wonder and they don't realise yet, and nor do we, though: ARISE and SHINE YOUR LIGHT HAS COME!

People are going to be both attracted and repelled by our Jesus light! The LIGHTS and the sparkles will get BRIGHT within us! We haven't seen nothing yet church! The meek will inherit the earth and reveal the new creation and new earth realm glories as we take over from heavenly dimensions. Our spirits fully possessed, owned, purchased by Holy Spirit are coming back down from Heaven and we will get the help needed sent from the sanctuary! Wells will be unblocked, pain released, repented of and let go of as more and more glory fills us and floods us!

HIGH WITH THE MOST HIGH

The LOVE OF GOD for ourselves and for each other is paramount and it will be made manifest IN JESUS!

Appreciation and gratitude and Thanksgiving are just a few of the foundation keys that unlock the revelation realms and greater glory! You can soar instead of bore! You will not be bored in Revival Glory Realms— that is for sure. I want more!!

Blessed [be] the God and Father of our Lord Jesus Christ, who hath blessed us with all spiritual blessings in heavenly [places] in Christ: According as he hath chosen us in him before the foundation of the world, that we should be holy and without blame before him in love: Having predestinated us unto the adoption of children by Jesus Christ to himself, according to the good pleasure of his will, To the praise of the glory of his grace, wherein he hath made us accepted in the beloved."

—(Ephesians 1:3—6)

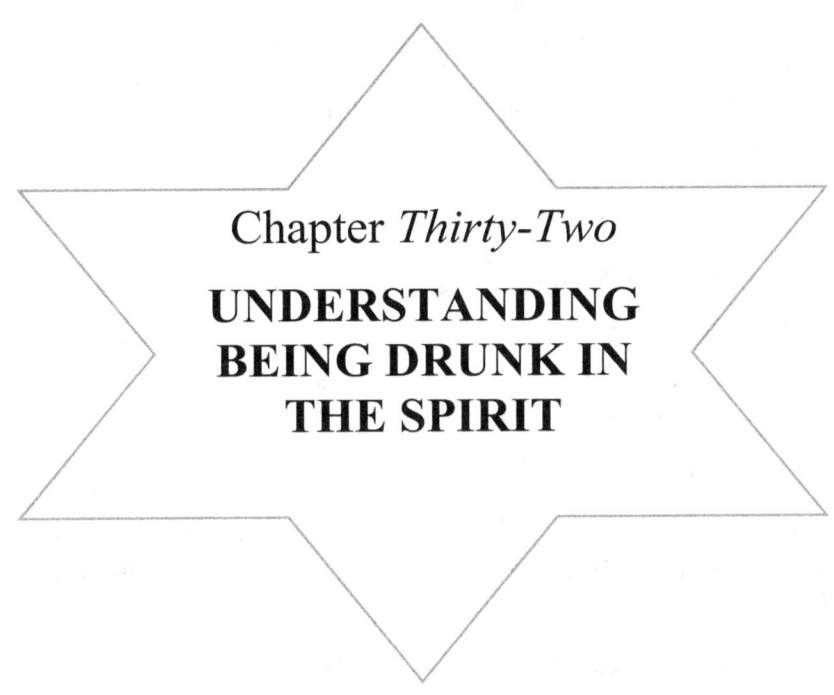

Chapter *Thirty-Two*

UNDERSTANDING BEING DRUNK IN THE SPIRIT

13th September

The last few days were out of this world and it took time to recover from what God did to me. Talk about a good Father! This books 'nuts and bolts' came together in less than 10 days in real time, but it took months to digest it and then get it written and edited and ready for print. It is so loaded in revelations and I really appreciate your time in hearing or reading this.

So what is real time I ask? Answer: God says 'REAL TIME IS WHAT YOU THINK IS REALITY BUT OH DEAR YOU ARE COMPLETELY UNAWARE OF MY NEW GLORY TIME THAT IS COMING!'

HIGH WITH THE MOST HIGH

He knows exactly what we need and how to cheer us up! Now I understand the charismatic phrase, 'take another drink!' I was somewhat confused by the whole drunken in the spirit movement for a number of different reasons:

1. I was sceptical that it was actually God.

2. I couldn't see the fruit of such experiences other than a few cases (other than Heidi baker for example)

3. I equated drinking alcohol with my parents and from my past and I certainly didn't want anything to do with that!

4. I just plain did not understand it.

5. I was frustrated as I knew it involved faith and personal visitation and I was going through too many problems so I shelved knowing about it.

6. I stayed ignorant because I couldn't see its relevance during suffering.

7. I had unbelief, preconceived ideas and judgements about not understanding it at all nor wanting to!

8: I had a bunch of religious spirits preventing me from seeing the fun and glory of really being high with the Most High or drunk as a crazy ass chipmunk on some glory acid! I had no idea God would be interested in making our culture more cool and more hip and more whack with His heavenly glory stack! I had no idea He was this COOL!

I was amazed when I was made an honorary Doctor of the Church when I really didn't like the idiotic drunk in the spirit antics, nor did I want to be associated with them. It felt forced and like false joy. I wanted real joy but I had completely missed the revelation of being drunk in the spirit. The verse in Acts which I am now going to call FACTS instead of ACTS said:

UNDERSTANDING BEING DRUNK IN THE SPIRIT

"But Peter, standing up with the eleven, lifted up his voice, and said unto them, Ye men of Judæa, and all [ye] that dwell at Jerusalem, be this known unto you, and hearken to my words: For these are not drunken, as ye suppose, seeing it is [but] the third hour of the day."

—(Acts 2:14—15)

This was my verse that I subconsciously used for justification why I shouldn't be involved with such nonsense. Guess what? I must have had a terrible religious spirit because I had taken offense and not even known it! I suppose this is why an ex sceptic must write this book! Now, that really is God's sense of humour! I understand now that I was wrong and I repented. I want to experience God and just because charismatics call it 'drunk' in the spirit' It doesn't mean that it's bad or evil. Just because I have had bad experiences with alcohol and the people who drink and do drugs does not mean that God can't get through any of that junk, shine His light through it all and set me free from controlling and judgemental thinking. Now I have my revelation, I am free to enjoy the realms of limitless glory!

I also didn't realise that a portal opening (or a gate if you prefer the old language) could or would involve being drunk in the spirit without even engaging in it! And did you know how alive the clouds of glory are? How fun they are! How they lift you far above your circumstances, how they can give you such wild giddy experiences and how realms of infinite joy are your portion? Did you know? Did you know how to access them? Or did you think it's just for a Revival time in church and then they pass, and then it's all over!

I had no idea I could just sit down at my desk where I write my books, pray and praise, and without barely engaging the spirit realms I can be caught up in external bliss! Whether I see it all or feel it all does not matter, the spiritual experience is absolutely undeniable! I am quite shocked and I need much more greater capacity than I thought I had already built up to be able to cope with the onslaught of a supernatural life! Do we really know the cost of a supernatural existence? God does!

I was listening today to 'Mantles require preparation' on YouTube by Eric Melwain. I found his work when I found out that he is an anointed author and former Hindu. My friends in India are also born again and they renounced Hinduism and religious thinking. Now they do revival crusades and have invited me to join them and for many years as they have always seen the prophet potential in me, even when I did not! They never judged me, they know exactly where I was, in a previous gay relationship and they accepted me with Christ's unconditional love including my partner at the time. Now, that is outrageous love! I'm single now and I could go to India but I will only ever do anything when it is the right time and never before! That is how God fearing I am, I just will not step out unless I see that I have the go ahead and the provisions from God.

It's ok to be in a place of waiting, and **waiting patiently** on the Lord for the Promised Land. Pastor Eric talks about the necessity of preparation and character building before exposure. I couldn't agree more.

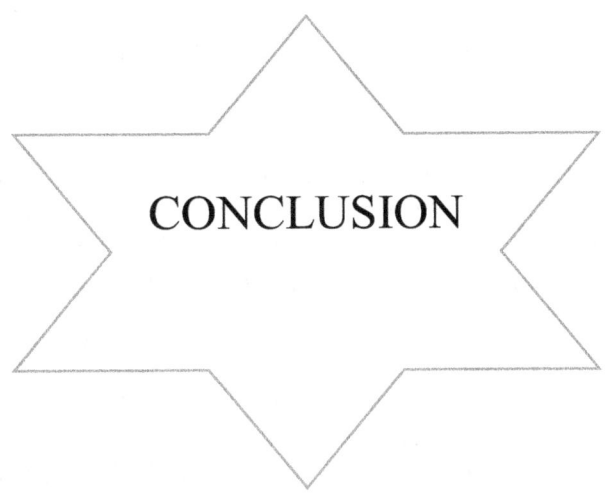

CONCLUSION

I am going to bring this book to a close here so I do not overwhelm you, my reader or my hearer! I have taken you on some of my journey and there is so much to say, but I would like to leave that for another day. I have to explain to you that you too can experience your own revival if you will keep an open heart and an open mind about it. You will have to humble yourselves daily and want to get rid of old sinful thinking that no longer serves you!

The religious spirit will even try to hinder you and distract you daily and the accuser. Well, he always tries it on, by trying to attack and weary the saints, but hold fast to your confession of faith and hold onto your revelations but more than that, hold fast onto Christ who is the author and the finisher of your faith journey! Learn to laugh at the Devil and learn to laugh at yourselves and learn to laugh at your mistakes and failures! That means learn to laugh a lot and while you are at it. Learn to revelate and learn to celebrate, then you'll become revival's glory gate! These are exciting times and scary times, so we have to focus on God, His vision daily and learn to let everything else go.

If you are a student, learn to let it go. If you are unemployed, learn to let it go. If you are in a relationship, learn to let it go. I assure you that if you surrender all to Christ you will gain all for Christ. This is one of the old costly kingdom keys but well worth knowing.

> *"For whosoever will save his life shall lose it: and whosoever will lose his life for my sake shall find it. For what will it profit a man if he gains the whole world and forfeits his soul? Or what will a man give in exchange for his soul?"*
>
> —(Mathew 16:25—26)

I read once that we should learn to 'hold life loosely' this means by not having a care in the world! God wants us to take on His burden which is made of light so that we begin to see that we have become the light in Him! Arise and shine, but by all means, take your time to awaken from the deepest slumber and see that God will always love you and care for you. We are having an awakening and we are getting ready. We must switch out of survival mode and into revival mode so that God can bless our 'goings in and coming out'

Learn to let go and be in the know, but not arrogant about it. Be refreshed in the river of Heaven and let the Holy Spirit wash over you every single day! It can be achieved and you will be more than blessed and refreshed, revival consciousness is just the beginning. We have so much in store for you just you wait.

Wait on God and He will revive you. He will surprise you. He will reveal to you greater mysteries and give you powerful visions. You will learn discernment and you will learn how to feel energy and sense energetic shifts and you will learn to work with the angels and higher heavenly harmonics so that you experience greater levels of daily freedom!

We can trust God with every area of our lives and live on the highway of holiness, not religion and be blessed to be a blessing for others. God is going to surprise you. I said that before, but I am saying it again for repetition and meditation effect, GOD IS GOING TO SURPRISE YOU. SO LET GO BE IN THE KNOW, BE IN THE FLOW, BE IN

CONCLUSION

THE GLOW AND BE REVIVED BY THE RIVER OF JOY AND PEACE IN HOLY SPIRIT!

Thank you so much for picking this book and I really hope and pray that you will get a powerful impartation! Every day is a choice to rejoice, so get ready to PASS your next test. You can do it, Christ is interceding for you and He believes in you too. I believe in the fullness and the future glory of the true Church Ecclesia and we are going to see it fully manifest! To God Almighty be the glory forever and ever. Amen.

ABOUT THE AUTHOR

Jonathan Kania is a young Apostolic and Prophetic voice for the endtime! He is a Minister of the Gospel and is head of Heaven to Earth Apostolic Ministries which is an online based ministry. He is a God chaser who worships JESUS CHRIST without any shame and ignores Man's concepts of normality when he believes he must pioneer a new 'normal' which is Heavenly Kingdom mentality.

This means to burn with love and passion always and endure all things for the sake of the Gospel. His prophetic ministry has touched many lives around the world, and he has been awarded an Honorary Degree as a Doctor of Divinity from Nigeria!

Jonathan is a British born man with an anointing for Africa and the nations! He has a Healing ministry being set up by the Spirit of God and he is a Prophet as you will read from a lot of his writings.

He is also an artist who loves to illustrate and author - both of nonfiction and fiction. He is considered a Revivalist and a controversial man with a heart of love and compassion. He was a Missionary in Uganda where a church has been planted and he has many spiritual sons and daughters mostly from Ghana where he had a wonderful revival in 2020 during Coronavirus!

Heaven to Earth Ministries do their very best to support orphans and the poor and needy across the nations and also providing help, support and encouragement, when possible, to the Prophets and Pastors and Evangelists. In fact anyone that is doing Kingdom work to the Lord's Glory. Until he and his team are called home, they will continue to preach the Gospel and do crusades and bring in the Great Last Days Harvest. This will be achieved not by might, nor power, but by the Holy Spirit of the Living God!

You can find him online:

Heaven to Earth Ministries: Podbean.

YouTube: Jon Kania - Heaven to Earth Ministries

Facebook: Heaven To Earth Apostolic Ministries group

WhatsApp: Private group.

Instagram: heaventoearthjonny

TikTok: heaventoearthministries

Email: heaventoearthjonny@gmx.co.uk

Huge thanks for all of your support and our wonderful typist teams and intercessors. Love always wins! Love you all! GLORY TO JESUS CHRIST!! OUR LIVES ARE HIDDEN IN HIM! REVIVAL IS YOUR INHERITANCE! PRAY & BE SAVED!

www.ingramcontent.com/pod-product-compliance
Lightning Source LLC
Chambersburg PA
CBHW071447220526
45472CB00003B/697